# EATCS
# Monographs on Theoretical Computer Science

Volume 15

Editors:  W. Brauer  G. Rozenberg  A. Salomaa

---

Advisory Board:  G. Ausiello  M. Broy  S. Even
J. Hartmanis  N. Jones  M. Nivat  C. Papadimitriou
D. Scott

*Authors*
Professor S. Sippu
Department of Computer Science, University of Jyväskylä
Seminaarinkatu 15, SF-40100 Jyväskylä, Finland

Professor E. Soisalon-Soininen
Department of Computer Science, University of Helsinki
Teollisuuskatu 23, SF-00510 Helsinki, Finland

*Editors*
Prof. Dr. Wilfried Brauer
Institut für Informatik, Technische Universität München
Arcisstr. 21, D-8000 München 2, Germany

Prof. Dr. Grzegorz Rozenberg
Institute of Applied Mathematics and Computer Science
University of Leiden, Niels-Bohr-Weg 1, P.O. Box 9512
NL-2300 RA Leiden, The Netherlands

Prof. Dr. Arto Salomaa
Department of Mathematics, University of Turku
SF-20500 Turku 50, Finland

ISBN 3-540-13720-3 Springer-Verlag Berlin Heidelberg New York
ISBN 0-387-13720-3 Springer-Verlag New York Heidelberg Berlin

Library of Congress Cataloging-in-Publication Data
Sippu, Seppo, 1950–
Parsing theory / Seppo Sippu, Eljas Soisalon-Soininen.
p.    cm. – (EATCS monographs on theoretical computer science ; v. 15)
Bibliography: p.
Included index.
Contents: v. 1. Languages and parsing.
ISBN 0-387-13720-3 (U.S.: v. 1)
1. Parsing (Computer grammar) 2. Formal languages. I. Soisalon-
Soininen, Eljas, 1949– II. Title. III. Series
QA267.3.S59 1988   511.3–dc 19   88-20091 CIP







Typesetting: Macmillan India Ltd, Bangalore
Offsetprinting: Color-Druck, Berlin. Bookbinding: Lüderitz & Bauer, Berlin.
2145/3020-543210

# Preface

The theory of parsing is an important application area of the theory of formal languages and automata. The evolution of modern high-level programming languages created a need for a general and theoretically clean methodology for writing compilers for these languages. It was perceived that the compilation process had to be "syntax-directed", that is, the functioning of a programming language compiler had to be defined completely by the underlying formal syntax of the language. A program text to be compiled is "parsed" according to the syntax of the language, and the object code for the program is generated according to the semantics attached to the parsed syntactic entities.

Context-free grammars were soon found to be the most convenient formalism for describing the syntax of programming languages, and accordingly methods for parsing context-free languages were developed. Practical considerations led to the definition of various kinds of restricted context-free grammars that are parsable by means of efficient deterministic linear-time algorithms.

Today, the theory of parsing is a well-established area of computer science. The most notable individual achievements in the area date from as early as the 1960s. These include the two major deterministic parsing methods now used in programming language compilers: $LR(k)$ parsing and $LL(k)$ parsing. However, since the invention of these methods, a great deal of research has been done on their analysis and on the practical issues involved in implementing parsers. As a result of this research, constructing a parser for a programming language is no longer an ad hoc task but a completely automatic process executed by a compiler writing system.

This monograph is intended as an up-to-date reference work on the theory of deterministic parsing of context-free grammars. The material included is treated in depth, with emphasis on the $LR(k)$ and $LL(k)$ methods, which are developed in a uniform way. Special attention is paid to the efficient implementation of $LR(k)$ and $LL(k)$ parsers. Construction algorithms for parsers are derived from general graph-theoretic methods, and complexity questions about parsable grammars are analyzed.

The treatment is mathematical in spirit, and contributes to the analysis of algorithms. The work tries to be self-contained in that relevant results from the general theory of formal languages and computational complexity are cited explicitly in the text (usually as propositions). For some of these results, a proof is also provided.

"Parsing Theory" appears in two volumes, "Volume I: Languages and Parsing" (Chapters 1 to 5) and "Volume II: LR $(k)$ and LL $(k)$ Parsing" (Chapters 6 to 10). The two volumes form an integrated work, with chapters, theorems, lemmas, etc. numbered consecutively.

Volume I provides an introduction to the basic concepts of languages and parsing. It also contains the relevant mathematical and computer science background needed in the development of the theory of deterministic parsing. In Chapter 1, concepts from discrete mathematics, formal languages and computational complexity are reviewed. Chapter 2 contains the basic algorithms on relations and graphs needed later in constructing parsers. In Chapter 3, the main classical results on regular languages are reviewed, with emphasis on the complexity of algorithms. Chapter 4 is a short introduction to context-free grammars and related concepts. Volume I ends with Chapter 5, which introduces the concepts of a pushdown automaton, pushdown transducer, left parser, right parser, strong LL $(k)$ parser, and simple precedence parser. In this chapter, the emphasis is on the analysis of strong LL $(k)$ parsing and on the efficient construction and implementation of strong LL $(1)$ parsers.

Volume II contains a thorough treatment of the theory of LR $(k)$ and LL $(k)$ parsing. The topics covered are: LR $(k)$, LALR $(k)$, and SLR $(k)$ parsers and grammars (Chapter 6), construction and implementation of LR $(1)$ parsers (Chapter 7), LL $(k)$ parsers and grammars, and non-left-recursive grammatical covers (Chapter 8), syntax error recovery and reporting (Chapter 9), and the complexity of testing grammars for parsability (Chapter 10).

This work is intended to be used as a textbook at graduate and senior undergraduate levels. A suitable background for a student would be an elementary knowledge of formal language theory, complexity, data structures and analysis of algorithms.

Some of the material has been used in a one-semester course on parsing theory at the University of Helsinki. A one-semester course on the basic theory of languages and parsing can be taught from Volume I. The whole material in both volumes can perhaps most conveniently be covered in an advanced two-semester course on parsing theory.

Numerous exercises are provided at the end of each chapter. The bibliographic notes attempt to point to a published source for exercises that are more difficult than average or that cover topics not discussed in the text.

Jyväskylä and Helsinki, March 1988    Seppo Sippu
Eljas Soisalon-Soininen

*Acknowledgements*
The work was supported by the Academy of Finland, the Finnish Cultural Foundation, and the Ministry of Education of Finland.

# Contents

# 1. Elements of Language Theory

In this chapter we shall review the mathematical and computer science background on which the presentation in this book is based. We shall discuss the elements of discrete mathematics and formal language theory, emphasizing those issues that are of importance from the point of view of context-free parsing. We shall devote a considerable part of this chapter to matters such as random access machines and computational complexity. These will be relevant later when we derive efficient algorithms for parsing theoretic problems or prove lower bounds for the complexity of these problems. In this chapter we shall also discuss a general class of formal language descriptors called "rewriting systems" or "semi-Thue systems". Later in the book we shall consider various language descriptors and language recognizers as special cases of a general rewriting system. As this approach is somewhat unconventional, we advise even the experienced reader to go through the definitions given in this chapter if he or she wishes to appreciate fully the presentation in this book.

The first two sections of this chapter contain a brief introduction to relations, directed graphs, trees, functions, countable sets, monoids, strings, homomorphisms and languages. Section 1.3 deals with the abstract model of a computer on which the algorithms presented in this book are intended to run. This model coincides with the conventional random access machine model except that we allow nondeterministic programs. Section 1.4 deals with decision problems and solvability, and Section 1.5 discusses the complexity of programs in our model of computation. Finally, Section 1.6 defines a general rewriting system and related concepts such as derivations, time complexity, and space complexity in rewriting systems.

## 1.1 Mathematical Preliminaries

Let $A$ and $B$ be sets. A *relation $R$ from $A$ to $B$*, denoted by $R: A \rightarrow B$, is any subset of the Cartesian product of $A$ and $B$, i.e. $R \subseteq A \times B$. $A$ is the *domain* and $B$ the *range* of $R$. $R$ is a relation *on $A$* if $A = B$. If a pair $(a, b)$ is in $R$, we say that $a$ is *R-related to b*, and write $a\, R\, b$.

If $A'$ is a subset of $A$, we call the set

$$R(A') = \{b \in B \mid a\, R\, b \text{ for some } a \in A'\}$$

the *image of A' under R*. In the case of a singleton set $\{a\}$ we may write $R(a)$ for $R(\{a\})$.

The relation $R^{-1}$ from $B$ to $A$ defined by

$$R^{-1} = \{(b, a) \in B \times A \mid a\,R\,b\}$$

is called the *inverse* of $R$.

The (*relational*) *product* of relations $R_1 : A \to B$ and $R_2 : B \to C$, denoted by $R_1 R_2$, is the relation from $A$ to $C$ defined by

$$R_1 R_2 = \{(a, c) \in A \times C \mid a\,R_1\,b \text{ and } b\,R_2\,c \text{ for some } b \in B\} \ .$$

The relational product $R_1 R_2$ is sometimes called the *composition* of $R_1$ and $R_2$ and may also be denoted by $R_2 \circ R_1$ (note the reversed order).

**Fact 1.1** Multiplication of relations is an associative binary operation on the set of all relations. That is, for any relations $R_1 : A \to B$, $R_2 : B \to C$ and $R_3 : C \to D$, we have

$$R_1(R_2 R_3) = (R_1 R_2)R_3 \ .$$

Thus we may omit the parentheses and write $R_1 R_2 R_3$.  $\square$

We say that a relation $R$ on a set $A$ is

(1) *reflexive*, if $a\,R\,a$ for all $a \in A$—in other words, $R$ includes the *identity relation* $\mathrm{id}_A = \{(a, a) \mid a \in A\}$ on $A$;

(2) *symmetric*, if $a\,R\,b$ always implies $b\,R\,a$—in other words, $R^{-1} = R$;

(3) *antisymmetric*, if $a\,R\,b$ and $b\,R\,a$ always imply $a = b$—in other words, $R^{-1} \cap R \subseteq \mathrm{id}_A$;

(4) *transitive*, if $a\,R\,b$ and $b\,R\,c$ always imply $a\,R\,c$—in other words, $RR \subseteq R$.

Let $R$ be a relation on $A$ and $n$ a natural number. The $n^{\mathrm{th}}$ *power of $R$* (or *n-fold product of $R$*), denoted by $R^n$, is defined inductively by

(1) $R^0 = \mathrm{id}_A$;

(2) $R^n = RR^{n-1}$, for $n > 0$.

**Fact 1.2** $a\,R^n\,b$ if and only if for some $a_0, \ldots, a_n \in A$, $a = a_0$, $a_n = b$ and $a_i\,R\,a_{i+1}$ for all $i = 0, \ldots, n-1$.  $\square$

The *transitive closure* of $R$, denoted by $R^+$, is the relation on $A$ defined by

$$R^+ = \bigcup_{n=1}^{\infty} R^n \ .$$

The *reflexive transitive closure* of R, denoted by $R^*$, is the relation on $A$ defined by

$$R^* = \bigcup_{n=0}^{\infty} R^n \ .$$

Thus $R^* = R^0 \cup R^+ = \mathrm{id}_A \cup R^+ \ .$

**Lemma 1.3** *Let R be a relation on a set A. Then $R^+$ is the smallest transitive relation on A that includes R, and $R^*$ is the smallest reflexive and transitive relation on A that includes R. In other words, the following statements hold:*

(1) $R^+$ *is transitive and* $R \subseteq R^+$.
(2) $R^+ \subseteq R'$ *whenever $R'$ is a transitive relation on A such that $R \subseteq R'$.*
(3) $R^*$ *is reflexive and transitive and* $R \subseteq R^*$.
(4) $R^* \subseteq R'$ *whenever $R'$ is a reflexive and transitive relation on A such that* $R \subseteq R'$. □

Let $A'$ be a subset of $A$. Then $R^+(A')$, the image of $A'$ under $R^+$, is called the *positive closure of $A'$ under R*, and $R^*(A')$, the image of $A'$ under $R^*$, is called the *closure of $A'$ under R*.

A pair $G = (A, R)$ is a *directed graph* (or *graph* for short) if $A$ is a set and $R$ is a relation on $A$. The elements of $A$ are called *nodes* (or *vertices*) of $G$ and the elements of $R$ *edges* (or *arcs*) of $G$. An edge $(a, b)$ is said to *leave* node $a$ and to *enter* node $b$. If $(a, b)$ is an edge, node $a$ is called a *predecessor* of node $b$, and node $b$ a *successor* of node $a$. In the figures in this book we usually represent an edge $(a, b)$ by an arrow that goes from $a$ to $b$ (see Figure 1.1).

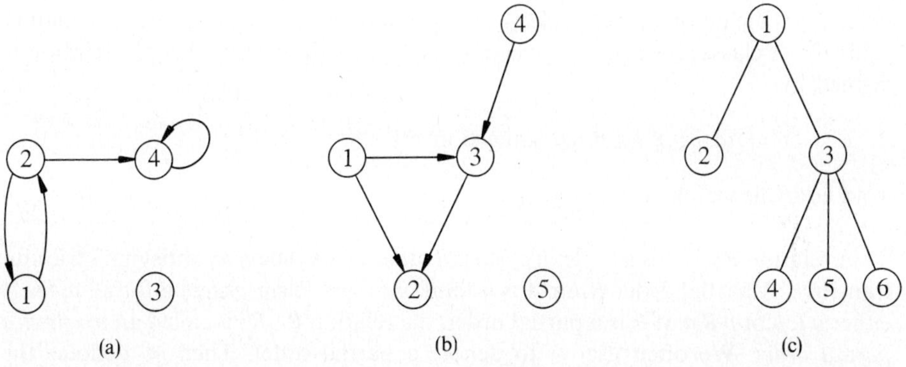

(a)                                        (b)                                        (c)

**Figure 1.1** Examples of graphs. **(a)** A cyclic directed graph $(\{1, 2, 3, 4\}, \{(1, 2), (2, 1), (2, 4), (4, 4)\})$. **(b)** An acyclic directed graph $(\{1, 2, 3, 4, 5\}, \{(1, 2), (1, 3), (3, 2), (4, 3)\})$. **(c)** A tree $(\{1, 2, 3, 4, 5; 6\}, \{(1, 2), (1, 3), (3, 4), (3, 5), (3, 6)\})$

A sequence of nodes $(a_0, a_1, \ldots, a_n)$, $n \geq 0$, is a *path of length n from $a_0$ to $a_n$* in a graph $G$ if for all $i = 0, \ldots, n-1$ $(a_i, a_{i+1})$ is an edge of $G$.

**Fact 1.4** The following statements hold for all $n \geq 0$ and nodes $a$, $b$ of a graph $G = (A, R)$:

(1) $a R^n b$ if and only if there is a path of length $n$ from $a$ to $b$ in $G$.
(2) $a R^* b$ if and only if there is a path from $a$ to $b$ in $G$.
(3) $a R^+ b$ if and only if there is a path of positive length from $a$ to $b$ in $G$.    $\square$

Let $G = (A, R)$ be a graph. The graph $(A, R^+)$ is called the *transitive closure* of $G$ and is denoted by $G^+$, and the graph $(A, R^*)$ is called the *reflexive transitive closure* of $G$ and is denoted by $G^*$. A *subgraph* of $G$ is any graph $(A', R')$ where $A' \subseteq A$ and $R' = (A' \times A') \cap R$.

A *cycle* is a path of positive length from a node to itself. A graph is said to be *cyclic* if it contains a cycle, otherwise it is *acyclic*.

An acyclic graph is a *tree* if there is a node $r$, called the *root*, such that for any other node $a$ there is exactly one path from $r$ to $a$. If $(a, b)$ is an edge of a tree, $a$ is called the *father* of $b$, and $b$ a *son* of $a$. If there is a path of positive length from node $a$ to node $b$, we say that $a$ is an *ancestor* of $b$, and $b$ is a *descendant* of $a$. A node having no sons is called a *leaf*. A *subtree* of a tree $(A, R)$ is any tree $(A', R')$ which is a subgraph of $(A, R)$ and in which no node is an ancestor of any node in $A \setminus A'$. In the figures, we usually represent a tree so that the root is at the top and the leaves at the bottom. Sons are connected to their fathers by plain lines (without arrowheads: see Figure 1.1c).

A relation $R$ on a set $A$ is an *equivalence* if it is reflexive, symmetric and transitive. The image $R(a)$ of a singleton set $\{a\}$ under an equivalence $R$ on $A$ is called the *equivalence class of $a$ under $R$* and is denoted by $[a]_R$. (We may drop the subscript $R$ and write $[a]$ if there is no ambiguity.)

**Fact 1.5** For any equivalence $R$ on a set $A$, the set $\{[a]_R | a \in A\}$ is a *partition* of $A$, that is, $A$ is the union of the sets $[a]_R$, $a \in A$, and the intersection of any two distinct equivalence classes is empty. Conversely, if $\mathbb{P}$ is a partition of a set $A$, the relation $R$ defined by

$$R = \{(a, b) | a, b \in B \text{ for some } B \text{ in } \mathbb{P}\}$$

is an equivalence on $A$ with $\{[a]_R | a \in A\} = \mathbb{P}$.    $\square$

A relation $R$ on $A$ is a *(reflexive) partial order* if it is reflexive, antisymmetric and transitive. A partial order $R$ on $A$ is a *total order* (or *linear order*) if for all $a, b \in A$ either $a R b$ or $b R a$. If $R$ is a partial order, the relation $R \setminus R^0$ is called an *irreflexive partial order*. We often use $\leqslant$ to denote a partial order. Then $<$ denotes the corresponding irreflexive partial order $\leqslant \setminus \leqslant^0$. Thus $a < b$ if and only if $a \leqslant b$ and $a \neq b$. Furthermore, we may denote $\leqslant^{-1}$ by $\geqslant$ and $<^{-1}$ by $>$.

If $\leqslant$ is a partial order on a set $A$, the pair $(A, \leqslant)$ is called a *partially ordered set*. If $\leqslant$ is a total order, $(A, \leqslant)$ is a *totally ordered set*.

An element $a \in A$ is *maximal* with respect to a partial order $\leqslant$ on $A$ if $a < b$ is false for all $b \in A$, and *minimal* if $b < a$ is false for all $b \in A$. If $\leqslant$ is a total order, $A$ can have at most one maximal element and at most one minimal element. When these exist, we call them the *maximum* and *minimum* of $A$ with respect to $\leqslant$ and denote them by $\max_{\leqslant} A$ and $\min_{\leqslant} A$ (or $\max A$ and $\min A$ for short).

A relation $f$ from a set $A$ to a set $B$ is a *partial function* (or *partial mapping*) if for all $a \in A$, $f(a)$ contains at most one element. If in addition $f$ is *defined* for all $a \in A$, i.e., if $f(a)$ is nonempty for all $a \in A$, then $f$ is called a *(total) function* (or *mapping*).

If $f$ is a partial function and $f(a) = \{b\}$ then we write $f(a) = b$.

Let $f$ be a function from $A$ to $B$ and $A'$ a subset of $A$. The *restriction of $f$ to $A'$* is the function $f'$ from $A'$ to $B$ that agrees with $f$ on $A'$, i.e., $f'(a) = f(a)$ for all $a \in A'$. The restriction $f'$ is sometimes denoted by $f|A'$.

A function $f$ from $A$ to $B$ is an *injection* (or *one-to-one*) if its inverse $f^{-1}$ is a partial function from $B$ to $A$, or, equivalently, if $f(a) = f(b)$ always implies $a = b$. $f$ is a *surjection* (or *onto*) if $f(A) = B$. A function that is both an injection and a surjection is called a *bijection*.

**Fact 1.6** The following statements hold for all sets $A$, $B$ and $C$:

(1) $\mathrm{id}_A$ is a bijection from $A$ to $A$.

(2) If $f$ is a bijection from $A$ to $B$, then $f^{-1}$ is a bijection from $B$ to $A$.

(3) If $f$ is a bijection from $A$ to $B$ and $g$ is a bijection from $B$ to $C$, then $fg$ is a bijection from $A$ to $C$.   $\square$

Let $\mathbb{U}$ be a collection of sets. ($\mathbb{U}$, the "universe", is assumed to contain all sets under discussion.) We say that a set $A$ in $\mathbb{U}$ is *isomorphic with* a set $B$ in $\mathbb{U}$, written $A \cong B$, if there is a bijection from $A$ to $B$.

Fact 1.6 immediately implies

**Fact 1.7** The set isomorphism $\cong$ is an equivalence relation on $\mathbb{U}$.   $\square$

The equivalence classes under set isomorphism are called *cardinal numbers*. A cardinal number $[A]_\cong$ is denoted by $|A|$ and is called the *size* (or *cardinality*) of set $A$.

A set is *finite* if it has the same size as the set $\{1, 2, \ldots, n\}$ for some natural number $n$. (We take $\{1, 2, \ldots, n\}$ to mean the empty set $\varnothing$ if $n = 0$.) A set is *infinite* if it is not finite.

Since $|\{1, 2, \ldots, m\}| = |\{1, 2, \ldots, n\}|$ if and only if $m = n$, we can denote $|\{1, 2, \ldots, n\}|$ by $n$. Thus the size of a finite set is the number of elements in the set.

We say that a set $A$ is *countable* (or *denumerable*) if it has the same size as some subset of $\mathbb{N}$, the set of all natural numbers. A set is *uncountable* (or *nondenumerable*) if it is not countable. A countable infinite set is called *countably infinite*.

**Proposition 1.8** *Any countably infinite set is of size $|\mathbb{N}|$.*   $\square$

If a set is countable, we can enumerate its elements and write $\{a_0, a_1, \ldots\}$; if it is finite, we can write it as $\{a_0, a_1, \ldots, a_n\}$ for some $n$.

**Lemma 1.9** Let $\{A_n \mid n = 0, 1, \ldots\}$ *be a collection of pairwise disjoint finite sets. Then the set*

$$\bigcup_{n=0}^{\infty} A_n$$

*is countable.*   □

If $A$ and $B$ are sets, we define

$$A^B = \{f \mid f \text{ is a function from } B \text{ to } A\} \ .$$

The elements in $A^\mathbb{N}$ are called *infinite strings* (or *sequences*) *over* $A$ (or *of* elements in $A$). If $f \in A^\mathbb{N}$ and $f(i) = a_i$, $i = 0, 1, \ldots$, we write

$$f = (a_0, a_1, \ldots) \ .$$

We now show that $\{0, 1\}^\mathbb{N}$, the set of all infinite strings over $\{0, 1\}$, is uncountable. We use a method of proof known as *Cantor's Diagonal Argument*. This involves assuming that the set is countable and deriving a contradiction. So, assuming that $\{0, 1\}^\mathbb{N}$ is countable, we can write

$$\{0, 1\}^\mathbb{N} = \{f_0, f_1, \ldots\}$$

for some infinite strings $f_i$ over $\{0, 1\}$, $i \in \mathbb{N}$. Each $f_i$ can be written as

$$f_i = (a_{i0}, a_{i1}, \ldots) \ ,$$

where $a_{ij} \in \{0, 1\}$ for all $j \in \mathbb{N}$. Using the "diagonal elements" $a_{ii}$, $i \in \mathbb{N}$, we can then construct $f$, another infinite string over $\{0, 1\}$:

$$f = (b_0, b_1, \ldots) \ ,$$

where the elements $b_i$ are defined by

$$b_i = \begin{cases} 0, \text{ if } a_{ii} = 1 \ ; \\ 1, \text{ if } a_{ii} = 0 \ ; \end{cases}$$

Now $f$ is not equal to $f_i$ for any $i \in \mathbb{N}$, because

$$f(i) = b_i \neq a_{ii} = f_i(i) \ .$$

Thus $f$ is not in the set $\{f_0, f_1, \ldots\}$, which is a contradiction.
We therefore have

**Theorem 1.10** $\{0, 1\}^\mathbb{N},$ *the set of all infinite strings over* $\{0, 1\}$, *is uncountable.*   □

## 1.2 Languages

A language whose sentences are written using letters from an alphabet $V$ is defined mathematically as a subset of an algebraic structure called the "free monoid generated by $V$". In what follows we shall define this structure and other algebraic concepts needed in the formal treatment of languages.

A pair $(M, \cdot)$ is a *semigroup* if $M$ is a set and $\cdot$ is an associative binary operation on $M$. That is, $\cdot$ is a function from $M \times M$ to $M$ that satisfies

$$x \cdot (y \cdot z) = (x \cdot y) \cdot z$$

for all $x, y, z \in M$. Here we have used the infix notation $x \cdot y$ for the image $\cdot(x, y)$. If no ambiguity arises, we may even abbreviate this to $xy$.

An element $e \in M$ is an *identity* of a semigroup $(M, \cdot)$ if for all $x \in M$

$$ex = xe = x \ .$$

**Lemma 1.11** *A semigroup has at most one identity.*   $\square$

A triple $(M, \cdot, e)$ is a *monoid* (or *semigroup with identity*) if $(M, \cdot)$ is a semigroup and $e$ its identity. If no ambiguity arises, we may denote a semigroup $(M, \cdot)$ or a monoid $(M, \cdot, e)$ simply by $M$.

**Fact 1.12** Let $A$ be a set and let $\cdot$ be the multiplication of relations on $A$. Then $(2^{A \times A}, \cdot, \mathrm{id}_A)$ is a monoid. (Here $2^{A \times A}$ denotes the set of all subsets of $A \times A$, i.e., the set of all relations on $A$.)   $\square$

Let $M$ be a monoid, $x$ an element of $M$ and $n$ a natural number. The $n^{\mathrm{th}}$ *power of* $x$, denoted by $x^n$, is defined inductively by
(1)  $x^0 = e$;
(2)  $x^n = xx^{n-1}$, for $n > 0$.
Let $A$ and $B$ be subsets of a monoid $(M, \cdot, e)$. The operation $\cdot$ induces in a natural way a binary operation $\cdot$ on $2^M$, the set of all subsets of $M$. This binary operation is defined by

$$A \cdot B = \{x \cdot y \mid x \in A \text{ and } y \in B\}$$

for all subsets $A$ and $B$ of $M$.

**Fact 1.13** Let $(M, \cdot, e)$ be a monoid. Then $(2^M, \cdot, \{e\})$, where $\cdot$ is the induced operation, is also a monoid.   $\square$

The monoid $(2^M, \cdot, \{e\})$ is called the monoid *induced by* $(M, \cdot, e)$ *on* $2^M$.

If $A$ is a subset of $M$ and $x$ is an element of $M$, we may write (in the induced monoid) $xA$ in place of $\{x\}A$ and $Ax$ in place of $A\{x\}$.

A subset $A$ of a monoid $M$ is *closed* if for all natural numbers $n$

$$x_1, \ldots, x_n \in A \text{ always implies } x_1 \ldots x_n \in A \ .$$

We take $x_1 \ldots x_n$ to mean the identity $e$ if $n = 0$. $A$ is *positively closed* if the above implication is true for all positive $n$.

**Fact 1.14** Let $A$ be a subset of a monoid. Then
(1)  $A$ is positively closed if and only if $x, y \in A$ always implies $xy \in A$.

(2) $A$ is closed if and only if $A$ is positively closed and contains the identity $e$.  $\square$

**Fact 1.15** Let $A$ be a closed subset of a monoid $(M, \cdot, e)$. Then $(A, \cdot, e)$, where $\cdot$ is the restriction of the operation of $M$ to $A \times A$, is also a monoid.  $\square$

Such a monoid $(A, \cdot, e)$ is called a *submonoid* of $(M, \cdot, e)$.

Let $A$ be any subset of a monoid $(M, \cdot, e)$. The *positive closure* of $A$, denoted by $A^+$, is defined by

$$A^+ = \bigcup_{n=1}^{\infty} A^n \ .$$

The *closure* of $A$, denoted by $A^*$, is defined by

$$A^* = \bigcup_{n=0}^{\infty} A^n \ .$$

Here $A^n$ means the $n^{th}$ power of $A$ in the induced monoid $(2^M, \cdot, \{e\})$. We have

$$A^* = A^0 \cup A^+ = \{e\} \cup A^+ \ .$$

**Lemma 1.16** *Let $A$ be a subset of a monoid $M$. Then $A^+$ is the smallest positively closed subset of $M$ that includes $A$, and $A^*$ is the smallest closed subset of $M$ that includes $A$. In other words, the following statements hold:*

(1) $A^+$ *is positively closed and* $A \subseteq A^+$.
(2) $A^+ \subseteq B$ *whenever $B$ is a positively closed subset of $M$ such that* $A \subseteq B$.
(3) $A^*$ *is closed and* $A \subseteq A^*$.
(4) $A^* \subseteq B$ *whenever $B$ is a closed subset of $M$ such that* $A \subseteq B$.  $\square$

Note the analogy between Lemmas 1.3 and 1.16.

A subset $B$ of a monoid $M$ *generates* (or *spans*) $M$ if $B^* = M$. $B$ is then called a *basis* (or *generator*) of $M$.

If $B$ generates $M$ then, by definition, any $x \in M$ has a representation as a product $x_1 \ldots x_n$ of elements $x_1, \ldots, x_n$ of $B$ for some $n \geq 0$. We say that $B$ generates $M$ *freely* if this representation is always unique, i.e., for all $x \in M$ there is exactly one natural number $n$ and exactly one sequence of elements $x_1, \ldots, x_n$ of $B$ such that $x = x_1 \ldots x_n$. $M$ is called a *free monoid* if it contains a subset $B$ which freely generates it.

**Lemma 1.17** *Let $M$ be a free monoid. Then $M$ has left and right cancellation, i.e., for all $x, y, z \in M$*

(1) $zx = zy$ *implies* $x = y$.
(2) $xz = yz$ *implies* $x = y$.  $\square$

Let $V$ be a set and $n$ a natural number. The elements of $V^{\{1,\ldots,n\}}$, i.e., the functions from $\{1,\ldots,n\}$ to $V$, are called *strings* (or *sequences*) *of length n over V* (or *of* elements in $V$). If $x$ is a string of length $n$ over $V$ and $x(i)=a_i$, $i=1,\ldots,n$, we write $x=(a_1,\ldots,a_n)$. We recall that $\{1,\ldots,n\}$ means the empty set $\varnothing$ when $n=0$. Because $V^{\varnothing}=\{\varnothing\}$, the empty set $\varnothing$ is the only string of length 0 over $V$. We call this string the *empty string* and denote it by $\varepsilon$.

The elements in the set

$$\text{Strings}(V)=\bigcup_{n=0}^{\infty} V^{\{1,\ldots,n\}}$$

are called (*finite*) *strings* (or *sequences*) *over V* (or *of* elements in $V$).

We define a binary operation, called *string concatenation*, on $\text{Strings}(V)$ as follows. If $x=(a_1,\ldots,a_m)$ is a string of length $m$ over $V$ and $y=(b_1,\ldots,b_n)$ is a string of length $n$ over $V$, let

$$x \cdot y = (a_1,\ldots,a_m, b_1,\ldots,b_n)\ .$$

That is, $x \cdot y$ is the string of length $m+n$ over $V$ with

$$(x \cdot y)(i)=\begin{cases} a_i, & \text{for } 1\leqslant i\leqslant m\ ; \\ b_{i-m}, & \text{for } m+1\leqslant i\leqslant m+n\ . \end{cases}$$

**Fact 1.18** For any set $V$, $(\text{Strings}(V), \cdot, \varepsilon)$ is a monoid, where $\cdot$ denotes string concatenation. $\square$

The following lemma says that $(\text{Strings}(V), \cdot, \varepsilon)$ is a free monoid generated by $V^{\{1\}}$, the set of all strings of length 1 over $V$.

**Lemma 1.19** *Let $V$ be a set and $n$ a natural number. Then the following statements hold*:

(1) $(V^{\{1\}})^n = V^{\{1,\ldots,n\}}$.
(2) $(V^{\{1\}})^+ = \text{Strings}(V)\setminus\{\varepsilon\}$.
(3) $(V^{\{1\}})^* = \text{Strings}(V)$.
(4) *The generation of $\text{Strings}(V)$ by $V^{\{1\}}$ is free.* $\square$

The function $g$ from $V$ to $V^{\{1\}}$ defined by

$$g(a)=(a), \quad a\in V\ ,$$

is a bijection. Thus we may identify $(a)$, a string of length 1 over $V$, with its only element $a$. This means that we can regard the sets $V^{\{1\}}$ and $V$ as identical. Lemma 1.19 then implies

**Theorem 1.20** *Any set can be embedded as a basis into a free monoid.* $\square$

Note that if nondeterminism is allowed the properties "halts correctly", "halts incorrectly", and "loops forever" are not mutually exclusive. Even if a program halts correctly on $w$ it may also halt incorrectly on $w$ and loop forever on $w$. Similarly, a program may produce several outputs for a given string $w$.

A RAM program $M$ that is deterministic and halts correctly on all inputs can be viewed as a *transformation* in that it defines a total function $f_M$ from the set of all input strings to the set of all output strings. Given a string $w$, $f_M(w)$ is the unique output produced by $M$ for $w$. The function $f_M$ is called the *function defined* (or *computed*) *by M*. We also say that $M$ *transforms* string $w$ *into* string $f_M(w)$ or that $M$ *constructs* (or *computes*) $f_M(w)$ *from w*.

A Pascal compiler for a RAM is an example of a transformation that transforms any syntactically correct Pascal program into an equivalent RAM program, and any syntactically incorrect program into a list of error messages.

A function $f$ is *recursive* (or *computable*) if it is the function defined by some transformation, i.e., if $f = f_M$ for some transformation $M$.

Any RAM program can be viewed as a *language recognizer*. We say that a RAM program $M$ *accepts* a string $w$ if it produces output 1 for $w$, i.e., $M$ has a correctly terminated computation on $w$ in which the final configuration is of the form $(i, M, F_{in}, (1))$. Such a computation is called an *accepting computation* of $M$. The *language accepted* (or *recognized*) *by M*, denoted by $L(M)$, consists of the strings accepted by $M$. In other words,

$$L(M) = \{w \mid M \text{ produces output 1 for } w\} \ .$$

Again, note that, since $M$ can be nondeterministic, there may exist computations on some sentence $w$ in $L(M)$ that do not lead to acceptance of $w$. Thus for some string $w$ all the following can be true simultaneously: (1) $M$ accepts $w$; (2) $M$ produces output $w' \neq 1$ for $w$; (3) $M$ halts incorrectly on $w$; and (4) $M$ loops forever on $w$.

A language $L_1$ is *recursively enumerable* if it is the language accepted by some RAM program $M$. A language is *recursive* if it is the language accepted by some deterministic RAM program that halts correctly on all inputs.

Henceforth, rather than using explicit RAM instructions, we shall express our algorithms using self-explaining high-level programming language constructs together with prose. The reader should find it easy to convince him- or herself that these algorithms can be translated into effective RAM programs. We will also feel free to apply to our algorithms any concepts defined in this and in the following sections for RAM programs.

## 1.4 Decision Problems

In this book we shall present several algorithms that solve some "decision problem" in parsing theory. Informally, a decision problem is a yes-or-no question such as

$P_{pal}$: "Is string $w$ a palindrome?"

A *palindrome* is a string $w$ that is the same whether it is written forwards or backwards, i.e., for which $w^R = w$. An algorithm that solves this decision problem takes as its input any string $w$ (over some fixed alphabet $V$) and produces output "yes" if and only if $w$ is a palindrome.

Formally, a *decision problem P over* alphabet $V$ is any partial function from $V^*$ to $\{0, 1\}$. Any element in the set $P^{-1}(\{0, 1\})$ is called an *instance* of $P$. An instance is a *yes-instance* if it is in $P^{-1}(1)$, and a *no-instance* otherwise. The set of yes-instances of $P$ is called the *language associated with P* and denoted by $L(P)$.

In $P_{pal}$ the set of instances comprises all strings over the underlying alphabet $V$. The set of yes-instances consists of all palindromes in $V^*$, and the set of no-instances consists of all non-palindromes in $V^*$. The decision problem here is thus a total function from $V^*$ to $\{0, 1\}$. This is not the case in general, however.

The *complement* of a decision problem $P$ over $V$, denoted by $\bar{P}$, is the decision problem over $V$ that has exactly the same instances as $P$ but in which the set of yes-instances is precisely the set of no-instances of $P$ and vice versa. More formally,

$$L(\bar{P}) = P^{-1}(\{0, 1\}) \setminus L(P) \ .$$

A *partial solution* to a decision problem $P$ over $V$ is any recognizer for the associated language $L(P)$, i.e., any RAM program $M$ for which $L(M) = L(P)$. A partial solution to $P$ is a *(total) solution* if it is deterministic and halts correctly on all inputs. A decision problem is *partially solvable* (or *partially decidable*) if it has a partial solution, and *(totally) solvable* (or *decidable*) if it has a total solution. A decision problem is *unsolvable* (or *undecidable*) if it is not solvable.

Clearly $P_{pal}$ is solvable. The decision problem

$$P_{Pascal}: \text{``Is string } w \text{ a syntactically correct Pascal program?''}$$

is also solvable. Any Pascal compiler can be taken as a solution to this problem if we ignore code generation and consider only the syntax checking part.

The following lemma says that the question of solvability is nontrivial only when the set of instances is infinite.

**Lemma 1.25** *Any decision problem that has only a finite number of instances is solvable.*

*Proof.* If $\{w_1, \ldots, w_n\}$ is the set of instances of the decision problem $P$ in question, let $b_i$ denote the value **true** if $P(w_i) = 1$ and the value **false** if $P(w_i) = 0$, for $i = 1, \ldots, n$. Then the following procedure $M$ provides a solution for $P$:

```
boolean procedure M (string w);
if w = w₁ then return b₁ else
if w = w₂ then return b₂ else
    ⋮
if w = wₙ then return bₙ else return false  .
```

We assume here that the string $w$, initially located in the input file, is read and then passed as a parameter to the procedure $M$. If $M$ returns **true**, this is interpreted as writing 1 into the output file, and if $M$ returns **false**, this is interpreted as writing 0 into the output file.    □

Note, however, that we have only proved the *existence* of a solution. The solution cannot be *constructed* because there are decision problems for which we do not know whether or not $P(w) = 1$ for a given instance $w$ (cf. Exercise 1.40).

For any alphabet $V$, the number of distinct functions $P$ from $V^*$ to $\{0, 1\}$ is uncountable. (This follows from Proposition 1.8, Theorem 1.10, Fact 1.23 and Exercise 1.11.) On the other hand, the set of distinct Pascal programs is countable (see Exercise 1.12). This means that there are not enough potential partial solutions to cover all possible decision problems. Thus we have

**Lemma 1.26** *For any alphabet $V$, there are decision problems over $V$ that are not partially solvable.*    □

Consider now the decision problem

$$P_{\text{halt}}: \text{``Does procedure } M \text{ halt correctly on input } w?\text{''}$$

This problem (when stated for Turing machines) is known in the literature as the *halting problem*. The set of instances consists of all strings (over, say, the ASCII alphabet) of the form $M \# w$, where $M$ is a syntactically correct procedure and $w$ is any string over the alphabet.

$P_{\text{halt}}$ turns out to be partially solvable but not totally solvable. The following procedure $M_{\text{halt}}$ provides a partial solution for $P_{\text{halt}}$:

```
boolean procedure M_halt (procedure M, string w);
begin
      M(w);
      return true
end.
```

We assume here that the programming language compiler is used to translate the string $M \# w$, initially located in the input file, into "procedure $M$" and "string $w$", which are then passed as parameters to $M_{\text{halt}}$. Now $M_{\text{halt}}$ is a partial solution to $P_{\text{halt}}$ because it returns **true** on input $(M, w)$ if and only if $M$ halts correctly on input $w$. Although $M_{\text{halt}}$ is deterministic, it is not a total solution to $P_{\text{halt}}$ because it halts incorrectly on input $(M, w)$ whenever (and only when) $M$ halts incorrectly on input $w$, and loops forever on input $(M, w)$ whenever (and only when) $M$ loops forever on input $w$.

To prove that $P_{\text{halt}}$ is unsolvable we consider a restriction of $P_{\text{halt}}$, denoted by $P'_{\text{halt}}$:

$$P'_{\text{halt}}: \text{``Does procedure } M \text{ halt correctly on } M', \text{ another procedure?''}$$

The set of instances of $P'_{\text{halt}}$ is a subset of the set of instances of $P_{\text{halt}}$. Only those strings $M \# w$ in which both $M$ and $w$ are syntactically correct procedures are instances of $P'_{\text{halt}}$. Clearly, if $P'_{\text{halt}}$ is unsolvable then so is $P_{\text{halt}}$.

We use a technique very similar in spirit to Cantor's Diagonal Argument, which we used to prove the uncountability of $\{0, 1\}^{\mathbb{N}}$ in Section 1.1. We assume for the sake of contradiction that $P'_{\text{halt}}$ is solvable. Then $P'_{\text{halt}}$ has a solution $M'_{\text{halt}}$, a deterministic program that halts correctly on all inputs and produces output 1 for input $M \# M'$ if and only if $M$ halts correctly on input $M'$. We can assume that $M'_{\text{halt}}$ is a procedure that takes two parameters, procedures $M$ and $M'$, and returns **true** if $M$ halts correctly on input $M'$ and **false** otherwise. But then we could write procedure $\hat{M}$:

> **procedure** $\hat{M}$ (**procedure** $M$);
> **if** $M'_{\text{halt}}(M, M)$ **then**
> **loop forever.**

Now since $M'_{\text{halt}}$ halts correctly on all inputs, $\hat{M}$ halts correctly on input $M$ when $M'_{\text{halt}}$ returns **false** on input $(M,\ M)$, and loops forever on $M$ when $M'_{\text{halt}}$ returns **true** on input $(M,\ M)$. But since $M'_{\text{halt}}$ was assumed to return **false** on input $(M, M')$ if and only if $M$ does not halt correctly on input $M'$, we conclude that for all $M$, $\hat{M}$ halts correctly on input $M$ if and only if $M$ does not halt correctly on input $M$. This, however, cannot be true for $M = \hat{M}$. Thus we must conclude that no procedure $M'_{\text{halt}}$ can exist, and so $P'_{\text{halt}}$ is unsolvable.

We summarize the above discussion in the following theorem.

**Theorem 1.27** *There exist partially solvable decision problems that are not totally solvable.* $\square$

Finally, consider the following version of the halting problem.

$P_{\text{exhalt}}$: "Does procedure $M$ halt correctly on some input?"

As in the case of $P_{\text{halt}}$, this decision problem is partially but not totally solvable. It is easily seen to have a nondeterministic partial solution, $M_{\text{exhalt}}$:

> **boolean procedure** $M_{\text{exhalt}}$ (**procedure** $M$);
> **begin string** $w$;
>     **guess** $w$;
>     $M(w)$;
>     **return true**
> **end**.

As it is considerably harder to show that $P_{\text{exhalt}}$ has a deterministic partial solution, this demonstrates the convenience of allowing nondeterministic programs. The following proposition guarantees that the restriction to deterministic programs does not reduce the class of partially solvable decision problems.

**Proposition 1.28** *Any partially solvable decision problem has a deterministic partial solution.* $\square$

Let $P_1$ and $P_2$ be decision problems. A deterministic RAM program $M$ that halts correctly on all inputs is a *reduction of $P_1$ to $P_2$* if it takes as input any instance of $P_1$ and transforms all yes-instances of $P_1$ into yes-instances of $P_2$ and all no-instances of $P_1$ into no-instances of $P_2$. If there exists a reduction of decision problem $P_1$ to decision problem $P_2$, we say that $P_1$ *reduces* (or *is reducible*) *to* $P_2$ and write $P_1 \leqslant P_2$.

**Fact 1.29** Given a decision problem $P$, any restriction $P'$ of $P$ reduces to $P$.

*Proof.* A program that simply copies the contents of the input file into the output file is a reduction of $P'$ to $P$.   $\square$

It follows that $P'_{\text{halt}}$ reduces to $P_{\text{halt}}$. As another example, consider the decision problem

$$P_{\text{accept}}: \text{``Does boolean procedure } M \text{ return \textbf{true} on input } w\text{?''}$$

In order to see that $P_{\text{halt}}$ reduces to $P_{\text{accept}}$, we note that there is a program $T$ that takes as input any instance $(M, w)$ of $P_{\text{halt}}$ and transforms it into an instance $f_T(M, w)$ of $P_{\text{accept}}$ defined by

$$f_T(M, w) =$$
**(boolean procedure $M'$(string $w$); begin $M(w)$; return true end**, $w$).

Now $M'$ returns **true** if and only if $M$ halts correctly on input $w$. This means that $(M, w)$ is a yes-instance of $P_{\text{halt}}$ if and only if $f_T(M, w)$ is a yes-instance of $P_{\text{accept}}$. So $P_{\text{halt}}$ reduces to $P_{\text{accept}}$. In fact the converse is also true, i.e., $P_{\text{accept}}$ reduces to $P_{\text{halt}}$ (Exercise 1.44).

**Lemma 1.30** *Let $P_1$ and $P_2$ be decision problems such that $P_1$ reduces to $P_2$. Then the following statements hold:*

(1) *If $P_2$ is solvable, then so is $P_1$.*
(2) *If $P_2$ is partially solvable, then so is $P_1$.*
(3) *If $P_1$ is unsolvable, then so is $P_2$.*
(4) *If $P_1$ is not partially solvable, then neither is $P_2$.*

*Proof.* First we note that statements (3) and (4) are merely restatements of (1) and (2). Statements (1) and (2) in turn follow from the observation that, if $M$ is a reduction of $P_1$ to $P_2$ and $M_2$ is a (partial) solution to $P_2$, then the procedure

```
boolean procedure M₁ (string w);
begin
      return M₂(M(w))
end
```

is a (partial) solution to $P_1$.   $\square$

## 1.5 Computational Complexity

In order to compare the efficiency of our algorithms, we need some measure of the computational resources needed by a RAM program in processing a given input. The resources we consider are the computation time and memory space used by the program. This leads us to the notion of "computational complexity" and, more specifically, to the notions of "time complexity" and "space complexity". The time complexity of a RAM program is a function on natural numbers that gives, for argument $n$, the maximum time needed to process an input of size $n$; similarly, the space complexity is a function that gives for argument $n$ the maximum memory space needed to process an input of size $n$.

When evaluating the time complexity of RAM programs, we need to know the number of time units the RAM is supposed to spend when executing a single instruction. There are two generally accepted criteria for evaluating the "computational cost" of RAM instructions. According to the *uniform cost criterion*, any RAM instruction is assumed to take one unit of time, no matter what the nature of the instruction is or what its arguments are. The time complexity of a RAM program is then simply the number of instructions executed.

A more realistic complexity measure is obtained using the *logarithmic cost criterion*, which takes into account the size of the arguments in the instruction. A cost

$$(\lfloor \log a \rfloor + 1) + (\lfloor \log \max\{1, |v|\} \rfloor + 1)$$

is charged every time a value $v$ is stored in or retrieved from a memory location $a$. Note that this cost is the number of bits needed to represent the value $v$ and the address of memory location $a$. The total logarithmic cost of an instruction is obtained by summing the costs of all store and retrieve operations performed by the instruction. For example, the logarithmic cost of the arithmetic instruction **add** $a, b, c$ is the sum of the costs of retrieving the contents of memory locations $a$ and $b$ and of storing the result in memory location $c$. The logarithmic cost of the nondeterministic instruction **guess** $a$ is the cost of storing the guessed value $v$ in memory location $a$.

Similar cost criteria are used to evaluate the space complexity of RAM programs. According to the uniform cost criterion, any integer stored in the memory is assumed to require one unit of space, whereas the logarithmic cost of storing integer $n$ is $\lfloor \log \max\{1, |n|\} \rfloor + 1$.

Let $\mathbb{C} = (C_0, \ldots, C_n)$ be a computation of a RAM. The *uniform cost time complexity* of $\mathbb{C}$ is $n$, and the *logarithmic cost time complexity* of $\mathbb{C}$ is $t_0 + \ldots + t_{n-1}$, where $t_i$ is the logarithmic cost of the instruction pointed to by the instruction pointer in configuration $C_i$, $i = 0, \ldots, n-1$. The *uniform cost workspace complexity* of $\mathbb{C}$ is $\max\{|C_0|, \ldots, |C_n|\}$, where $|C_i|$ is the number of used memory locations in $C_i$, i.e., the length of that portion of the memory which extends from location 1 up to the last location referenced by instructions executed in the preceding configurations $C_0, \ldots, C_{i-1}$, $i = 0, \ldots, n-1$. The *logarithmic cost workspace* complexity of $\mathbb{C}$ is $\max\{\|C_0\|, \ldots, \|C_n\|\}$, where $\|C_i\|$ is the sum of the logarithmic costs of the integers stored in the used portion of the memory in $C_i$. The *uniform cost space complexity* of $\mathbb{C}$ is obtained by adding to the uniform cost workspace complexity the length of the input file in $C_0$ and the length of the output file in $C_n$. The *logarithmic cost space complexity* of $\mathbb{C}$ is obtained by adding to the logarithmic cost workspace complexity the logarithmic costs of the integers in the input file in $C_0$ and in the output file in $C_n$.

Let $M$ be a transformation (i.e., a deterministic RAM program that halts correctly on all inputs). Further let $w$ be a string and $\mathbb{C}$ the terminated computation of $M$ on $w$. We say that $M$ *transforms* string $w$ *into* string $f_M(w)$ (or that $M$ *constructs* or *computes* $f_M(w)$ *from* $w$) (1) *in time* $t$ if the time complexity of $\mathbb{C}$ is at most $t$, (2) *in space* $s$ if the space complexity of $\mathbb{C}$ is at most $s$, and (3) *in workspace* $s$ if the workspace complexity of $\mathbb{C}$ is at most $s$. If we wish to emphasize the cost criterion, we may add the attribute "uniform cost" or "logarithmic cost" and say that $M$ transforms $w$ into $f_M(w)$ "in uniform cost time $t$", "in logarithmic cost time $t$", "in uniform cost space $s$", etc. This also applies to all similar definitions given below which do not specify the cost criterion.

Let $T$ and $S$ be functions from the set of natural numbers to the set of nonnegative real numbers. We say that a transformation $M$ is $T(n)$ *time-bounded* (or *runs in time* $T(n)$) if, for all natural numbers $n$ and strings $w$ of size $n$, $M$ transforms $w$ into $f_M(w)$ in time $T(n)$. Here the *size* of string $w$ is understood to be the length of $w$ if the uniform cost criterion is used, and the norm of $w$ if the logarithmic cost criterion is used. $M$ is $S(n)$ *(work)space-bounded* (or *runs in (work)space* $S(n)$) if, for all natural numbers $n$ and strings $w$ of size $n$, $M$ transforms $w$ into $f_M(w)$ in (work)space $S(n)$.

The *time complexity* of a transformation $M$ is the least function $T$ such that $M$ is $T(n)$ time-bounded. The *space complexity* of $M$ is the least function $S$ such that $M$ is $S(n)$ space-bounded, and the *workspace complexity* of $M$ is the least function $S$ such that $M$ is $S(n)$ workspace-bounded.

For language recognizers these concepts are defined somewhat differently because we are only interested in accepting computations. We say that a language recognizer $M$ *accepts* string $w$ *in time* $t$ (or *space* $s$ or *workspace* $s$) if $M$ has an accepting computation on $w$ of time complexity at most $t$ (or space complexity at most $s$ or workspace complexity at most $s$, respectively). $M$ accepts $w$ *simultaneously in time* $t$ *and in (work)space* $s$ if $M$ has an accepting computation on $w$ of time complexity at most $t$ and (work)space complexity at most $s$. Note that these definitions say nothing about the behaviour of $M$ in the case of non-sentences, i.e., strings in $V^* \backslash L(M)$. Also, as $M$ is allowed to be nondeterministic, it may happen that on some sentence of size $n$ there are computations whose time and space complexities are not bounded by $T(n)$ and $S(n)$.

A language recognizer $M$ is $T(n)$ *time-bounded* (or *runs in time* $T(n)$) if for all natural numbers $n$ and sentences $w$ of size $n$, $M$ accepts $w$ in time $T(n)$. $M$ is $S(n)$ *(work)space-bounded* (or *runs in (work)space* $S(n)$) if for all natural numbers $n$ and sentences $w$ of size $n$, $M$ accepts $w$ in (work)space $S(n)$. $M$ is *simultaneously* $T(n)$ *time-bounded and* $S(n)$ *(work)space-bounded* (or *runs simultaneously in time* $T(n)$ *and in (work)space* $S(n)$) if for all natural numbers $n$ and sentences $w$ of size $n$, $M$ accepts $w$ simultaneously in time $T(n)$ and in (work)space $S(n)$.

As in the case of transformations, the *time complexity* (or *space complexity* or *workspace complexity*) of a language recognizer $M$ is defined as the least function $T$

(or $S$) such that $M$ is $T(n)$ time-bounded (or $S(n)$ space-bounded or $S(n)$ workspace-bounded).

A decision problem $P$ is *solvable* (or *decidable*) *in nondeterministic time* $T(n)$ (or *space* $S(n)$ *or workspace* $S(n)$) if it has a $T(n)$ time-bounded (or $S(n)$ space-bounded or $S(n)$ workspace-bounded) partial solution. $P$ is *solvable* (or *decidable*) *in deterministic time* $T(n)$ (or *space* $S(n)$ *or workspace* $S(n)$) if it has a deterministic $T(n)$ time-bounded (or $S(n)$ space-bounded or $S(n)$ workspace-bounded) partial solution. $P$ is *solvable* (or *decidable*) *simultaneously in nondeterministic time* $T(n)$ *and* (*work*)*space* $S(n)$ if it has a simultaneously $T(n)$ time-bounded and $S(n)$ (work)space-bounded partial solution, and is *solvable* (or *decidable*) *simultaneously in deterministic time* $T(n)$ *and* (*work*)*space* $S(n)$ if it has a $T(n)$ time-bounded and $S(n)$ (work)space-bounded deterministic partial solution.

The following proposition relates these concepts to the solvability of decision problems as discussed in the previous section.

**Proposition 1.31** *Let $f$ be a recursive function on the set of natural numbers. If a decision problem is solvable in nondeterministic time $f(n)$ or in nondeterministic* (*work*)*space $f(n)$, then it is solvable.*    $\square$

Let $f$ and $g$ be functions from the set of positive integers to the set of positive reals. We say that $g(n)$ *is order* $f(n)$, written "$g(n)$ is $O(f(n))$", if there exist natural numbers $c$ and $n_0$ such that $g(n) \leqslant cf(n)$ for all $n \geqslant n_0$. Informally, $g$ does not grow much faster than $f$.

It is sufficient usually to consider only the order of the complexity of an algorithm rather than its exact complexity. Indeed, if we express our algorithms in a high-level language it is impossible to evaluate their exact complexity unless a specific implementation of the algorithm as a RAM program is given. The order of the complexity, on the other hand, may often be obtained rather easily.

**Lemma 1.32** *Let $f$ and $g$ be functions from the set of positive integers to the set of positive reals, and let $a$ and $b$ be positive reals. Then the following statements hold:*

(1)  $af(n) + b$ is $O(f(n))$.
(2)  $f(n) + g(n)$ is $O(\max\{f(n), g(n)\})$.    $\square$

The decision problem $P_{\text{pal}}$ described in the previous section is solvable in deterministic uniform cost time $O(n)$, and simultaneously in deterministic logarithmic cost time $O(n \log n)$ and (work)space $O(n)$. This can be seen as follows. Given a string $w = a_1 \ldots a_k$ over alphabet $V$, initially located in the input file, $w$ is first read and stored in successive memory locations. It is then tested for the palindrome property by comparing all pairs of symbols $a_i$ and $a_{k-i+1}$, $i = 1, \ldots, \lfloor k/2 \rfloor$. The workspace needed for this is $O(k)$ under the uniform cost criterion, and $O(k \log |V|)$ under the logarithmic cost criterion. The uniform cost time taken by the test is $O(k)$, because $k$ symbols are read and $\lfloor k/2 \rfloor$ symbol pairs are compared, each read operation and comparison requiring constant time. The logarithmic cost time is $O(k(\log k + \log |V|))$, because in each of the $k$ read

long as the complexities under the two criteria do not differ "essentially" from one another. In establishing reductions between decision problems and in deriving lower bounds for problem complexity, it is usually sufficient that a complexity which is uniform-cost polynomial remains polynomial even if the logarithmic cost criterion is used. Indeed, the algorithms given in this book all have the property that if the uniform cost complexity is $O(f(n))$, then the logarithmic cost complexity is $O(f(n(\log n)^k))$, for some constant $k \geq 0$.

## 1.6 Rewriting Systems

In this book we shall encounter various models for describing languages and their recognizers. These include context-free grammars, regular grammars, finite automata, pushdown automata and one-tape Turing machines. We shall define these models as special cases of a general model called a "rewriting system". In this way we avoid redefining for specific models those operations that are already available in the general model. The approach deviates from that generally adopted in the literature on formal language and parsing theory, but we feel that apart from the fact that it leads to concise definitions it also makes the comparison of models easier.

Formally, a *rewriting system* (or *semi-Thue system*) is a pair $G = (V, P)$, where $V$ is an alphabet and $P$ is a finite relation on the free monoid $V^*$. A pair $(\omega_1, \omega_2) \in P$ is called a *rule* (or *production*) of $G$ and denoted by $\omega_1 \to \omega_2$. The string $\omega_1$ is called the *left-hand side* and the string $\omega_2$ the *right-hand side* of the rule.

Rules are used to "rewrite" strings in $V^*$. If $\gamma$ is a string in $V^*$ that can be decomposed as $\alpha\omega_1\beta$, where $\omega_1$ is the left-hand side of some rule, then $\gamma$ can be rewritten as $\alpha\omega_2\beta$, where $\omega_2$ is the right-hand side of the rule. Formally, this means that $P$, the finite set of rules of the rewriting system, induces an infinite relation on $V^*$ in which two strings $\gamma_1$ and $\gamma_2$ are related if and only if $\gamma_1$ can be rewritten as $\gamma_2$ using some sequence or string of rules of the system. This relation on $V^*$ will be called the "derives" relation of the system. If we restrict the way in which the rewriting can be done, we get various subrelations of the "derives" relation. If in the rewriting only a single rule may be used, we have the relation "directly derives". If only a specific rule $r$ may be used, we have the relation "derives using rule $r$", and if only a specific rule string $\pi$ is allowed, we have the relation "derives using rule string $\pi$". In the following we give formal definitions of these relations.

Let $G = (V, P)$ be a rewriting system. If $r = \omega_1 \to \omega_2$ is a rule in $P$, we define a relation $\underset{G}{\overset{r}{\Longrightarrow}}$ (or $\overset{r}{\Longrightarrow}$ for short) on $V^*$ by

$$\underset{G}{\overset{r}{\Longrightarrow}} = \{(\alpha\omega_1\beta, \alpha\omega_2\beta) \mid \alpha, \beta, \in V^*\} \ .$$

If for strings $\gamma_1$ and $\gamma_2$ in $V^*$, $\gamma_1 \underset{G}{\overset{r}{\Longrightarrow}} \gamma_2$, then we say that *in $G$ $\gamma_1$ derives $\gamma_2$ using* rule $r$, and that rule $r$ *is applicable to* $\gamma_1$ (or *can be applied to* $\gamma_1$).

Let $\pi$ be a rule string of $G$, i.e., an element of the free monoid $P^*$. We define a relation $\xrightarrow[G]{\pi}$ (or $\xRightarrow{\pi}$ for short) on $V^*$ by induction on the length of $\pi$ as follows:

(1) $\xrightarrow[G]{\varepsilon} = \mathrm{id}_{V^*}$;

(2) $\xrightarrow[G]{\pi} = \xrightarrow[G]{r} \xrightarrow[G]{\pi'}$ where $\pi = r\pi'$ for some rule $r$ and rule string $\pi'$.

If for strings $\gamma_1$ and $\gamma_2$ in $V^*$, $\gamma_1 \xrightarrow[G]{\pi} \gamma_2$, then we say that *in $G$ $\gamma_1$ derives $\gamma_2$ using* rule string $\pi$, and that rule string $\pi$ *is applicable to* $\gamma_1$ (or *can be applied to* $\gamma_1$).

We denote by $\xRightarrow[G]{}$ (or $\Rightarrow$ for short) the union of all relations $\xrightarrow[G]{r}$, where $r$ is a rule of $G$. In other words,

$$\xRightarrow[G]{} = \bigcup_{r \in P} \xrightarrow[G]{r} .$$

If for strings $\gamma_1$ and $\gamma_2$ in $V^*$, $\gamma_1 \xRightarrow[G]{} \gamma_2$, then we say that $\gamma_1$ *directly derives* $\gamma_2$ *in $G$.*

If for strings $\gamma_1$ and $\gamma_2$ in $V^*$, $\gamma_1 \xRightarrow[G]{}^* \gamma_2$, then we say that $\gamma_1$ *derives* $\gamma_2$ *in $G$,* and that $\gamma_2$ is a *sentential form* of $\gamma_1$.

A string sequence $(\gamma_0, \ldots, \gamma_n)$, $n \geqslant 0$, is a *derivation of length $n$ of $\gamma_n$ from $\gamma_0$ in $G$* if it is a path of length $n$ from node $\gamma_0$ to node $\gamma_n$ in the directed graph $(V^*, \xRightarrow[G]{})$. In other words, if $n > 0$ then $\gamma_i$ directly derives $\gamma_{i+1}$ in $G$, for $i = 0, \ldots, n-1$.

**Fact 1.43** A string $\gamma_1$ derives a string $\gamma_2$ in $G$ if and only if $\gamma_2$ has a derivation from $\gamma_1$ in $G$.  $\square$

As an example, consider the rewriting system

$$G_{\mathrm{match}} = (\{S, 0, 1\} , \quad \{S \to \varepsilon, S \to 0S1\}) .$$

($G_{\mathrm{match}}$ is what will be called a context-free grammar in Chapter 4.) The following statements hold in $G_{\mathrm{match}}$, where $r_1$ denotes the rule $S \to \varepsilon$ and $r_2$ the rule $S \to 0S1$:

$$\alpha S \beta \xRightarrow{r_1} \alpha\beta \text{ for all } \alpha, \beta \in \{S, 0, 1\}^* ,$$

i.e., $\alpha S \beta$ derives $\alpha\beta$ using rule $r_1$ .

$$\alpha S \beta \xRightarrow{r_2} \alpha 0 S 1 \beta \text{ for all } \alpha, \beta \text{ in } \{S, 0, 1\}^* ,$$

i.e., $\alpha S \beta$ derives $\alpha 0 S 1 \beta$ using rule $r_2$ .

$$S \xRightarrow{r_2} 0S1 \xRightarrow{r_2} 00S11 \xRightarrow{r_1} 0011 .$$

$$S \overset{r_2}{\Rightarrow} 0S1 \overset{r_2}{\Rightarrow} 00S11 \overset{r_2}{\Rightarrow} \ldots \overset{r_2}{\Rightarrow} 0^n S 1^n \overset{r_1}{\Rightarrow} 0^n 1^n \text{ for all } n \geq 0 \ .$$

$$S \overset{r_2^n r_1}{\Rightarrow} 0^n 1^n \text{ for all } n \geq 0 \ ,$$

i.e., $S$ derives $0^n 1^n$ using rule string $r_2^n r_1$ .
$S \Rightarrow^{n+1} 0^n 1^n$ for all $n \geq 0$ .
$S \Rightarrow^* 0^n 1^n$ for all $n \geq 0$ ,
i.e., $S$ derives $0^n 1^n$ .

In fact we have

$$L(G_{\mathrm{match}}) = L_{\mathrm{match}} \ ,$$

where $L(G_{\mathrm{match}})$ and $L_{\mathrm{match}}$ denote the languages

$$L(G_{\mathrm{match}}) = \{w \in \{0, 1\}^* \mid S \Rightarrow^* w \text{ in } G_{\mathrm{match}}\} \ .$$

$$L_{\mathrm{match}} = \{0^n 1^n \mid n \geq 0\} \ .$$

We shall prove the equality of the languages $L(G_{\mathrm{match}})$ and $L_{\mathrm{match}}$ using
(*mathematical*) *induction*. We have already used induction in definitions. For
example, the $n^{th}$ power $R^n$ of a relation $R$ was defined in Section 1.1 using induction
on $n$, while we defined the relation $\underset{G}{\overset{\pi}{\Rightarrow}}$ above using induction on the length of $\pi$. As
we shall see, *proof by induction* is a major technique used to prove properties of
rewriting systems. The principle of proof by induction is stated in the following fact.

**Fact 1.44** (Principle of Proof by Induction) Let $P(n)$ be a statement that is either
true or false, depending on the natural number $n$. Assume that the following
statements are true:

(B) $P(0)$ .
(I) For all $n > 0$, the statements $P(0), \ldots, P(n-1)$ together imply $P(n)$ .

Then $P(n)$ is true identically, i.e., for all natural numbers $n$.      $\square$

A proof by induction thus consists of two parts. In the *base case* we prove that
$P(0)$ is true. In the *induction step* we prove that, for all $n > 0$, $P(n)$ is true assuming
$P(0), \ldots, P(n-1)$ are all true. The assumption that statements $P(0), \ldots, P(n-1)$
are true is called the *induction hypothesis*.
To prove the equality of $L(G_{\mathrm{match}})$ and $L_{\mathrm{match}}$ we first prove the inclusion

$$L_{\mathrm{match}} \subseteq L(G_{\mathrm{match}}) \ .$$

This inclusion holds if the statement

$$P(n): \text{“} S \Rightarrow^* 0^n S 1^n \text{”}$$

is true for all $n$, because then

$$S \Rightarrow^* 0^n S 1^n \Rightarrow 0^n 1^n \quad \text{for all } n .$$

Note that this implies

$$S \Rightarrow^* 0^n 1^n \quad \text{for all } n ,$$

which means that $L(G_{\text{match}})$ contains all strings of the form $0^n 1^n$. So it suffices to prove that $P(n)$ is true identically, which we do using induction on $n$. The base case is immediate because $P(0)$ only states that $S \Rightarrow^* S$, which is always true. In the induction step we assume that $n > 0$ and, as an induction hypothesis, that $P(0), \ldots, P(n-1)$ are true. Since $P(n-1)$ is true, we have

$$S \Rightarrow^* 0^{n-1} S 1^{n-1} .$$

Applying the rule $S \rightarrow 0S1$ we then have

$$S \Rightarrow^* 0^{n-1} S 1^{n-1} \Rightarrow 0^{n-1} 0 S 1 1^{n-1} = 0^n S 1^n .$$

In other words, $P(n)$ is true. Therefore, by Fact 1.44, $P(n)$ is true for all $n$.

Note that in this case it was not necessary to assume in the induction hypothesis that all of the statements $P(0), \ldots, P(n-1)$ are true: assuming only the truth of $P(n-1)$ would have been sufficient. Indeed, the principle of proof by induction is sometimes stated in this restricted form, i.e., with statement (I) in Fact 1.44 replaced by

$(I')$ For all $n > 0$, $P(n-1)$ implies $P(n)$ .

However, in many cases it is harder or even impossible to formulate the claim to be proved in such a way that this form of induction can be used. That is why we prefer the form given in Fact 1.44.

We now proceed to prove, again by induction, the inclusion

$$L(G_{\text{match}}) \subseteq L_{\text{match}} .$$

In this case the statement $P(n)$ takes the form

$P(n)$: "For all strings $\gamma$, $S \Rightarrow^n \gamma$ implies
$$\gamma = 0^n S 1^n \quad \text{or} \quad \gamma = 0^{n-1} 1^{n-1} " .$$

Now if $n = 0$, $S \Rightarrow^n \gamma$ implies $\gamma = S$. Since $S = 0^0 S 1^0$, we see that $P(0)$ is true, which concludes the proof of the base case. In the induction step we assume that $n > 0$ and, as an induction hypothesis, that $P(n-1)$ is true. Now if $S \Rightarrow^n \gamma$, there exist strings $\alpha$ and $\beta$ in $\{S, 0, 1\}^*$ such that either

$$(1) \quad S \Rightarrow^{n-1} \alpha S \beta \Rightarrow \alpha \beta = \gamma$$

or

$$(2) \quad S \Rightarrow^{n-1} \alpha S \beta \Rightarrow \alpha 0 S 1 \beta = \gamma .$$

This follows immediately from the definition of $\Rightarrow$ because $n>0$. What we have done is to display the final step in the derivation of $\gamma$ from $S$: there are two cases depending on which of the rules $S\to\varepsilon$ and $S\to0S1$ is applied in this step. Because $P(n-1)$ is true, we have in particular

$$S\Rightarrow^{n-1}\alpha S\beta \text{ implies } \alpha S\beta=0^{n-1}S1^{n-1} \quad\text{or}\quad \alpha S\beta=0^{n-2}1^{n-2} \ .$$

Here we have applied the induction hypothesis to the string $\alpha S\beta$. Clearly, $\alpha S\beta=0^{n-2}1^{n-2}$ is never true. Moreover, $\alpha S\beta=0^{n-1}S1^{n-1}$ implies, by Lemma 1.17, that $\alpha=0^{n-1}$ and $\beta=1^{n-1}$. So we have

$$S\Rightarrow^{n-1}\alpha S\beta \quad\text{implies}\quad \alpha=0^{n-1} \quad\text{and}\quad \beta=1^{n-1} \ .$$

By statements (1) and (2) above, we can then conclude that either

$$\gamma=\alpha\beta=0^{n-1}1^{n-1}$$

or

$$\gamma=\alpha0S1\beta=0^{n-1}0S11^{n-1}=0^nS1^n \ .$$

But this means that we have proved $P(n)$. Thus, by Fact 1.44, $P(n)$ is true for all $n$. This in turn implies immediately

$$S\Rightarrow^n\gamma\in\{0,1\}^* \quad\text{implies}\quad \gamma=0^{n-1}1^{n-1} \quad\text{for all}\quad n>0 \ .$$

In other words, the inclusion $L(G_{\text{match}})\subseteq L_{\text{match}}$ holds. This completes the proof of the equality of these languages.

Several algorithms presented in this book have as their input some rewriting system. This raises the questions of how to represent a rewriting system as a string of symbols and what is the size of this representation. Remember that, in analyzing the complexity of an algorithm, it is the length (or norm) of the string located initially in the input file of a RAM that is used as the measure of input size.

The *size* of a rewriting system $G=(V,P)$, denoted by $|G|$, is defined as the sum of the lengths of the rules in $P$, or the size of $V$, whichever is larger. In other words,

$$|G|=\max\left\{\sum_{\substack{\omega_1\to\omega_2\\ \in P}}|\omega_1\omega_2|,\ |V|\right\} \ .$$

The *norm* of $G$, denoted by $\|G\|$, is defined by

$$\|G\|=|G|\log|V| \ .$$

**Lemma 1.45** *Any rewriting system $G=(V,P)$ can be encoded uniquely as a binary string of length $O(\|G\|)$.*

*Proof.* Let $\#$ be a symbol not found in $V$. $V$ can then be represented as the string $\#\alpha\#$, where $\alpha$ contains exactly one occurrence of each symbol in $V$. Any rule $\omega_1\to\omega_2$ in $P$ can be represented as the string $\#\omega_1\#\omega_2$. A unique representation is then obtained for $G$ by concatenating the representation of $V$ and the representations of individual rules into a single string over $V \cup \{\#\}$. By Fact 1.24, this string can again be encoded uniquely as a binary string of length $O(|G|\log|V|)$.    $\square$

Apart from the fact that they offer a means of language description, rewriting systems can be viewed as programs for a primitive computer in which the instruction set contains only string rewriting instructions. In this case, however, a "program" is an unordered set from which any (applicable) instruction can be selected at any moment. Sentential forms can be thought of as configurations of the computer, and derivations as computations. The initial sentential form in a derivation represents the input to the program, while any intermediate sentential form represents the current contents of the memory and the final sentential form represents the output produced by the program. These programs are usually nondeterministic because a given sentential form can contain the left-hand side of more than one rule or simply because there can be two rules with the same left-hand side.

Many of the concepts defined in Sections 1.3 and 1.5 for RAM programs lend themselves, in a simplified form, to rewriting systems. We conclude this section by defining for rewriting systems some notions analogous to those pertaining to the time and space complexity of RAM programs. These issues will be developed further in Chapters 4, 5 and 10 when we study the complexity of context-free grammars, parsers and Turing-machines.

Let $D = (\gamma_0, \ldots, \gamma_n)$ be a derivation of length $n$ in a rewriting system $G = (V, P)$. The length $n$ of $D$ is also called the *time complexity* of $D$ and denoted by TIME($D$). The length of the longest of the strings $\gamma_0, \ldots, \gamma_n$ is in turn called the *space complexity* of $D$ and denoted by SPACE($D$).

Let $\gamma_1$ and $\gamma_2$ be strings over $V$ such that $\gamma_1$ derives $\gamma_2$ in $G$. The *time complexity of deriving $\gamma_2$ from $\gamma_1$ in $G$*, denoted by $\text{TIME}_G(\gamma_1, \gamma_2)$, is defined by

$$\text{TIME}_G(\gamma_1, \gamma_2) = \min\{\text{TIME}(D) | D \text{ is a derivation of } \gamma_2 \text{ from } \gamma_1 \text{ in } G\} \ .$$

**Fact 1.46**

$$\text{TIME}_G(\gamma_1, \gamma_2) = \min\{n \geqslant 0 \,|\, \gamma_1 \Rightarrow^n \gamma_2 \text{ in } G\}. \quad \square$$

The *space complexity of deriving $\gamma_2$ from $\gamma_1$ in $G$*, denoted by $\text{SPACE}_G(\gamma_1, \gamma_2)$, is defined by

$$\text{SPACE}_G(\gamma_1, \gamma_2) = \min\{\text{SPACE}(D) | D \text{ is a derivation of } \gamma_2 \text{ from } \\ \gamma_1 \text{ in } G\}.$$

If no ambiguity can arise, we will drop the "$G$" from $\text{TIME}_G$ and $\text{SPACE}_G$.

We say that $\gamma_1$ *derives* $\gamma_2$ *in time* $t$ if $\text{TIME}(\gamma_1, \gamma_2) \leqslant t$, *in space* $s$ if $\text{SPACE}(\gamma_1, \gamma_2) \leqslant s$, and *simultaneously in time t and in space s* if for some derivation $D$ of $\gamma_2$ from $\gamma_1$ $\text{TIME}(D) \leqslant t$ and $\text{SPACE}(D) \leqslant s$.

For example, in $G_{\text{match}}$ we have

$$TIME(S, 0^n1^n) = n+1 \qquad \text{for all} \quad n \geqslant 0 \; ,$$
$$SPACE(S, 0^n1^n) = 2n+1 \qquad \text{for all} \quad n \geqslant 0 \; .$$

## Exercises

1.1   Let **male**, **female**, **married-to**, **child-of**, and **sibling-of** be relations on the set of all people defined by:

(1)  $x$ **male** $x$, if $x$ is male.
(2)  $x$ **female** $x$, if $x$ is female.
(3)  $x$ **married-to** $y$, if $x$ and $y$ are married.
(4)  $x$ **child-of** $y$, if $x$ is a child of $y$.
(5)  $x$ **sibling-of** $y$, if $x$ and $y$ are siblings.

Which of these relations are (a) reflexive, (b) symmetric, (c) antisymmetric, (d) transitive?

1.2   Given the relations of Exercise 1.1, express the following statements in English:

a)  $x$ **child-of**$^{-1}$ **male** $y$.
b)  $x$ **married-to child-of male** $y$.
c)  $x$ **sibling-of married-to male** $\cup$ **married-to sibling-of male** $y$.
d)  $x$ (**child-of**$^{-1}$)$^+$ $y$.

1.3   Express the following statements using the relations of Exercise 1.1:

a)  $y$ is $x$'s son-in-law.
b)  $y$ is $x$'s second cousin.
c)  $y$ is $x$'s grandfather's grandmother.
d)  $y$'s uncle descends from $x$ down the male line.

1.4   Prove Lemma 1.3.

1.5   Show that the following statements hold for all relations $R$ on $A$:

a)  $R = R^+$ if and only if $R$ is transitive.
b)  $R = R^*$ if and only if $R$ is reflexive and transitive.

1.6   Let $R$ be a relation on a set $A$. Show that $R^* \cap (R^{-1})^*$ is an equivalence on $A$. For nodes $a$ and $b$ of a graph $(A, R)$, what does it mean if $a \; R^* \cap (R^{-1})^* \; b$?

1.7   Draw the graph $(A, R)$, where
$A = \{0, 1, 2, 3, 4, 5, 6, 7\}$ ,
$R = \{(0, 5), \quad (1, 0), \quad (2, 7), \quad (4, 5), \quad (3, 3), \quad (3, 6), \quad (5, 1),$
$\quad (5, 2), \quad (6, 5), \quad (7, 4)\}$.
Give the equivalence classes under $R^* \cap (R^{-1})^*$.

1.8   Show that, for any set $A$, the set inclusion $\subseteq$ is a partial order on $2^A$, the set of all subset of $A$. When is it a total order?

1.9   Let $(A, \leqslant)$ be a partially ordered finite set. The *Hasse diagram* of $(A, \leqslant)$ is a directed graph $(A, R)$, where

$$R = \{(x, y) \in < \,|\, x < z < y \text{ does not hold for any } z\} \ .$$

Show that $(A, R)$ is acyclic and that $R^* = \leqslant$. Draw the Hasse diagram for the partially ordered set $(2^{\{0,1,2,3\}}, \subseteq)$.

1.10  Show that $|2^A| = |\{0, 1\}^A|$ for any set $A$.

1.11  Let $A_1, A_2, B_1$ and $B_2$ be any sets. Show that

$$|B_1^{A_1}| = |B_2^{A_2}| \text{ whenever } |A_1| = |A_2| \text{ and } |B_1| = |B_2| \ .$$

1.12  Show that the set of all Pascal programs is countable.

1.13  Prove Proposition 1.8.

1.14  Prove Lemma 1.9 and use this to show that $\mathbb{N} \times \mathbb{N}$ is countably infinite.

1.15  Show that the set

$$\{f \in \mathbb{N}^{\mathbb{N}} \,|\, f(n+1) > f(n) \text{ for all } n \in \mathbb{N}\}$$

is uncountable.

1.16  Show that the set of all real numbers $x$ with $0 \leqslant x \leqslant 1$ is uncountable.

1.17  Prove Lemma 1.11.

1.18  Show that, for any set $A$, $(2^A, \cap, A)$ and $(2^A, \cup, \varnothing)$ are monoids. Here $\cap$ denotes set intersection and $\cup$ set union on subsets of $A$.

1.19  Let $n$ be a positive integer. A *boolean $n \times n$-matrix* is any function from the set $\{1, \ldots, n\} \times \{1, \ldots, n\}$ to the set of truth values. The *sum* of boolean $n \times n$-matrices $A$ and $B$, denoted by $A + B$, is the boolean $n \times n$-matrix that satisfies

$$(A + B)(i, j) = A(i, j) \quad \textbf{or} \quad B(i, j)$$

for all $i$, $j=1, \ldots, n$. The *product* of $A$ and $B$, denoted by $A \cdot B$, is the boolean $n \times n$-matrix that satisfies

$$
\begin{aligned}
(A \cdot B)(i, j) = \;& A(i, 1) \quad \textbf{and} \quad B(1, j) \quad \textbf{or} \\
& A(i, 2) \quad \textbf{and} \quad B(2, j) \quad \textbf{or} \\
& \qquad\qquad \vdots \\
& A(i, n) \quad \textbf{and} \quad B(n, j)
\end{aligned}
$$

for all $i, j = 1, \ldots, n$. Let $M_n$ be the set of all boolean $n \times n$-matrices. Show that $(M_n, +, 0_n)$ and $(M_n, \cdot, D_n)$ are monoids, where $0_n$ is the matrix for which $0_n(i, j) = \textbf{false}$ for all $i, j = 1, \ldots, n$, and $D_n$ is the matrix for which $D_n(i, j) = \textbf{true}$ if and only if $i = j$. Matrix $0_n$ is called the *null matrix*, and $D_n$ the *diagonal matrix* in $M_n$.

**1.20** An element $y$ is an *inverse* of an element $x$ in a monoid if $x \cdot y = y \cdot x = e$. A monoid in which each element has an inverse is called a *group*. When has an element $R$ in the monoid $(2^{A \times A}, \cdot, \text{id}_A)$ an inverse? What is this inverse?

**1.21** Prove Lemma 1.16.

**1.22** Show that the following statements hold for all monoids $M$ and subsets $A$ of $M$:

a) $A = A^+$ if and only if $A$ is positively closed.
b) $A = A^*$ if and only if $A$ is closed.

**1.23** Show that $(\mathbb{N}, +, 0)$ is a monoid generated freely by $\{1\}$. Here $+$ denotes addition of natural numbers.

**1.24** Are any of the monoids given in Exercises 1.18 and 1.19 free?

**1.25** Prove Lemma 1.17.

**1.26** Prove Fact 1.18 and Lemma 1.19.

**1.27** Is there any set $V$ for which the free monoid $V^*$ is a group?

**1.28** Let $(M, \cdot, e)$ be a monoid, $A$, $B$ and $C$ subsets of $M$, and $k$ a natural number. Which of the following statements are (1) always true, (2) always false, (3) sometimes true and sometimes false?

a) $A^k = \{x^k \mid x \in A\}$     b) $\varnothing^* = \{e\}$
c) $A^{**} = A^*$     d) $(A \cup B)^* = A^* \cup B^*$
e) $A(B \cap C) = AB \cap AC$     f) $(A^*B^*)^* = (A \cup B)^*$

**1.29** Prove Lemmas 1.21 and 1.22.

1.30  Show that the function $f$ defined by

$$f(x) = 2^x$$

is a homomorphism from the monoid $(\mathbb{R}, +, 0)$ to the monoid $(\mathbb{R}, \cdot, 1)$. Here $\mathbb{R}$ denotes the set of real numbers, and $+$ and $\cdot$ real number addition and multiplication respectively. Is $f$ an isomorphism?

1.31  Show that the following statements hold for all monoids $M, M_1, M_2$ and $M_3$:

    a) $id_M$ is an isomorphism from $M$ to $M$.
    b) If $h$ is an isomorphism from $M_1$ to $M_2$, then $h^{-1}$ is an isomorphism from $M_2$ to $M_1$.
    c) If $h$ is an isomorphism from $M_1$ to $M_2$ and $g$ is an isomorphism from $M_2$ to $M_3$, then $hg$ is an isomorphism from $M_1$ to $M_3$.
Hence monoid isomorphism is an equivalence relation.

1.32  Describe in English the following languages over $\{0, 1\}$:
    a) $\{0, 1\}^* \{1, 0\}$          b) $\{00, \varepsilon\}^+$
    c) $\{1, 01, 001\}^* \{\varepsilon, 0, 00\}$
    d) $(\{00, 11\} \cup \{01, 10\} \{00, 11\}^* \{01, 10\})^*$

1.33  Write expressions that denote the following languages over $\{0, 1\}$. You may use in these expressions only finite sets and the operations $\cup$ (union), $\cdot$ (concatenation), and $*$ (closure).

    a) All strings that end with two zeros.
    b) All strings that contain at most two zeros.
    c) All strings in which the number of zeros is even.

1.34  Let $h$ be a homomorphism from $\{0, 1\}^*$ to $\{0, 1\}^*$ such that $h(0) = \varepsilon$ and $h(1) = 100$. Give expressions for the following sets:

    a) $h(\{\varepsilon\})$                 b) $h(\{011001, 100, \varepsilon\})$
    c) $h^{-1}(\{\varepsilon\})$             d) $h^{-1}(\{0\})$
    e) $h^{-1}(\{100\})$          f) $h(\{0, 1\}^*)$

1.35  Let $f$ and $g$ be recursive functions on $V^*$. Show that $fg$ is recursive.

1.36  Show that a language $L_1$ is recursively enumerable if and only if there is a deterministic RAM program $M$ that *enumerates* its sentences. That is, $M$ takes as input a natural number $i$ and produces as output a sentence $w_i$ in $L_1$ such that $\{w_0, w_1, \ldots\} = L_1$.

1.37  Give a total solution to the decision problem $P_{pal}$ given in Section 1.4 using a high-level programming language. What is the most convenient data structure to use as a workspace?

1.38  A string over alphabet $V$ is a *palindrome with centre marker c* if it is of the form $xcx^R$, where $x$ does not contain $c$. Consider the decision problem

$P_{cpal}$: "Is string $w$ a palindrome with centre marker $c$?"

where $c$ is a fixed symbol in $V$. Give a deterministic algorithm that is a total solution to this problem. The algorithm may use as workspace a stack of symbols. In handling the stack, only the stack operations PUSH, POP, TOP, and ISEMPTY can be used. Here PUSH($a$) pushes symbol $a$ onto the stack, POP deletes the topmost symbol, TOP returns the topmost symbol, and ISEMPTY returns **true** if the stack is empty and **false** otherwise. The stack is initially empty.

1.39  Give a nondeterministic algorithm that is a partial solution to the decision problem $P_{pal}$. The algorithm may use as workspace a stack of symbols as in Exercise 1.38.
*Hint*: guess the centre of the palindrome.

1.40  Explain why the decision problem

"Will a nuclear war break out within 10 years?"

is trivially solvable.

1.41  Show that a decision problem $P$ is solvable if and only if both $P$ and its complement $\bar{P}$ are partially solvable.
*Hint*: Use the result of Exercise 1.36. Note that $P$ is partially solvable if and only if its associated language $L(P)$ is recursively enumerable.

1.42  In the procedure $M_{exhalt}$ presented in Section 1.4 we used the nondeterministic statement "guess $w$" for strings $w$, although in our RAM model only integers can be guessed. Implement the statement "guess $w$" using statements "guess $n$" and "guess $c$", where $n$ is an integer variable and $c$ is a character variable. (The statement "guess $c$" is implemented in the RAM as a guess of the character code for $c$.)

1.43  Show that reducibility of decision problems is a reflexive and transitive relation.

1.44  Show that the decision problem $P_{accept}$ reduces to the decision problem $P_{halt}$.

1.45  Show that the decision problem

$P_{unhalt}$: "Does procedure $M$ halt on all inputs?"

is not partially solvable.
*Hint*: Apply a diagonal argument to the result of Exercise 1.36.

1.46  Prove Lemma 1.32.

1.47  Prove Lemma 1.33.

1.48  Evaluate the complexity of the algorithms of Exercises 1.38 and 1.39 under (a) the uniform cost criterion, (b) the logarithmic cost criterion.

1.49  Evaluate the complexity of your implementation of the "guess $w$" statement (Exercise 1.42).

1.50  Give an algorithm that sorts a set of $n$ positive integers in uniform cost time $O(n)$. What is the logarithmic cost complexity of your algorithm?

1.51  Prove Lemma 1.42.

1.52  Consider the rewriting system $(\{S, a, b\}, \{S \to a, S \to bSS\})$.

a)  Describe the language

$$\{w \in \{a, b\}^* \mid S \Rightarrow^* w \text{ in } G\} \ .$$

b)  Prove by induction that your description is correct.

1.53  The definitions of the partial functions TIME and SPACE for rewriting systems do not involve any cost criterion. Redefine these partial functions so as to correspond as closely as possible to the logarithmic cost time and space complexity of RAM programs.

## Bibliographic Notes

The issues discussed in this chapter are found in one form or another in most monographs on the theory of formal languages and computation, e.g., Aho and Ullman (1972), Harrison (1978), Hopcroft and Ullman (1979), Lewis and Papadimitriou (1981) and Salomaa (1973). An introduction to the discrete mathematics needed here is found in Arbib, Kfoury and Moll (1981), amongst others. The RAM model of computation and its relationship to Turing machines is discussed in detail by Aho, Hopcroft and Ullman (1974). The deterministic RAM model we have used is essentially theirs, whereas the nondeterministic RAM model is defined by analogy with the nondeterministic Turing machine model used by Garey and Johnson (1979). The theory of computability is treated in a way similar to ours by Kfoury, Moll and Arbib (1982). Most of the propositions presented without proof in Section 1.5 can be found in Hopcroft and Ullman (1979), where they are stated and proved for the Turing machine model. The approach based on rewriting systems which we have adopted was inspired by Salomaa (1973). This approach has been used in parsing theory by Deussen (1979) and Waite and Goos (1984).

# 2. Algorithms on Graphs

In this chapter we shall develop some basic algorithms for directed graphs and relations which will be of use in later chapters, where the efficient construction of parsers is considered. The constructions needed can be expressed as the computing of certain "relational expressions". These are expressions whose operands are relations and whose operators are chosen from among multiplication, closure, union and inverse. For this purpose we need to develop an algorithm for computing the closure of a relation. In view of the nature of our applications, the most appropriate way to do this is by a depth-first traversal of the graph that corresponds to the given relation. Other ways of computing the closure of a relation are considered in the exercises.

In Section 2.1 the basic algorithms for searching graphs are given, and in Section 2.2 an efficient algorithm for finding the strongly connected components of a directed graph is presented. Using the algorithm of Section 2.2, a certain set-valued function which includes the closure of a relation as a special case is computed in Section 2.3, and Section 2.4 deals with the computation of general relational expressions.

## 2.1 Basic Algorithms

Let $R$ be a relation on a finite set $A$. Given a subset $B$ of $A$, we often wish to compute the set $R^*(B)$, the closure of $B$ under $R$. We might also wish to construct the whole reflexive transitive closure $R^*$ of $R$, which is obtained by determining the sets $R^*(a)$ for all $a \in A$. This can be done by interpreting $R$ as a directed graph $(A, R)$ and making use of known graph algorithms.

In order to be able to evaluate the complexity of our algorithms, we need to specify how the relations are represented. Obviously, any relation $R$ on a finite set $A$ can be represented uniquely as a string over $A \cup \{\#\}$, where $\#$ is a new symbol not belonging to $A$. This string is made up of substrings $a \# b \#$, where $(a, b)$ is in $R$. We therefore have

**Lemma 2.1** *Any relation $R$ on a finite set $A$ can be encoded uniquely as a binary string of length $O(|R|\log|A|)$.*

*Proof.* Cf. the proof of Lemma 1.45. $\square$

We first present an algorithm that computes the closure under $R$ of a singleton set, i.e., $R^*(a)$ for some element $a$ of $A$. By Fact 1.4, $R^*(a)$ is composed of the nodes of $(A, R)$ that appear in some path from $a$ in $(A, R)$. Thus $R^*(a)$ can be computed by traversing all possible paths that begin at $a$. One way of doing this is to take any node $b$ such that $a\ R\ b$ and recursively traverse all paths beginning at $b$, and then take the next node $c$ such that $a\ R\ c$ and traverse all paths beginning at $c$, provided that $c$ has not previously been visited. The process continues until all nodes appearing in some path from $a$ in $(A, R)$ have been visited. It is possible to arrange the traversal such that no node is visited more than once by marking each node when it is first visited. A graph traversal as described above is called a "depth-first traversal". This term comes from the order in which the nodes are visited: if node $b$ has just been visited, then all nodes in $R^*(b)$ will be visited before any other node.

In Figure 2.1 (a), a procedure TRAVERSE is given that traverses $R^*(a)$. It should be clear that the effect of the call TRAVERSE(a) is to mark exactly those elements $b$ of $A$ for which there is a path in $(A, R)$ from $a$ to $b$. Thus the set $R^*(a)$ is obtained as the subset of $A$ consisting of the marked elements. TRAVERSE runs in time linear in $|R|$, because, as a result of the marking, there is at most one call TRAVERSE($a'$) for a given $a'$, and in one call TRAVERSE ($a'$) each edge $(a', b')$ is inspected only once. Note that to achieve the linear time bound a suitable data structure for storing $R$ is needed. This data structure must be of size $O(|R|)$, and must allow the next edge to be traversed to be found in constant time (see the exercises).

```
procedure TRAVERSE (node a);
begin
    mark a;
    for each edge (a, b) ∈ R do
        if b is unmarked then
            TRAVERSE (b)
end.
```

(a)

```
begin
    unmark all nodes in A;
    for each node a ∈ B do if a is unmarked then
        TRAVERSE(a)
end.
```

(b)

**Figure 2.1** Traversal of a graph $(A, R)$. (a) Traversal of $R^*$ $(a)$. (b) Traversal of $R^*(B)$, where $B \subseteq A$

The procedure TRAVERSE can be used to compute the set $R^*(B)$ for a given subset $B$ of $A$ by adding the main program of Figure 2.1(b). Again it is clear that $R^*(B)$ is obtained as the subset of $A$ consisting of the marked elements. It is also clear that the algorithm runs in time linear in $\max\{|R|, |A|\}$. We therefore have

**Theorem 2.2** *Let $R$ be a relation on a finite set $A$. Given a subset $B$ of $A$, $R^*(B)$ can be computed in time $O(\max\{|R|, |A|\})$.* $\square$

If we want to construct the entire closure $R^*$, we can proceed by computing $R^*(a)$ for each $a \in A$, using the procedure TRAVERSE. We therefore have

**Theorem 2.3** *If $R$ is a relation on a finite set $A$, then $R^*$ can be computed in time* $O(|A| \cdot |R|)$.  $\square$


## 2.2 Finding Strongly Connected Components

In computing $R^*$ by the method presented in the previous section, some portions of $(A, R)$ may be traversed several times unnecessarily because the recursive computation of sets $R^*(a)$ may mean that some set $R^*(b)$ is computed more than once. However, we can avoid multiple traversals of portions of $(A, R)$ if we properly recognize its "strongly connected components".

By the *strongly connected component* of an element $a$ of $A$, denoted SCC($a$), we mean the equivalence class of $a$ under the equivalence relation $R^* \cap (R^{-1})^*$ on $A$ (see Exercise 1.6). Thus SCC($a$) = SCC($b$) if and only if $a \, R^* \, b$ and $b \, R^* \, a$.

In finding the strongly connected components of $(A, R)$ we make use of the algorithm of Figure 2.1(b). A *depth-first traversal of $(A, R)$ induced by* this algorithm with $B = A$ is a permutation of the $2|A|$ symbols **enter**($a$) and **exit**($a$), $a \in A$, that indicates the order in which the procedure TRAVERSE enters and exits nodes during the execution of the algorithm. Note that there are in general many depth-first traversals of a graph: the procedure TRAVERSE can fix arbitrarily the order in which it handles the edges leaving a node.

A substring of a depth-first traversal that begins with **enter**($a$) and ends with **exit**($a$) is called a *depth-first traversal of $a$.*

Let $(A, R)$ be a graph and $\pi$ its depth-first traversal. By the corresponding *depth-first order of $(A, R)$ with respect to $\pi$* we mean the total order $\leqslant$ on $A$ in which $a < b$ if and only if **enter**($a$) appears in $\pi$ before **enter**($b$), or equivalently if and only if $a$ is marked before $b$.

As an example, consider the graph shown in Figure 2.2, which also serves to illustrate the following simple facts.

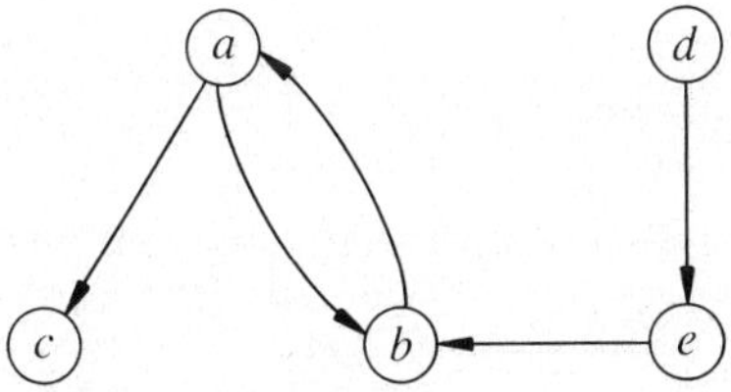

**Figure 2.2** A directed graph. One possible depth-first traversal is

**enter**($a$) **enter**($b$) **exit**($b$) **enter**($c$) **exit**($c$) **exit**($a$) **enter**($d$) **enter**($e$) **exit**($e$) **exit**($d$).

The corresponding depth-first order is: $a < b < c < d < e$

**Fact 2.4** A depth-first traversal is *properly nested*, i.e., whenever $a$ and $b$ are two distinct nodes then any depth-first traversal takes one of the following forms:

(1) ... **enter**$(a)$ ... **exit**$(a)$ ... **enter**$(b)$ ... **exit**$(b)$ ...
(2) ... **enter**$(b)$ ... **exit**$(b)$ ... **enter**$(a)$ ... **exit**$(a)$ ...
(3) ... **enter**$(a)$ ... **enter**$(b)$ ... **exit**$(b)$ ... **exit**$(a)$ ...
(4) ... **enter**$(b)$ ... **enter**$(a)$ ... **exit**$(a)$ ... **exit**$(b)$ ...

In other words, either the depth-first traversals of $a$ and $b$ do not interleave or one of them is a substring of the other.    $\square$

We say that $a$ is *traversed before* $b$ if the traversal is of form (1) above, *during* the traversal of $b$ if the traversal is of form (4), and *after* $b$ if the traversal is of form (2).

**Fact 2.5** Let $\pi$ be a depth-first traversal of the graph $(A, R)$ and $\leqslant$ the depth-first order with respect to $\pi$. Then $\pi$ is of the form

$$\ldots \textbf{enter}(a) \ldots \textbf{enter}(b) \ldots \textbf{exit}(b) \ldots \textbf{exit}(a) \ldots$$

if and only if $a\ (R \cap <)^+\ b$.    $\square$

**Lemma 2.6** *For all* $a$, $b$, $c \in A$, *the conditions* $a \leqslant b \leqslant c$ *and* $a\ (R \cap <)^*\ c$ *imply* $a\ (R \cap <)^*\ b$.

*Proof.* The cases in which $a = b$ or $b = c$ are trivial, so assume that $a < b < c$. Then the nodes $a$, $b$, $c$ are visited in the order

$$\ldots \textbf{enter}(a) \ldots \textbf{enter}(b) \ldots \textbf{enter}(c) \ldots \tag{2.1}$$

The conditions $a\ (R \cap <)^*\ c$ and $a \neq c$ imply, by Fact 2.5, that the depth-first traversal is of the form

$$\ldots \textbf{enter}(a) \ldots \textbf{enter}(c) \ldots \textbf{exit}(c) \ldots \textbf{exit}(a) \ldots$$

Combining this with (2.1) we see that **enter**$(b)$ must lie between **enter**$(a)$ and **exit**$(a)$, which means, by Fact 2.4, that the depth-first traversal is of the form

$$\ldots \textbf{enter}(a) \ldots \textbf{enter}(b) \ldots \textbf{exit}(b) \ldots \textbf{exit}(a) \ldots$$

Hence Fact 2.5 implies that $a\ (R \cap <)^*\ b$, as required.    $\square$

The following three lemmas demonstrate, among other things, how two $R^*$-related elements are related with respect to $\leqslant$.

**Lemma 2.7** *Let* $(a_0, \ldots, a_n)$ *be a path of length $n$ in $(A, R)$. Then at least one of the following two statements holds:*
(1) $a_0\ (R \cap <)^*\ a_n$.
(2) *For some $i$ with* $0 \leqslant i < n$, $a_0\ (R \cap <)^*\ a_i$ *and* $a_{i+1} < a_0$.

*Proof.* Let $k$ be the number of "back edges" in $(a_0, \ldots, a_n)$, i.e., edges $(a_i, a_{i+1})$ for which $a_{i+1} \leqslant a_i$. The proof uses induction on $k$. First, if $k=0$ then $a_i < a_{i+1}$ for all $i = 0, \ldots, n-1$, which means that $a_0 \,(R \cap <)^n\, a_n$ and statement (1) is true. We may thus assume that $k > 0$ and, as an induction hypothesis, that the lemma holds for all paths in $(A, R)$ with less than $k$ back edges. Let

$$j = \min\{i \mid i = 0, \ldots, n-1, a_{i+1} \leqslant a_i\} \ .$$

Then $a_0 \,(R \cap <)^*\, a_j$ and $a_{j+1} \leqslant a_j$. If $a_{j+1} < a_0$, then choose $j+1$ as the index $i$ mentioned in the lemma. Otherwise, $a_0 \leqslant a_{j+1}$ and we conclude from Lemma 2.6 that $a_0 \,(R \cap <)^*\, a_{j+1}$. Hence there is a path $(b_0, \ldots, b_m)$ in $(A, R \cap <)$ such that $b_0 = a_0$ and $b_m = a_{j+1}$. Then $(b_0, \ldots, b_m, a_{j+2}, \ldots, a_n)$ is a path in $(A, R)$ from $a_0$ to $a_n$ with only $k-1$ back edges. Thus by the induction hypothesis either $a_0 \,(R \cap <)^*\, a_n$ or, for some $i_1$ with $j+1 \leqslant i_1 < n$, $a_0 \,(R \cap <)^*\, a_{i_1}$ and $a_{i_1+1} < a_0$. This completes the proof.   $\square$

**Lemma 2.8** *Let* $(a_0, \ldots, a_n)$ *be a path in* $(A, R)$. *Then at least one of the following two statements holds*:
  (1) $a_0 \,(R \cap <)^*\, a_n$.
  (2) *For some* $j$ *with* $0 < j \leqslant n$, $a_j < a_0$ *and* $a_j \,(R \cap <)^*\, a_n$.

*Proof.* The proof uses induction on $n$. If $n=0$, then statement (1) holds trivially. Assume then that $n > 0$ and as an induction hypothesis that the lemma holds for paths shorter than $n$. By Lemma 2.7, either statement (1) is true or, for some $i$ with $0 \leqslant i < n$, $a_0 \,(R \cap <)^*\, a_i$ and $a_{i+1} < a_0$. In the latter case we apply the induction hypothesis to the path $(a_{i+1}, \ldots, a_n)$. We then have either $a_{i+1} \,(R \cap <)^*\, a_n$, or for some $j$ with $i+1 < j \leqslant n$, $a_j < a_{i+1}$ and $a_j \,(R \cap <)^*\, a_n$. Since $a_{i+1} < a_0$, statement (2) is true in both cases.   $\square$

The proof of the following lemma is somewhat complicated because the conditions $a\,R^*\,b$ and $a < b$ do not necessarily imply that $a \,(R \cap <)^*\, b$, as is illustrated in Figure 2.3.

**Lemma 2.9** *For all* $a, b, c \in A$, *the conditions* $a \leqslant b \leqslant c$ *and* $a\,R^*\,c$ *imply* $a\,R^*\,b$.

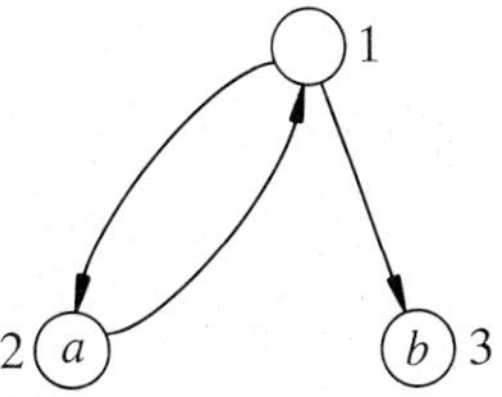


**Figure 2.3** $a\,R^*\,b$ and $a < b$ are both true, but $a \,(R \cap <)^*\, b$ does not hold. The order in which the nodes are visited is indicated by the numbers

**Theorem 2.16**  *The strongly connected components of a graph $(A, R)$ can be found in time $O(max\{|A|, |R|\})$.*   $\square$


## 2.3 Computing Functions Defined on Graphs

In this section we shall show how the results of the previous section can be used to derive a practical algorithm for computing $R^*$. Actually we shall compute a more general function which includes $R^*$ as a special case.

Let $A$ and $B$ be finite sets, $R$ a relation on $A$ and $F_0: A \rightarrow 2^B$ a function which can be computed easily. We shall consider the computation of the function $F: A \rightarrow 2^B$ defined by the equation

$$F(a) = \bigcup_{aR^*b} F_0(b) \ .$$

As an example, consider the graph in Figure 2.8. If $F_0(i) = \{i\}$ for $i = 1, \ldots, 6$, then $F(1) = \{1, 2, 3, 4, 5, 6\}$, $F(2) = \{2\}$, $F(3) = F(4) = F(5) = \{3, 4, 5\}$, and $F(6) = \{3, 4, 5, 6\}$.

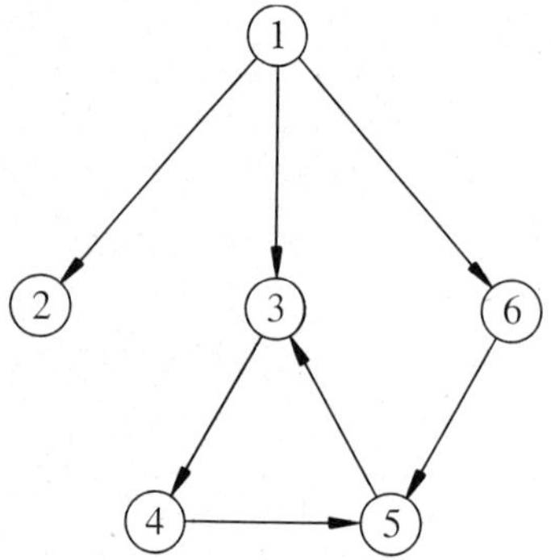

**Figure 2.8** A graph

The procedure TRAVERSE given in Figure 2.1(a) can be used to compute the values of $F$. As $F(a)$ is the union of all $F(b)$ with $b \in R^*(a)$, $F(a)$ can be computed during the depth-first traversal of $R^*(a)$ performed by the procedure TRAVERSE.

Let us consider the depth-first traversal of a graph $(A, R)$ by the algorithm of Figure 2.1(b). We shall augment this algorithm with the recursive computation of a function $\hat{F}$, such that $\hat{F}(a) = F(a)$ if all nodes in $R^*(a)$ are unmarked when node $a$ is entered in the depth-first traversal. The modified algorithm is given in Figure 2.9.

**Lemma 2.17**  *For $\hat{F}$ computed using the algorithm of Figure 2.9,*

$$\hat{F}(a) = \bigcup_{a(R \cap <)^*b} F_0(b)$$

*for all $a \in A$.*

```
procedure COMPUTE1 (node a);
begin
    mark a;
    F̂(a) := F₀(a);
    for each edge (a, b) ∈ R do
        if b is unmarked then begin
            COMPUTE1(b);
            F̂(a) := F̂(a) ∪ F̂(b)
        end
end.
```

**(a)**

```
begin
    unmark all nodes in A;
    for each node a ∈ A do if a is unmarked then
    COMPUTE1(a)
end.
```

**(b)**

**Figure 2.9** Computation of a function $\hat{F}$. **(a)** Procedure COMPUTE1. **(b)** Main program

*Proof.* The proof uses induction on the number of **exit**-operations that precede **exit**($a$) in the depth-first traversal of $(A, R)$ corresponding to $\leqslant$. In the base case we assume that **exit**($a$) is the first **exit**-operation. Then there are no edges $(a, b)$ in $(A, R)$ for which $b$ is unmarked, i.e., no $b$ for which $a\ (R \cap <)\ b$. Thus the algorithm computes

$$\hat{F}(a) = F_0(a) = \bigcup_{a(R\,\cap\,<)^*b} F_0(b) \ .$$

Assume then that the lemma holds for all $b$ such that **exit**($b$) precedes **exit**($a$). The algorithm computes $\hat{F}(a)$ as

$$\hat{F}(a) = F_0(a) \cup \bigcup_{a(R\,\cap\,<)b} \hat{F}(b) \ .$$

Thus we get by the induction hypothesis that

$$\hat{F}(a) = F_0(a) \cup \bigcup_{a(R\,\cap\,<)b} \left( \bigcup_{b(R\,\cap\,<)^*c} F_0(c) \right)$$

$$= F_0(a) \cup \bigcup_{a(R\,\cap\,<)^+c} F_0(c)$$

$$= \bigcup_{a(R\,\cap\,<)^*b} F_0(b),$$

as required. $\square$

We now construct a graph $G_E = (V_E, R_E)$ from a relational expression $E$ such that $R(E)$ will be obtained from a certain subset of $R_E^*$ (see Figure 2.13). Moreover, this computation can be done in time $O(\text{size}(E))$.

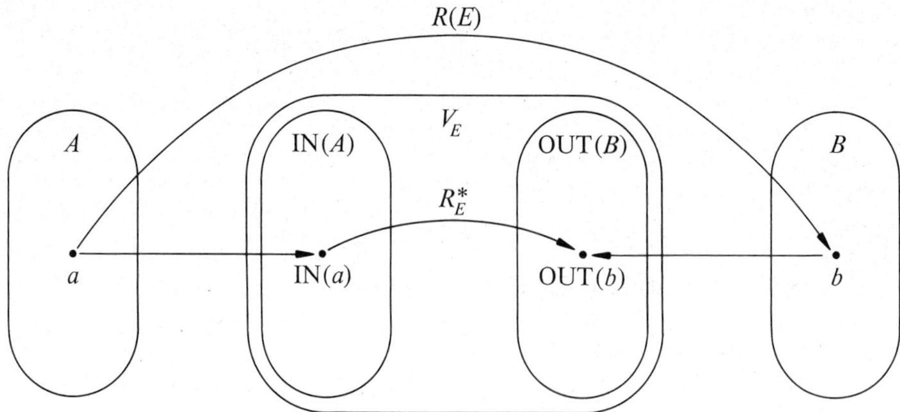


**Figure 2.13** The graph $G_E = (V_E, R_E)$ corresponding to a relational expression $E$ with domain $A$ and range $B$. For all $a \in A$ and $b \in B$, $a\ R(E)\ b$ if and only if $\text{IN}(a)\ R_E^*\ \text{OUT}(b)$

**Lemma 2.27** *Let $E$ be a relational expression with domain $A$ and range $B$ such that $\text{size}(E)$ is finite. Then there exist a directed graph $G_E = (V_E, R_E)$ and injections $IN: A \to V_E$ and $OUT: B \to V_E$ satisfying the following conditions:*

*(1) $IN(A)$, the set of input nodes, and $OUT(B)$, the set of output nodes, are disjoint.*
*(2) $R_E(V_E) \cap IN(A) = \varnothing$, i.e., no input node has an edge entering it.*
*(3) $R_E^{-1}(V_E) \cap OUT(B) = \varnothing$, i.e., no output node has an edge leaving it.*
*(4) For all $a \in A$ and $b \in B$*

$$a\ R(E)\ b \text{ if and only if } IN(a)\ R_E^*\ OUT(b)\ .$$

*Moreover, the graph $G_E$ and the injections $IN$ and $OUT$ can be constructed from $E$ in time $O(\text{size}(E))$.*

*Proof.* We prove the lemma by induction on the length of the relational expression $E$.

*Base Case.* $E$ is a relational expression of length 1. Then $E$ is simply a relation from $A$ to $B$. In this case, we construct two injections $IN: A \to V_E$ and $OUT: B \to V_E$, such that $|V_E| = |A| + |B|$ and $IN(A) \cap OUT(B) = \varnothing$. The graph $G_E = (V_E, R_E)$, where

$$R_E = \{(\text{IN}(a), \text{OUT}(b)) \mid (a, b) \in E\}\ ,$$

satisfies the conditions of the lemma. The time needed to construct $G_E$ (and $IN$ and $OUT$) is clearly $O(\text{size}(E))$.

*Induction Step.* Assume that the length of $E$ is $n > 1$. As an induction hypothesis, assume that the lemma holds for relational expressions shorter than $E$. By definition, $E$ has one of the forms $(E_1)$, $E_1^*$, $E_1^{-1}$, $E_1 E_2$, or $E_1 \cup E_2$, where $E_1$ and $E_2$ are relational expressions of length less than $n$. Thus in all cases the induction hypothesis can be applied to $E_1$ and $E_2$, the corresponding graphs being $G_{E_1} = (V_{E_1}, R_{E_1})$ and $G_{E_2} = (V_{E_2}, R_{E_2})$, and the injections $IN_1$, $OUT_1$, $IN_2$, $OUT_2$. We may also assume that $V_{E_1} \cap V_{E_2} = \varnothing$, since we can always choose new symbols to represent nodes if necessary.

*Case 1.* $E = (E_1)$. Then take $IN = IN_1$, $OUT = OUT_1$, and $G_E = G_{E_1}$.

*Case 2a.* $E = E_1^*$. Then $A = B$ and $E_1$ is a relational factor over $A$. Construct two injections $IN : A \to V_E$ and $OUT : B \to V_E$, such that $V_{E_1} \subseteq V_E$, $|V_E| = |V_{E_1}| + |A| + |B|$, and $IN(A)$, $OUT(B)$ and $V_{E_1}$ are pairwise disjoint. Then construct the graph $G_E = (V_E, R_E) = (V_E, R_{E_1} \cup R_{in} \cup R_{back} \cup R_{out} \cup R_{id})$, where

$$R_{in} = \{(IN(a), IN_1(a)) \mid a \in A\} \ ,$$

$$R_{back} = \{(OUT_1(a), IN_1(a)) \mid a \in A\} \ ,$$

$$R_{out} = \{(OUT_1(a), OUT(a) \mid a \in A\} \ ,$$

$$R_{id} = \{(IN(a), OUT(a) \mid a \in A\} \ .$$

By construction, $IN(a) \, R_E^* \, OUT(b)$ if and only if

$$IN(a) \, R_{id} \, OUT(b), \text{ or}$$

$$IN(a) \, R_{in}(R_{E_1}^* \, R_{back})^* \, R_{E_1}^* \, R_{out} \, OUT(b) \ .$$

(See Figure 2.14.) Thus the definitions of $R_{in}$, $R_{back}$, $R_{out}$ and $R_{id}$, together with the induction hypothesis imply that $IN(a) \, R_E^* \, OUT(b)$ if and only if $a \, R(E) \, b$, so that the construction is correct. Since by the induction hypothesis $IN_1$, $OUT_1$ and $G_{E_1}$ can be constructed in time $O(\text{size}(E_1))$, we conclude that $IN$, $OUT$ and $G_E$ can be constructed in time $O(\text{size}(E))$.

*Case 2b.* $E = E_1^{-1}$. Then $E_1$ is a relational factor with domain $B$ and range $A$. Thus if we set $IN = OUT_1$, $OUT = IN_1$, and $G_E = (V_{E_1}, R_{E_1}^{-1})$, the conditions of the lemma are satisfied.

*Case 3.* $E = E_1 E_2$. Then for some finite set $C$, $E_1$ is a relational term with domain $A$ and range $C$ and $E_2$ is a relational factor with domain $C$ and range $B$. Now take $IN = IN_1$ and $OUT = OUT_2$, and define $G_E = (V_{E_1} \cup V_{E_2}, R_{E_1} \cup R_{E_2} \cup R_{mul})$, where

$$R_{mul} = \{(OUT_1(a), IN_2(a)) \mid a \in C\}$$

The definition of relational multiplication and the induction hypothesis imply the correctness of the construction of $G_E$. Also, the time bound for computing $G_E$ is easily seen to be $O(\text{size}(E))$. The construction for this case is illustrated in Figure 2.15.

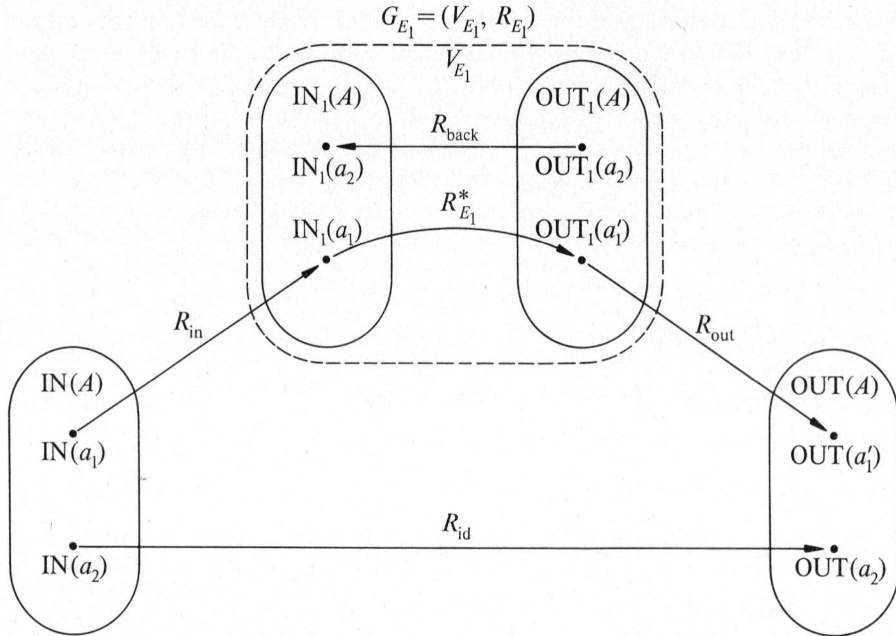



**Figure 2.14** The graph $G_E = (V_E, R_E)$ corresponding to the relational expression $E = E_1^*$, where $G_{E_1} = (V_{E_1}, R_{E_1})$ is the graph corresponding to $E_1$

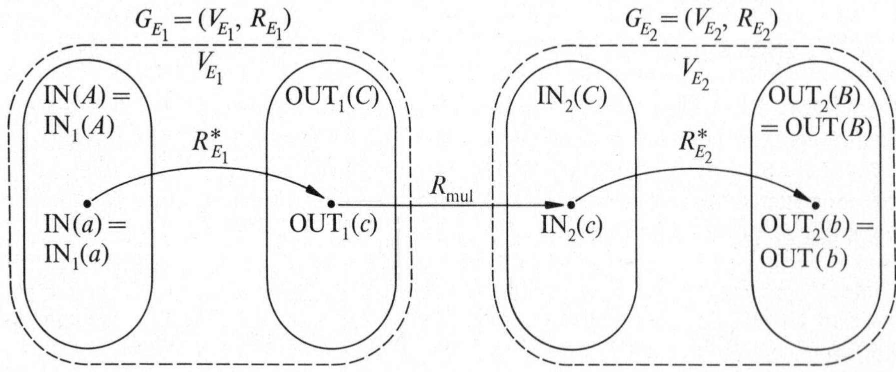



**Figure 2.15** The graph $G_E = (V_E, R_E)$ corresponding to the relational expression $E = E_1 E_2$, where $G_{E_1} = (V_{E_1}, R_{E_1})$ is the graph corresponding to $E_1$, and $G_{E_2} = (V_{E_2}, R_{E_2})$ is the graph corresponding to $E_2$

*Case 4.* $E = E_1 \cup E_2$. Then $E_1$ is a relational expression with domain $A$ and range $B$, and $E_2$ is a relational term with domain $A$ and range $B$. Construct two injections IN: $A \to V_E$ and OUT: $B \to V_E$, such that $V_{E_1} \subseteq V_E$, $V_{E_2} \subseteq V_E$, $|V_E| = |V_{E_1}| + |V_{E_2}| + |A| + |B|$, and $IN(A)$, $OUT(B)$, $V_{E_1}$ and $V_{E_2}$ are pairwise disjoint. The graph $G_E = (V_E, R_{E_1} \cup R_{E_2} \cup R_{in1} \cup R_{in2} \cup R_{out1} \cup R_{out2})$, where

$$R_{\text{in}1} = \{(\text{IN}(a), \text{IN}_1(a)) \mid a \in A\} \ ,$$

$$R_{\text{in}2} = \{(\text{IN}(a), \text{IN}_2(a)) \mid a \in A\} \ ,$$

$$R_{\text{out}1} = \{(\text{OUT}_1(b), \text{OUT}(b)) \mid b \in B\} \ ,$$

$$R_{\text{out}2} = \{(\text{OUT}_2(b), \text{OUT}(b)) \mid b \in B\} \ ,$$

clearly satisfies the conditions of the lemma. Since by the induction hypothesis $\text{IN}_1$, $\text{OUT}_1$, $\text{IN}_2$, $\text{OUT}_2$, $G_{E_1}$ and $G_{E_2}$ can be constructed in time $O(\text{size}(E_1))$ or $O(\text{size}(E_2))$, we conclude that $\text{IN}$, $\text{OUT}$ and $G_E$ can be constructed in time $O(\text{size}(E))$. The construction is illustrated in Figure 2.16.    $\square$

Theorem 2.2 and Lemma 2.27 together imply

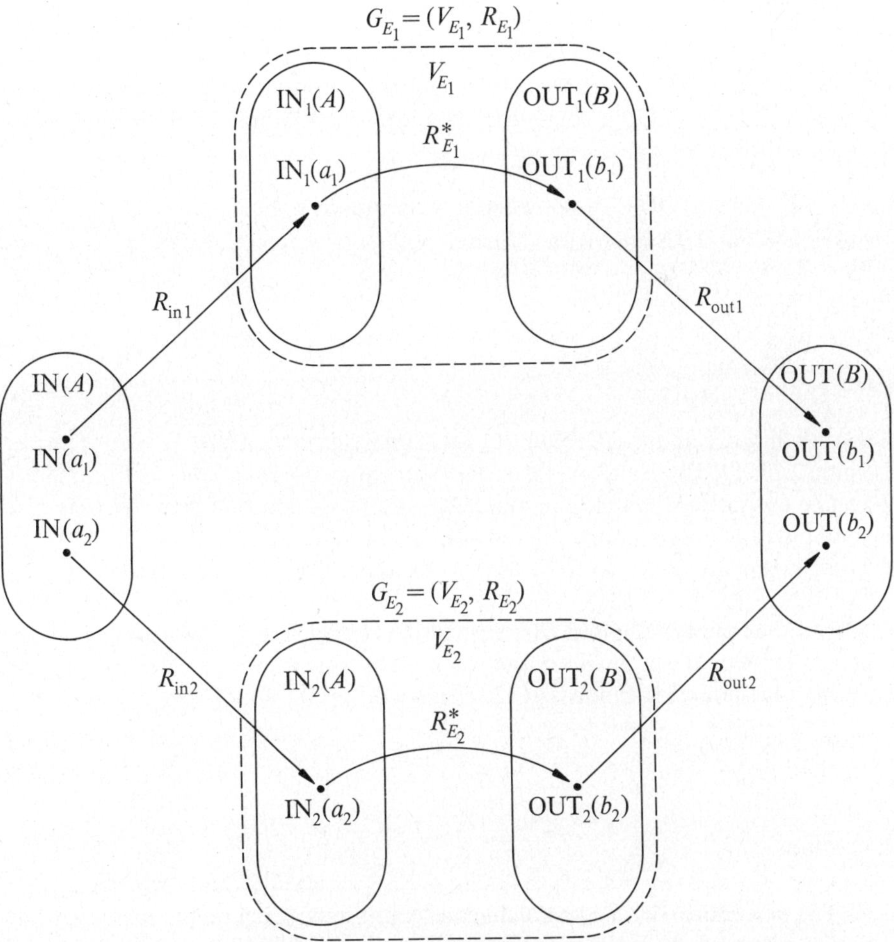


**Figure 2.16** The graph $G_E = (V_E, R_E)$ corresponding to the relational expression $E = E_1 \cup E_2$, where $G_{E_1} = (V_{E_1}, R_{E_1})$ is the graph corresponding to $E_1$, and $G_{E_2} = (V_{E_2}, R_{E_2})$ is the graph corresponding to $E_2$

**Theorem 2.28** *Let E be a relational expression with domain A and range B such that size(E) is finite. Then for any subset A' of A, R(E)(A') can be computed in time O(size(E)).*   □

From Theorem 2.24 and Lemma 2.27 we get

**Theorem 2.29** *Let E be a relational expression with domain A and range B such that size (E) is finite. Then the relation R(E) can be computed in time $O(t \cdot size\,(E))$, where t is the time required for a single set operation (union, assignment) on sets of size $min\{|A|, |B|\}$. Moreover, this computation can be performed during a single traversal of the directed graph $G_E$.*

*Proof.* Assume that $|B| \leqslant |A|$. (If $|A| < |B|$, consider the relational expression $E^{-1}$, compute the relation $R(E^{-1}) = R(E)^{-1}$, and take its inverse.) First note that the standard depth-first traversal (Figure 2.1) of $G_{E^{-1}}$ readily gives an $O(|B| \cdot size\,(E))$ algorithm (cf. Theorem 2.3): for each $b \in B$, compute the set $R(E^{-1})\,(b)$. However, this algorithm is inefficient in that portions of the graph $G_E = (V_E, R_E)$ are traversed several times. To obtain a single-traversal, $O(t \cdot size(E))$ time-bounded algorithm, define a function $F_0 : V_E \to 2^B$ by setting

$$F_0(u) = \begin{cases} \{OUT^{-1}(u)\}, & \text{when } u \text{ is an output node ;} \\ \varnothing, & \text{otherwise ,} \end{cases}$$

and a function $F : V_E \to 2^B$ by

$$F(u) = \bigcup_{u R_E^* v} F_0(v) \ .$$

Then for all $a \in A$ and $b \in B$, $IN(a)\ R_E^+\ OUT(b)$ if and only if $b \in F\,(IN(a))$. Thus by Lemma 2.27, $a\ R(E)\ b$ if and only if $b \in F\,(IN(a))$. Since by Theorem 2.24 the function $F$ can be constructed in time $O(t \cdot max\{|R_E|, |V_E|\})$, we conclude that $R(E)$ can also be computed within this time bound. The construction of $G_E = (V_E, R_E)$ takes time $O(size(E))$ (Lemma 2.27), so $R(E)$ can be constructed in time $O(t \cdot size(E))$.   □

Note that the time bound $O(t \cdot |E|)$ can be regarded as being linear in $size(E)$ when either $A$ or $B$ is a small set and when vector operations are available. In any case the time bound is $O(min\{|A|, |B|\} \cdot size(E))$.

## Exercises

2.1   The procedure TRAVERSE defines a "depth-first" order on the set of nodes of the graph $(A, R)$. Write a procedure that traverses $(A, R)$ in a "breadth-first" order, i.e., for any node $a \in A$, all nodes in $R(a)$ are visited before any node in $R^*(a) \backslash R(a)$ which was not already visited before $a$.

2.2  a)  Design a data structure for storing a relation (and a directed graph) such
         that the procedure TRAVERSE given in Figure 2.1(a) can be implemented
         in linear time.
     b)  Represent the directed graph in Figure 2.17 using this data structure.
     c)  Write a program to implement the algorithm of Figure 2.1 using this data
         structure.

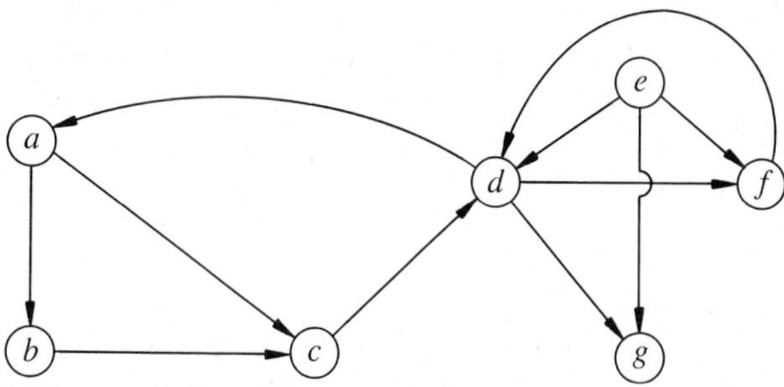

**Figure 2.17**  Directed graph

2.3  Give algorithms for computing the sum and the product of two boolean $n \times n$-
     matrices (see Exercise 1.19). What are the time complexities of your al-
     gorithms?

2.4  Give an efficient algorithm for computing the $k^{\text{th}}$ power $A^k$ of a boolean $n \times n$-
     matrix $A$ using the algorithms from the previous exercise. Note that only
     $O(\log k)$ matrix multiplications are needed. What is the time complexity of the
     algorithm?

2.5  A relation $R$ on an $n$-element set $\{a_1, \ldots, a_n\}$ can be represented by a boolean
     $n \times n$-matrix $\hat{R}$ such that

$$\hat{R}(i, j) = \textbf{true} \text{ if and only if } a_i \, R \, a_j \, .$$

     The matrix $\hat{R}$ is called the *adjacency matrix* of R.
     a)  Show by induction on $k$ that the adjacency matrix of $R^k$ is $\hat{R}^k$.
     b)  Show that the adjacency matrix of $R^*$ is $\hat{R}^0 + \hat{R}^1 + \ldots + \hat{R}^{n-1}$.

2.6  Give an algorithm for computing the transitive closure of a relation on a finite
     set. Use the results of Exercises 2.3, 2.4 and 2.5.

2.7  Let $R$ be a relation on an $n$-element set $\{a_1, \ldots, a_n\}$, and let $\hat{R}$ be its adjacency
     matrix. Let $A_0, A_1, \ldots, A_n$ be $n \times n$-matrices such that $A_0 = \hat{R}$, and for
     $k = 1, \ldots, n$

$$A_k(i, j) = A_{k-1}(i, j) \ \textbf{or} \ (A_{k-1}(i, k) \ \textbf{and} \ A_{k-1}(k, j))$$

     for $i = 1, \ldots, n$ and $j = 1, \ldots, n$. Prove that $A_n$ is the adjacency matrix of $R^*$.

2.8  Give an algorithm for computing $A_n$ as defined in the previous exercise. What is the time complexity of your algorithm? Note that for all $k, i, j$ $A_k(i, j) = A_{k-1}(i, k)$ and $A_k(k, j) = A_{k-1}(k, j)$, which implies that the algorithm need no more workspace than that required to store the adjacency matrix of the input relation.

2.9  Give all depth-first traversals of the graph in Figure 2.17 that begin with **enter**($a$).

2.10  Prove Fact 2.4.

2.11  Prove Fact 2.5.

2.12  Consider a modification to the procedure FINDSCC in which the statement in line 11 is changed to

$$\hat{f}(a) := \min\{\hat{f}(a), \hat{f}(c)\}$$

Show that the procedure FINDSCC still works correctly after this change (i.e., it finds the strongly connected components). Note that after this change the assignments to $\hat{f}(a)$ in lines 9 and 11 are the same, and thus the procedure can be shortened a little. Work out how this can be done.

2.13  Give the values of $\hat{f}$ for the graph in Figure 2.17, both for FINDSCC as given in Figure 2.5 and when FINDSCC has been modified as suggested in the previous exercise.

2.14  Let $(A, R)$ be a directed graph, and let $\pi$ be a depth-first traversal. Let $\leqslant_\pi$ be the total order on $A$ such that $a <_\pi b$ if **exit**($a$) precedes **exit**($b$) in $\pi$. Further, let $\rho$ be a depth-first traversal of $(A, R^{-1})$ and $\leqslant_\rho$ the corresponding depth-first order such that, for each **enter**($a$) which does not lie inside any substring **enter**($b$) . . . **exit**($b$) of $\rho$,

$$a >_\pi \max{}_{\leqslant_\pi} \{b \,|\, \textbf{enter}(b) \text{ appears after } \textbf{enter}(a) \text{ in } \rho\} \ .$$

Thus $\rho$ starts with the maximal element in $A$ with respect to $\leqslant_\pi$, and when the depth-first traversal of the starting element ends, the maximal element with respect to $\leqslant_\pi$ among the untraversed elements is chosen as the new starting element. This process is repeated until all elements in $A$ have been traversed. Show that the sets $(R^{-1} \cap \leqslant_\rho)^*(a)$, where $a \in A$ and no edge in $(A, R^{-1} \cap \leqslant_\rho)$ enters $a$, i.e., $\rho$ is not of the form

$$\ldots \ \textbf{enter}(b) \ldots \textbf{enter}(a) \ \ldots \textbf{exit}(b) \ldots \ ,$$

are precisely the strongly connected components of $(A, R)$.

2.15  Implement the method for finding the strongly connected components of a directed graph described in the previous exercise. What is the time complexity of your algorithm?

2.16  Let $A$ and $B$ be finite sets, $R$ a relation on $A$, and $F_0: A \to 2^B$ a function whose values $F_0(b) \subseteq B$ for $b \in A$, are known. Let $R$ be a relation on $A$ and $G: A \to 2^B$ any function that satisfies the equation

$$G(a) = F_0(a) \cup \bigcup_{aRb} G(b) \; .$$

Show that this equation does not uniquely define $G$.

2.17  Let $\mathbb{G}$ be the set of functions $G$ as defined in the previous exercise. Show that the function $F: A \to 2^B$ defined by

$$F(a) = \bigcup_{aR^*b} F_0(b)$$

is a member of $\mathbb{G}$, and moreover, for all $G \in \mathbb{G}$, $F(a) \subseteq G(a)$ for all $a \in A$.

2.18  Show that, for $\hat{F}$ computed by the algorithm of Figure 2.9, $\hat{F} = F$ whenever the graph $(A, R)$ is a tree.

2.19  Show that, for $\hat{F}$ computed by the algorithm of Figure 2.10, $\hat{F} = F$ whenever the graph $(A, R)$ is acyclic.

2.20  Prove Fact 2.22.

2.21  In the procedure CONSTRUCTF shown in Figure 2.11 some unnecessary assignments to $\hat{F}$ may be performed. In a call CONSTRUCTF$(a)$ the assignment

$$\hat{F}(a) := \hat{F}(a) \cup \hat{F}(c)$$

is not needed if $c < a$ and $a \in \mathrm{SCC}(c)$, because the value of $\hat{F}(c)$ will later be assigned to $\hat{F}(a)$. Implement this modification to the procedure CONSTRUCTF.

2.22  Modify the procedure CONSTRUCTF so that the algorithm of Figure 2.12 computes the transitive closure $R^+$ of $R$ when $F_0$ is defined appropriately. What will be the values of $F_0$?

2.23  Assume that the definition of a relational factor over a finite set $A$ is extended as follows. $E$ is a relational factor over $A$ if it is a relational primary over $A$ or has one of the forms $E_1^*$, $E_1^+$, or $E_1^{-1}$, where $E_1$ is a relational factor over $A$. Extend the proof of Lemma 2.27 to cover the case $E = E_1^+$.

## Bibliographic Notes

The algorithm for finding the strongly connected components of a directed graph comes from Tarjan (1972). Eve and Kurki-Suonio (1977) give a complete analysis of the algorithm which is similar to ours, and also explicitly embed the computation of the transitive closure of a relation into the strongly connected components algorithm. DeRemer and Pennello (1982) adapted this method for computing the function $F$ defined in Section 2.3. Relational expressions are defined in Hunt, Szymanski and Ullman (1977). This is the source of Lemma 2.27 and its proof.

The algorithm outlined in Exercises 2.7 and 2.8 for computing the transitive closure of a relation is the well-known algorithm of Warshall (1962). The method for determining the strongly connected components of a directed graph given in Exercise 2.14 comes from Aho, Hopcroft and Ullman (1983), who attribute it to R. Kosaraju.

General sources for graph algorithms and transitive closure computation are Aho, Hopcroft and Ullman (1974, 1983), Baase (1978), and Even (1980).

# 3. Regular Languages

In this chapter we shall consider a subfamily of the family of context-free languages known as the regular languages. The family of regular languages over an alphabet $V$ is the smallest family of languages over $V$ that contains all finite languages over $V$ and is closed under the operations closure, concatenation and finite union. We shall consider three equivalent ways of describing regular languages, namely regular expressions, finite automata and regular grammars. These are "equivalent" in the sense that each defines precisely the same family of regular languages. Moreover, there exist algorithms for transforming any regular expression, finite automaton or regular grammar into an equivalent language description belonging to either of the other two classes.

In Section 3.1 we introduce regular expressions and define regular languages as the languages which they describe. In Section 3.2 we introduce finite automata and show that any regular expression can be transformed into an equivalent finite automaton, and vice versa. In Section 3.3 we introduce regular grammars and show that any finite automaton can be transformed into an equivalent regular grammar, and vice versa. In Section 3.4 we consider a subclass of finite automata, deterministic finite automata, and show that any finite automaton can be transformed into an equivalent deterministic finite automaton. In Section 3.5 we derive algorithms for solving some important decision problems on regular languages and their descriptions. Finally, in Section 3.6 we demonstrate how the theory of regular languages can be applied in the design of lexical analyzers.


## 3.1 Regular Expressions

Let $L$ be a language over some alphabet $V$. A *language description* for $L$ is any finite means of specifying which strings in $V^*$ belong to $L$ and which do not. By finiteness here we mean that the description can be expressed using only a finite number of finitely structured elements. Given a language description $D$, we denote by $L(D)$ the language it describes.

Any language recognizer, as defined in Section 1.3, is a language description for the language it recognizes. Note that language recognizers, being RAM programs, always satisfy the finiteness requirement.

Finite languages can be described in a trivial manner by simply writing down all the sentences which they contain. In Section 1.6 we considered a language description, the context-free grammar $G_{match}$, that describes an infinite language, $L_{match}$. Rewriting systems satisfy the finiteness requirement because by definition both the alphabet and the set of rules are finite sets and any rule is in turn a pair of finite strings.

We may assume without loss of generality that descriptions of languages over an alphabet $V$ are themselves strings over another alphabet $W$, usually a superset of $V$. This makes sense because, whenever a structure is made up of a finite number of elements in a set $V$, it should be possible to represent the structure uniquely as a finite string over some finite superset of $V$. Thus any RAM program, being a finite sequence of instructions, can be represented as a finite string over some alphabet. Any rewriting system with alphabet $V$ can be represented as a finite string over $V \cup \{ \# \}$ (see Fact 1.45). As strings over any alphabet can be further encoded as binary strings, we may conclude that language descriptions can be viewed merely as finite strings over the binary alphabet $\{0, 1\}$.

This interpretation of language descriptions immediately implies that not all languages can be described. In fact, for any alphabet $V$ only a countably infinite number of languages over $V$ have descriptions, because $\{0, 1\}^*$, the set of possible language descriptions, is only countably infinite (see Theorem 1.23). On the other hand, $2^{V^*}$, the family of all languages over $V$, is uncountable: it has the same size as $\{0, 1\}^{\mathbb{N}}$, which we have shown to be uncountable (see Theorem 1.10 and Exercises 1.10 and 1.11). Since any language description $D$ describes only one language, namely $L(D)$, there are simply not enough such $D$s to cover all the languages in $2^{V^*}$.

One way to generate descriptions of infinite languages over an alphabet $V$ is to use expressions in which the arguments are finite languages over $V$ and the operators are chosen from among * (closure), · (concatenation), and $\cup$ (finite union). For example, we can describe the language

$$L_{end} = \{w \in \{0, 1\}^* \mid w \text{ is empty or ends in 01 or 100}\}$$

by the expression

$$\{\varepsilon\} \cup \{0, 1\}^* \{01, 100\} \ .$$

Here we have as usual omitted the concatenation operator ·, and assumed that the closure operator * has the highest precedence and the union operator $\cup$ the lowest.

Since only finite languages are allowed as arguments, we may as well write the expression in a form in which the arguments are all singleton (or empty) subsets of $V \cup \{\varepsilon\}$, i.e.,

$$\{\varepsilon\} \cup (\{0\} \cup \{1\})^* (\{0\}\{1\} \cup \{1\}\{0\}\{0\}) \ .$$

This expression can be simplified by omitting the braces from the singleton sets to give

$$\varepsilon \cup (0 \cup 1)^* (01 \cup 100) \ .$$

This is an example of a "regular expression" over $\{0, 1\}$.

Informally, a *regular expression over* an alphabet $V$ is thus any well-formed expression whose arguments are elements in $V \cup \{\varepsilon, \emptyset\}$ and whose operators are chosen from among * (closure), · (concatenation), and $\cup$ (union). Here $\varepsilon$ and $\varnothing$ are special symbols denoting the empty string $\varepsilon$ and the empty language $\varnothing$ respectively.

In what follows we formally define regular expressions over $V$ as certain strings over the extended alphabet

$$V \cup \{\underline{\varepsilon}, \varnothing, *, \cdot, \cup, ), (\}$$

where $\underline{\varepsilon}, \varnothing, *, \cdot, \cup, )$ and $($ are assumed to be new distinct symbols not found in $V$. The definition is inductive on the length of an expression, and defines not only regular expressions but also restricted kinds of regular expression called "regular terms", "regular factors" and "regular primaries", which reflect the precedence and associativity of the operators $\cup$, $\cdot$ and *. The definition is very similar to that of relational expressions given in Chapter 2. (As usual, we shall omit the concatenation operator when no confusion can arise.)

Let $E$ be a string over $V \cup \{\underline{\varepsilon}, \varnothing, *, \cdot, \cup, ), (\}$.

(1) $E$ is a *regular primary over* $V$ if it is a symbol in $V \cup \{\varepsilon, \varnothing\}$ or is of the form $(E_1)$, where $E_1$ is a regular expression over $V$.

(2) $E$ is a *regular factor over* $V$ if it is a regular primary over $V$ or is of the form $E_1^*$, where $E_1$ is a regular factor over $V$.

(3) $E$ is a *regular term over* $V$ if it is a regular factor over $V$ or is of the form $E_1 E_2$, where $E_1$ is a regular term and $E_2$ a regular factor over $V$.

(4) $E$ is a *regular expression over* $V$ if it is a regular term over $V$ or is of the form $E_1 \cup E_2$, where $E_1$ is a regular expression and $E_2$ a regular term over $V$.

If no ambiguity arises, we may write $\varepsilon$ for $\underline{\varepsilon}$ and $\varnothing$ for $\varnothing$ in regular expressions.

**Fact 3.1** Let $V$ be an alphabet.

(1) If $E_1$ and $E_1'$ are regular terms and $E_2$ and $E_2'$ regular factors over $V$ such that $E_1 E_2 = E_1' E_2'$, then $E_1 = E_1'$ and $E_2 = E_2'$.

(2) If $E_1$ and $E_1'$ are regular expressions and $E_2$ and $E_2'$ regular terms over $V$ such that $E_1 \cup E_2 = E_1' \cup E_2'$, then $E_1 = E_1'$ and $E_2 = E_2'$.   $\square$

The *language $L(E)$ denoted* (or *described*) by a regular expression $E$ over $V$ is defined inductively on the length of $E$ as follows:

(1a) $L(\varnothing) = \varnothing$.

(1b) $L(\varepsilon) = \{\varepsilon\}$.

(1c) $L(a) = \{a\}$ for all $a$ in $V$.

(1d) $L((E)) = L(E)$ for all regular expressions $E$ over $V$.

(2) $L(E^*) = L(E)^*$ for all regular factors $E$ over $V$.

(3) $L(E_1 E_2) = L(E_1)L(E_2)$ for all regular terms $E_1$ and regular factors $E_2$ over $V$.

(4) $L(E_1 \cup E_2) = L(E_1) \cup L(E_2)$ for all regular expressions $E_1$ and regular terms $E_2$ over $V$.

Note that Fact 3.1 guarantees that $L(E_1 E_2)$ and $L(E_1 \cup E_2)$ are well-defined. Thus the language denoted by the regular expression

$$\underline{\varepsilon} \cup (0 \cup 1)^*(01 \cup 100)$$

is obtained by applying the above definition repeatedly as follows:

$$
\begin{aligned}
&L(\varepsilon \cup (0 \cup 1)^*(01 \cup 100)) \\
&= L(\underline{\varepsilon}) \cup L((0 \cup 1)^*(01 \cup 100)) \\
&= \{\varepsilon\} \cup L((0 \cup 1)^*)L((01 \cup 100)) \\
&= \{\varepsilon\} \cup L((0 \cup 1))^* L(01 \cup 100) \\
&= \{\varepsilon\} \cup L(0 \cup 1)^* (L(01) \cup L(100)) \\
&= \{\varepsilon\} \cup (L(0) \cup L(1))^* (L(0)L(1) \cup L(1)L(0)L(0)) \\
&= \{\varepsilon\} \cup (\{0\} \cup \{1\})^* (\{0\}\{1\} \cup \{1\}\{0\}\{0\}) \\
&= \{\varepsilon\} \cup \{0, 1\}^* \{01, 100\}.
\end{aligned}
$$

A language $L_1$ over an alphabet $V$ is *regular* if it is the language denoted by some regular expression over $V$, i.e., if $L_1 = L(E)$ for some regular expression $E$ over $V$.

**Fact 3.2** Any finite language is regular.

*Proof.* A finite language $\{w_1, \ldots, w_n\}$, $n \geq 1$, is denoted by the regular expression $w_1 \cup \ldots \cup w_n$. The empty language is denoted by the regular expression $\emptyset$.  □

A language family $\mathbb{F}$ is said to be *effectively closed* under an $n$-ary operation $f$ if any $n$-tuple $D_1, \ldots, D_n$ of language descriptions (belonging to the class of descriptions used to describe languages in $\mathbb{F}$) can be transformed into a description of the language $f(L(D_1), \ldots, L(D_n))$. Clearly, $\mathbb{F}$ is closed under $f$ whenever it is effectively closed under $f$. ($\mathbb{F}$ is *closed* under $f$ if $L_1, \ldots, L_n \in \mathbb{F}$ always implies $f(L_1, \ldots, L_n) \in \mathbb{F}$.)

The following lemma states that the family of regular languages is effectively closed under the operations closure, concatenation and finite union.

**Lemma 3.3** *Any regular expression $E$ over an alphabet $V$ can be transformed in time $O(|E|)$ into a regular expression that denotes $L(E)^*$. Any pair of regular expressions $E_1$ and $E_2$ over $V$ can be transformed in time $O(|E_1| + |E_2|)$ into regular expressions that denote $L(E_1)L(E_2)$ and $L(E_1) \cup L(E_2)$.*

*Proof.* By definition, $(E)^*$ is a regular expression denoting $L(E)^*$, $(E_1)(E_2)$ is a regular expression denoting $L(E_1)L(E_2)$, and $(E_1) \cup (E_2)$ is a regular expression denoting $L(E_1) \cup L(E_2)$. Moreover, these expressions can obviously be constructed in time linear in the size of the original expressions.  □

**Theorem 3.4** (*Kleene*) *For any alphabet $V$, the family of regular languages over $V$ is the smallest family of languages over $V$ that contains all finite languages over $V$ and is (effectively) closed under closure, concatenation and finite union.*

*Proof.* First, the family of regular languages over $V$ contains all finite languages over $V$ and is effectively closed under closure, concatenation and finite union (Fact 3.2 and Lemma 3.3). Then let $\mathbb{F}$ be any family of languages over $V$ that contains all finite languages over $V$ and is closed under closure, concatenation and finite union. We have to prove that the family of regular languages over $V$ is contained in $\mathbb{F}$. Let $E$ be any regular expression over $V$. We prove by induction on the length of $E$ that $L(E)$ belongs to $\mathbb{F}$. First, if $|E|=1$ then $E \in V \cup \{\varepsilon, \varnothing\}$, so $L(E)$, being a finite language, belongs to $\mathbb{F}$. This proves the base case. To prove the induction step, we assume that $E$ has one of the forms $(E_1)$, $E_1^*$, $E_1 E_2$, or $E_1 \cup E_2$. Since both $E_1$ and $E_2$ are shorter than $E$, we can assume as an induction hypothesis that $L(E_1)$ and $L(E_2)$ belong to $\mathbb{F}$. But then $L(E)$ also belongs to $\mathbb{F}$, because by definition one of the statements $\quad L(E)=L(E_1), \quad L(E)=L(E_1)^*, \quad L(E)=L(E_1)L(E_2), \quad$ or $\quad L(E) = L(E_1) \cup L(E_2)$ holds, and because $\mathbb{F}$ is closed under closure, concatenation and finite union.  $\square$

The language

$$L_{\text{match}} = \{0^n 1^n \,|\, n \geqslant 0\} \,,$$

which was discussed in Section 1.6, is a prototypical example of a language that is not regular but is context-free (i.e., describable by a context-free grammar).

That $L_{\text{match}}$ is not regular is due to the fact that regular expressions "cannot count". Informally, we cannot use the closure operator * to introduce the leading zeros or the trailing ones in sentences $0^n 1^n$, because the language denoted by any such regular expression would then also contain strings that either have an unequal number of zeros and ones or have zeros and ones mixed. However, the only way to denote an infinite language is to use the closure operator. It should then be obvious that no regular expression denoting $L_{\text{match}}$ can exist.

We will be in a position to give more rigorous arguments for the nonregularity of $L_{\text{match}}$ in Section 3.2, where we establish that a language is regular only if it can be accepted by some finite automaton.

We say that two language descriptions $D_1$ and $D_2$ are *equivalent* if they describe the same language, i.e., if $L(D_1)=L(D_2)$. $D_1$ and $D_2$ are *inequivalent* if they are not equivalent.

**Fact 3.5** For any regular expression there exist a countably infinite number of equivalent regular expressions.

*Proof.* Given any regular expression $E$, the regular expressions $E, E \cup E, E \cup E \cup E$, $E \cup E \cup E \cup E, \ldots$ all denote $L(E)$.  $\square$

Thus any regular language has a countably infinite number of descriptions within the class of regular expressions.

The result of Fact 3.5 is not unusual. We shall see that, given any class of language descriptions $\mathbb{D}$, any description in $\mathbb{D}$ usually has a countably infinite number of equivalent descriptions (that differ from each other more than just in the naming of symbols).

We say that a language description $D$ is *ambiguous* if some sentence in $L(D)$ is described in two ways. (The precise meaning of the term "described in two ways" depends on the particular class of language descriptions in question, and we shall restate the definition of ambiguity for each particular class.) A description $D$ is *unambiguous* if it is not ambiguous.

For example, $0 \cup 0$, $(0 \cup 01)(\varepsilon \cup 1)$, $(0 \cup 000)^*$, and $\varepsilon^*$ are all ambiguous regular expressions over $\{0, 1\}$. Here $0 \cup 0$ describes 0 in two ways, $(0 \cup 01)(\varepsilon \cup 1)$ describes 01 in two ways, $(0 \cup 000)^*$ describes in at least two ways any string of more than two zeros, and $\varepsilon^*$ describes $\varepsilon$ in infinitely many ways. By contrast, the regular expression $\varepsilon \cup (0 \cup 1)^*(01 \cup 100)$ discussed above is unambiguous.

Formally, ambiguity of regular expressions over an alphabet $V$ is defined inductively as follows:

(1)  $\emptyset$, $\varepsilon$, $a$, and $(E)$ are *unambiguous* for all $a \in V$ and unambiguous regular expressions $E$ over $V$.

(2)  For any regular factor $E$ over $V$, $E^*$ is *unambiguous* if $E$ is unambiguous and for all $x \in L(E^*)$ there is exactly one $n \geqslant 0$ and exactly one sequence $(x_1, \ldots, x_n)$ of strings in $L(E)$ such that $x_1 \ldots x_n = x$. (In the case $n = 0$, $x_1 \ldots x_n$ is taken to be $\varepsilon$.)

(3)  For any regular term $E_1$ and regular factor $E_2$ over $V$, $E_1 E_2$ is *unambiguous* if either (a) $L(E_1 E_2) = \emptyset$, or (b) $E_1$ and $E_2$ are unambiguous and for all $x \in L(E_1 E_2)$ there is exactly one pair $(y, z) \in L(E_1) \times L(E_2)$ such that $yz = x$.

(4)  For any regular expression $E_1$ and regular term $E_2$ over $V$, $E_1 \cup E_2$ is *unambiguous* if $E_1$ and $E_2$ are unambiguous and $L(E_1) \cap L(E_2) = \emptyset$.


Ambiguity in language descriptions may sometimes be undesirable. Ambiguity cannot be allowed at all in language descriptions that are not only intended to describe the language but also to attach some unique meaning to the sentences. For example, in describing a programming language by means of an attribute grammar, the underlying context-free grammar is required to be unambiguous because otherwise some program might be assigned more than one meaning. However, ambiguous descriptions may often be more concise and easier to understand than equivalent unambiguous descriptions. The reader is invited to design an unambiguous regular expression that denotes the language

$$\{w \in \{0, 1\}^* \mid w \text{ contains } 000 \text{ or } 111 \text{ as a substring}\} \ .$$

This language is denoted by the ambiguous regular expression

$$(0 \cup 1)^*(000 \cup 111)(0 \cup 1)^* \ .$$

For some classes of language descriptions, the unambiguity requirement reduces the *descriptional power* of the class, in the sense that there are languages that have an ambiguous description but no unambiguous one. This is the case with, for example, the class of context-free grammars. It can be shown that there are *inherently ambiguous* context-free languages, i.e., languages that are generated by an ambiguous context-free grammar but not by any unambiguous one.

The descriptional power of unambiguous regular expressions, however, turns out to be equal to that of unrestricted regular expressions. In other words, any language over an alphabet $V$ that is denoted by some regular expression over $V$ is also denoted by an unambiguous regular expression over $V$. Hence there are no "inherently ambiguous" regular languages with respect to the class of regular expressions. This is stated in the following theorem.

**Theorem 3.6** *Any regular expression over an alphabet $V$ can be transformed into an equivalent unambiguous regular expression over $V$.*

*Proof.* We shall show in later sections (see Theorems 3.16 and 3.30) that any regular expression over an alphabet $V$ can be transformed into an equivalent deterministic $\varepsilon$-free finite automaton with input alphabet $V$. On the other hand, we shall show (Theorem 3.17) that any unambiguous finite automaton with input alphabet $V$ can be transformed into an equivalent unambiguous regular expression over $V$. Since any deterministic $\varepsilon$-free finite automaton is also unambiguous (Fact 3.29), we conclude that any regular expression over $V$ can be transformed into an equivalent unambiguous regular expression over $V$.    $\square$

Let $\mathbb{D}_1$ and $\mathbb{D}_2$ be any classes of language descriptions. We say that the descriptions in $\mathbb{D}_1$ are *at least as descriptive as* those in $\mathbb{D}_2$ if all descriptions in $\mathbb{D}_2$ have equivalent descriptions in $\mathbb{D}_1$. The descriptions in $\mathbb{D}_1$ are *more descriptive than* those in $\mathbb{D}_2$ if the descriptions in $\mathbb{D}_1$ are at least as descriptive as those in $\mathbb{D}_2$ and if there is a description in $\mathbb{D}_1$ that has no equivalent description in $\mathbb{D}_2$. The descriptions in $\mathbb{D}_1$ are *as descriptive as* (or *equivalent in descriptional power to*) those in $\mathbb{D}_2$ if the descriptions in $\mathbb{D}_1$ are at least as descriptive as those in $\mathbb{D}_2$ and vice versa.

Apart from descriptional power, classes of language descriptions may also differ in the *succinctness* of their descriptions. Let $\mathbb{D}_1$ and $\mathbb{D}_2$ be classes of language descriptions such that the descriptions in $\mathbb{D}_1$ are at least as descriptive as those in $\mathbb{D}_2$. We say that the descriptions in $\mathbb{D}_1$ are *at least as succinct as* those in $\mathbb{D}_2$ if for any description $D_2$ in $\mathbb{D}_2$ there is an equivalent description $D_1$ in $\mathbb{D}_1$ whose size is at most linear in the size of $D_2$. Let the descriptions in $\mathbb{D}_1$ be as descriptive as those in $\mathbb{D}_2$. Then the descriptions in $\mathbb{D}_1$ are *as succinct as* (or *equivalent in succinctness to*) those in $\mathbb{D}_2$ if the descriptions in $\mathbb{D}_1$ are at least as succinct as those in $\mathbb{D}_2$ and vice versa.

Let $f$ be a function from the natural numbers to the positive reals. We say that the descriptions in $\mathbb{D}_1$ *can be $f(n)$ more succinct than* those in $\mathbb{D}_2$ if there exists an infinite sequence of languages $L_1, L_2, \ldots$ such that each $L_n$ has a description of size $O(n)$ in $\mathbb{D}_1$ and some description in $\mathbb{D}_2$, but all descriptions of $L_n$ in $\mathbb{D}_2$ are of size at least $f(n)$.

Although equivalent in descriptional power, unambiguous regular expressions are not equivalent in succinctness to unrestricted regular expressions. In fact, unrestricted regular expressions can be exponentially more succinct than unambiguous regular expressions, as is stated in the following proposition.

**Proposition 3.7** *There exists a constant $c>0$ and an infinite sequence of regular languages $L_1, L_2, \ldots$ over $\{0, 1\}$ such that each $L_n$ is denoted by an ambiguous regular expression of length $O(n)$, but any unambiguous regular expression denoting $L_n$ must have length at least $2^{cn}$.*  $\square$


## 3.2  Finite Automata

In this section we shall discuss a subclass of rewriting systems called finite automata. A finite automaton can be thought of as a model of a primitive computer that runs in constant workspace. As a class of language descriptions, finite automata turn out to be equivalent in descriptional power to regular expressions. In other words, the languages described by finite automata are exactly the regular languages.

Let $M=(V, P)$ be a rewriting system, and let $Q$ and $T$ be disjoint nonempty subsets of an alphabet $V$ satisfying $V=Q \cup T$. Further, let $q_s$ be an element of $Q$ and $F$ a subset of $Q$. We say that $M$ is a *finite automaton* (or *finite-machine program*) *with state alphabet $Q$, input alphabet $T$, initial state $q_s$ and set of final states $F$, denoted by*

$$M=(Q, T, P, q_s, F) ,$$

if each rule in $P$ is of the form

$$q_1 x \to q_2 ,$$

where $q_1$ and $q_2$ are states, i.e., elements of $Q$, and $x$ is an input string, i.e., an element of $T^*$. A rule $q_1 x \to q_2$ is called an *x-transition* (or a *transition on x*) *from state $q_1$ to state $q_2$*.

A *configuration* (or an *instantaneous description*) of a finite automaton $M$ is a string of the form $qw$, where $q$ is a state and $w$ is an input string of $M$. Thus configurations are strings in $QT^*$. A configuration $qw$ is *initial for $w$* if $q$ is the initial state $q_s$. It is *accepting* if $w=\varepsilon$ and $q$ is a final state, i.e., belongs to $F$. A nonaccepting configuration to which no rule of $M$ is applicable is called an *error configuration*.

A *computation* (or *process*) *of* a finite automaton $M$ *on* input string $w$ is any derivation in $M$ from the initial configuration for $w$. A computation is *accepting* if it ends with an accepting configuration. $M$ *accepts* $w$ if it has an accepting computation on $w$.

The *language accepted* (or *recognized* or *described*) by a finite automaton $M$, denoted by $L(M)$, is the set of input strings accepted by $M$.

By Fact 1.43 we have

$$L(M)=\{w \in T^* \mid q_s w \Rightarrow^* q \text{ in } M \text{ for some } q \in F\} .$$

As an example, consider the finite automaton

$$M_{\text{end}}=(\{q_0, q_1, q_2\}, \quad \{0, 1\}, \quad P, \quad q_0, \quad \{q_0, q_2\}) ,$$

where $P$ consists of the rules

$$q_0 \rightarrow q_1, \quad q_1 0 \rightarrow q_1, \quad q_1 1 \rightarrow q_1, \quad q_1 01 \rightarrow q_2, \quad q_1 100 \rightarrow q_2 .$$

Thus $M_{\text{end}}$ is a finite automaton with state alphabet $\{q_0, q_1, q_2\}$, input alphabet $\{0, 1\}$, initial state $q_0$, and set of final states $\{q_0, q_2\}$, and with transitions on the empty string $\varepsilon$ from state $q_0$ to state $q_1$, on strings 0 and 1 from state $q_1$ to itself, and on strings 01 and 100 from state $q_1$ to state $q_2$.

The following statements hold for $M_{\text{end}}$:

$$q_0 \Rightarrow^0 q_0 ,$$
$$q_0 w01 \Rightarrow q_1 w01 \Rightarrow^{|w|} q_1 01 \Rightarrow q_2 \text{ for all } w \text{ in } \{0, 1\}^* ,$$
$$q_0 w100 \Rightarrow q_1 w100 \Rightarrow^{|w|} q_1 100 \Rightarrow q_2 \text{ for all } w \text{ in } \{0, 1\}^* .$$

In fact, we have

$$L(M_{\text{end}}) = \{w \in \{0, 1\}^* \mid w \text{ is empty or ends with 01 or 100}\} .$$

This is the language $L_{\text{end}}$ discussed in the previous section.

A finite automaton $M$ is often visualized by means of a *transition graph*. This is a directed graph whose set of nodes consists of all states of $M$ and whose edges are all pairs $(q_1, q_2)$ such that $q_1 x \rightarrow q_2$ is a rule of $M$ for some $x$. In addition, each edge $(q_1, q_2)$ is labeled by all those $x$ for which $q_1 x \rightarrow q_2$ is a rule of $M$.

The transition graph of the finite automaton $M_{\text{end}}$ given above is shown in Figure 3.1. The initial state is indicated by an unlabeled arrow and the final states by a double circle.

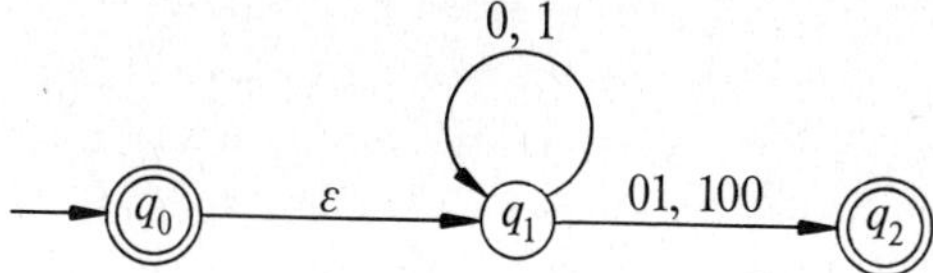

Figure. 3.1  Transition graph of the finite automaton $M_{\text{end}}$

A finite automaton is *ambiguous* if it accepts some sentence in two distinct ways, i.e., if there are at least two accepting computations on some sentence; otherwise, it is *unambiguous*. The automaton $M_{\text{end}}$ is unambiguous. An example of an ambiguous finite automaton is given in Figure 3.2.

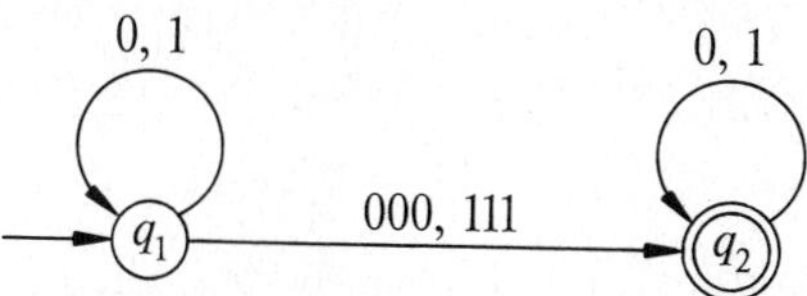

Figure 3.2  Transition graph of an ambiguous finite automaton that accepts the language denoted by the regular expression $(0 \cup 1)^*(000 \cup 111)(0 \cup 1)^*$

A state $p$ of a finite automaton $M$ is *reachable from* a state $q$ of $M$ *upon reading* input string $w$ if $qw$ derives $p$ in $M$. A state is *accessible upon reading $w$* if it is reachable from the initial state $q_s$ of $M$ upon reading $w$.

**Fact 3.8** A finite automaton accepts an input string $w$ if and only if some final state is accessible upon reading $w$.  □

A state that is accessible upon reading some string is called simply *accessible*. A state is *inaccessible* if it is not accessible. A finite automaton that has no inaccessible states is called *reduced*.

The inaccessible states play no role in the accepted language. We shall show that in fact any finite automaton $M$ can be transformed in time linear in $|M|$ into an equivalent reduced finite automaton. Here $|M|$ means the size of $M$, as defined in Section 1.6.

**Lemma 3.9** *The set of states reachable from a given state of a finite automaton $M$ can be computed in time $O(|M|)$.*

*Proof.* We define a relation **reaches** on the set of states of $M$ as follows: for states $q_1$ and $q_2$ of $M$, $q_1$ **reaches** $q_2$ if $M$ has a transition from $q_1$ to $q_2$. (In other words, **reaches** is the set of edges in the transition graph of $M$.) It can be shown by a simple induction that $q_1$ **reaches*** $q_2$ if and only if $q_2$ is reachable from $q_1$. Thus the set of states reachable from a given state $q$ of $M$ is obtained as the closure **reaches*** $(q)$. The relation **reaches** is of size $O(|M|)$ and can obviously be constructed from $M$ in time $O(|M|)$. By Theorem 2.2, the closure of $\{q\}$ under **reaches** can then be computed in time $O(|M|)$.  □

**Theorem 3.10** *Any finite automaton $M=(Q, T, P, q_s, F)$ can be transformed in time $O(|M|)$ into an equivalent reduced finite automaton $M'=(Q', T, P', q_s, F')$, where $Q'\subseteq Q$, $P'\subseteq P$, and $F'\subseteq F$.*

*Proof.* First find the set of states reachable from $q_s$. Then remove from $M$ all other states and all transitions from these. By Lemma 3.9, this algorithm produces a reduced finite automaton equivalent to $M$. Moreover, the algorithm runs in time $O(|M|)$.  □

A state $q$ of a finite automaton $M$ is *live* if some final state of $M$ is reachable from $q$. A state that is not live is *dead*.

**Lemma 3.11** *The set of live states of a finite automaton $M$ can be computed in time $O(|M|)$.*

*Proof.* The set of live states of $M$ is obtained as the closure $(\mathbf{reaches}^{-1})^*(F)$, where $F$ is the set of final states of $M$ and **reaches** is the relation defined in the proof of Lemma 3.9. The claim therefore follows from Theorem 2.2.  □

**Fact 3.12** Let $M$ be an unambiguous finite automaton. Then for any accessible live states $q_1$ and $q_2$, and any input string $x$, there is at most one derivation of $q_2$ from $q_1 x$ in $M$.  $\square$

A finite automaton is *normal-form* if it has transitions on single input symbols and the empty string only, i.e., each rule is of the form $q_1 x \to q_2$, where $x$ belongs to $T \cup \{\varepsilon\}$. A finite automaton is *$\varepsilon$-free* if it has no transitions on the empty string $\varepsilon$.

The following theorem says that normal-form finite automata are equivalent in descriptional power as well as in succinctness to unrestricted finite automata.

**Theorem 3.13** *Any finite automaton $M$ with input alphabet $T$ can be transformed in time $O(|M|)$ into an equivalent normal-form finite automaton $M'$ with input alphabet $T$. Moreover, $M'$ is unambiguous if and only if $M$ is, and $M'$ is $\varepsilon$-free if and only if $M$ is.*

*Proof.* The set of states of the transformed automaton $M'$ is

$$\{[q] \mid q \text{ is a state of } M\}$$
$$\cup \{[qx] \mid qxy \text{ is the left-hand side of some rule of } M, \text{ for some } y \neq \varepsilon\} .$$

The initial state of $M'$ is $[q_s]$, where $q_s$ is the initial state of $M$. The set of final states of $M'$ is

$$\{[q] \mid q \text{ is a final state of } M\} ,$$

and its set of rules is

$$\{[q_1] \to [q_2] \mid q_1 \to q_2 \text{ is a rule of } M\}$$
$$\cup \{[qx]a \to [qxa] \mid a \in T \text{ and } qxay \text{ is the left-hand side of some rule of } M,$$
$$\text{for some } y \neq \varepsilon\}$$
$$\cup \{[q_1 x]a \to [q_2] \mid a \in T \text{ and } q_1 xa \to q_2 \text{ is a rule of } M\} .$$

By the construction of $M'$, any positive-length derivation of the form $([q]x, \ldots, [p]y)$ in $M'$ is a concatenation of shorter derivations of the following forms

(1) $([q_1]w, [q_2]w)$.
(2) $([q_1]a_1 \ldots a_n w, [q_1 a_1]a_2 \ldots a_n w, \ldots, [q_1 a_1 \ldots a_{n-1}]a_n w, [q_2]w)$.

Here $w \in T^*$ and $a_1, \ldots, a_n \in T$. In (1), $q_1 \to q_2$ is a rule of $M$, and in (2) $q_1 a_1 \ldots a_n \to q_2$ is a rule of $M$. Conversely, if $q_1 \to q_2$ is a rule of $M$, then for all $w$, (1) is a derivation in $M'$, and if $q_1 a_1 \ldots a_n \to q_2$ is a rule of $M$, then for all $w$, (2) is a derivation in $M'$. This means that there is a bijective correspondence between derivations $([q]x, \ldots, [p]y)$ in $M'$ and derivations $(qx, \ldots, py)$ in $M$. But then clearly $L(M') = L(M)$, and $M'$ is unambiguous if and only if $M$ is. The construction of $M'$ in turn implies immediately that $M'$ is $\varepsilon$-free if and only if $M$ is.

Finally we note that $M'$ is of size at most $3|M|$, and that $M'$ can obviously be constructed from $M$ in time $O(|M|)$.  $\square$

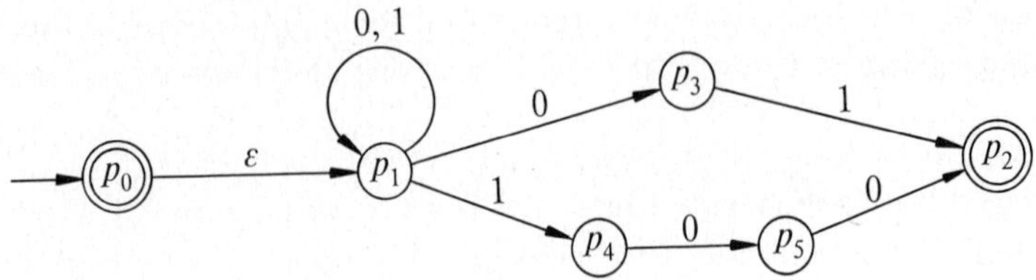


**Figure 3.3** A normal-form finite automaton equivalent to $M_{end}$ shown in Figure 3.1

As an example, the transformed automaton $M'_{end}$ for $M_{end}$ is shown in Figure 3.3, where $p_0$ denotes $[q_0]$, $p_1$ denotes $[q_1]$, $p_2$ denotes $[q_2]$, $p_3$ denotes $[q_1 0]$, $p_4$ denotes $[q_1 1]$, and $p_5$ denotes $[q_1 10]$.

Like transitions on strings longer than one, $\varepsilon$-transitions can also be eliminated, as is stated in the following lemma. However, this can only be done at the cost of increasing the size of the automaton by a factor of $|Q|$, the number of states.

**Lemma 3.14** *Any normal-form finite automaton $M$ with state alphabet $Q$ and input alphabet $T$ can be transformed in time $O(|Q| \cdot |M|)$ into an equivalent $\varepsilon$-free normal-form finite automaton $M''$ with input alphabet $T$. Moreover, if $M$ is unambiguous then so is $M''$.*

*Proof.* The set of states and the initial state of the transformed automaton $M''$ are as in $M$. The set of rules of $M''$ is

$$\{q_1 a \rightarrow q_2 \,|\, a \in T \text{ and for some } q \in Q, q_1 \Rightarrow^* q$$
$$\text{in } M \text{ and } qa \rightarrow q_2 \text{ is a rule of } M\} \ .$$

In other words, $M''$ has a transition on input symbol $a$ from state $q_1$ to state $q_2$ whenever $M$ has a transition on $a$ to $q_2$ from some state $q$ reachable from $q_1$ upon reading the empty string $\varepsilon$. The set of final states of $M''$ is

$$\{q \in Q \,|\, q \Rightarrow^* q' \text{ in } M \text{ for some final state } q' \text{ of } M\} \ ,$$

i.e., the set of states from which some final state of $M$ is reachable upon reading $\varepsilon$.

It can be shown by a straightforward induction that, for all states $q_1$ and states $q_2$ and input strings $w$, $q_1 w \Rightarrow^* q_2$ in $M$ if and only if

$$q_1 w \Rightarrow^* q \text{ in } M'' \quad \text{and} \quad q \Rightarrow^* q_2 \quad \text{in } M \text{ for some state } q.$$

Choosing here $q_1$ to be the initial state and $q_2$ some final state, we conclude that $L(M'') = L(M)$. Moreover, it is not hard to see that the transformation preserves unambiguity. (In fact, it may remove some degree of ambiguity.)

Now let **empty-trans** denote the restriction of the directly derives relation of $M$ to single states of $M$, i.e., for states $q_1$ and $q_2$, $q_1$ **empty-trans** $q_2$ if and only if $q_1 \rightarrow q_2$ is a rule of $M$. We then have $q_1$ **empty-trans*** $q_2$ if and only if $q_1 \Rightarrow^* q_2$ in $M$. Moreover, **empty-trans** is of size $O(|M|)$ and can be computed from $M$ in time $O(|M|)$. By Theorem 2.3, its closure **empty-trans*** can be computed in time

$O(|Q|\cdot|M|)$. This means that the set of rules and the set of final states of $M''$ can be constructed in time $O(|Q|\cdot|M|)$.   □

The transformed automaton for the automaton of Figure 3.3 is shown in Figure 3.4.

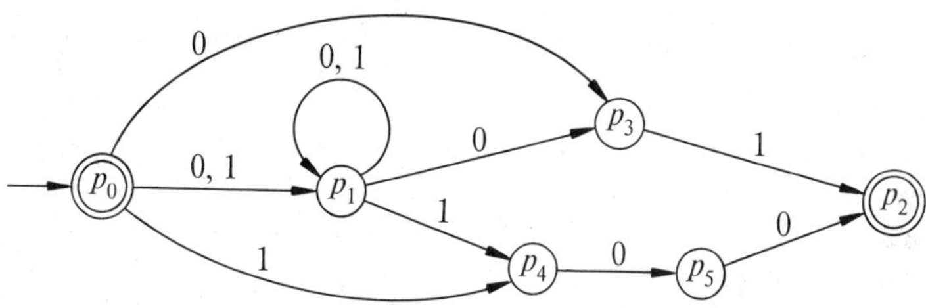

**Figure 3.4** An $\varepsilon$-free normal-form finite automaton equivalent to $M_{end}$ shown in Figure 3.1

In view of Theorem 3.13 and Lemma 3.14 we have

**Theorem 3.15** *Any finite automaton M can be transformed in time $O(|M|^2)$ into an equivalent $\varepsilon$-free normal-form finite automaton. Moreover, if M is unambiguous then so is the transformed automaton.*   □

The nonlinear time bound in Theorem 3.15 suggests that finite automata with $\varepsilon$-transitions can be more succinct than their $\varepsilon$-free counterparts. Indeed, it can be shown that there is an infinite sequence of regular languages $L_1, L_2, \ldots$ such that each $L_n$ is accepted by a non-$\varepsilon$-free normal-form finite automaton of size $O(n)$, but any $\varepsilon$-free normal-form finite automaton accepting $L_n$ must have size at least $3n(n+1)/2$ (see the exercises).

Next we shall show that finite automata are at least as descriptive as regular expressions.

**Theorem 3.16** *Any regular expression E over alphabet T can be transformed in time $O(|E|)$ into an equivalent finite automaton $M(E)$ with input alphabet T. Moreover, $M(E)$ is unambiguous if and only if E is.*

*Proof.* The transformed automaton $M(E)$ is defined inductively on the length of $E$, as indicated in Figure 3.5. For all $E$, $M(E)$ has only one final state. Moreover, it is distinct from the initial state and there are no transitions from it. Similarly, there are no transitions to the initial state. The automata $M(\varnothing)$, $M(\varepsilon)$, and $M(a)$, for $a\in T$, have only two states, the initial state and the final state. $M(\varnothing)$ has no transitions. $M(\varepsilon)$ has only an $\varepsilon$-transition, and $M(a)$ only an $a$-transition from the initial state to the final state. The automaton $M((E))$ is the same as $M(E)$. The automaton $M(E^*)$ is obtained from $M(E)$ by adding a new initial state, a new final state and $\varepsilon$-

(1a)    $M(\phi) =$    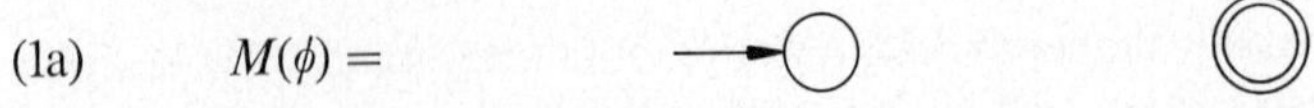

(1b)    $M(\varepsilon) =$

(1c)    $M(a) =$

(1d)    $M((E)) =$

(2)    $M(E^*) =$    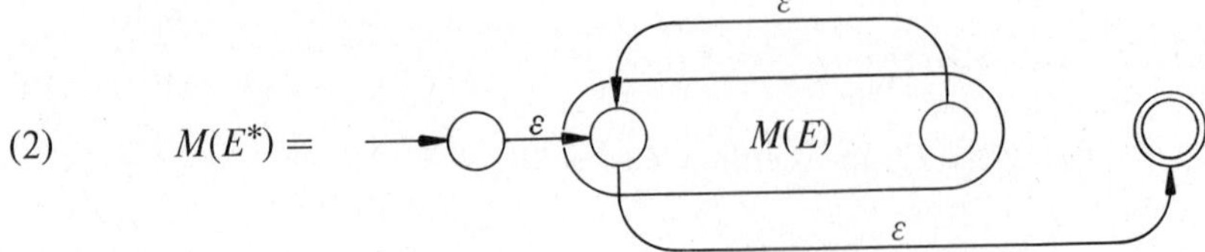

(3)    $M(E_1 E_2) =$

(4)    $M(E_1 \cup E_2) =$    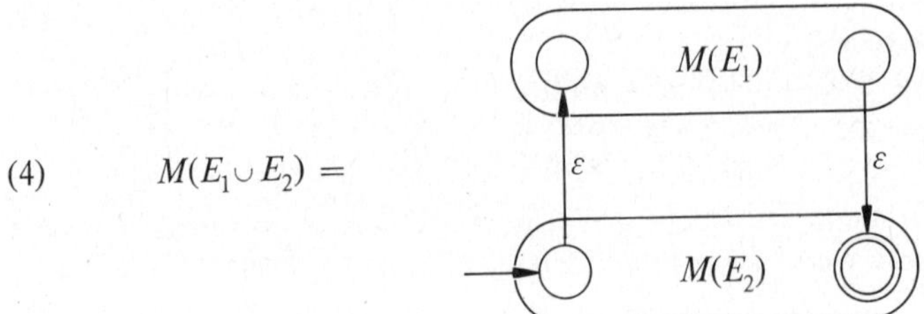

**Figure 3.5** An inductive definition of the finite automaton $M(E)$ corresponding to a regular expression $E$

transitions from the final state of $M(E)$ to the initial state of $M(E)$, from the initial state of $M(E)$ to the new final state, and from the new initial state to the initial state of $M(E)$. The automaton $M(E_1 E_2)$ is obtained from $M(E_1)$ and $M(E_2)$ by uniting the final state of $M(E_1)$ and the initial state of $M(E_2)$. The automaton $M(E_1 \cup E_2)$ is obtained from $M(E_1)$ and $M(E_2)$ by adding ε-transitions from the initial state of $M(E_2)$ to the initial state of $M(E_1)$ and from the final state of $M(E_1)$ to the final state of $M(E_2)$. See Figure 3.6 for a concrete example.

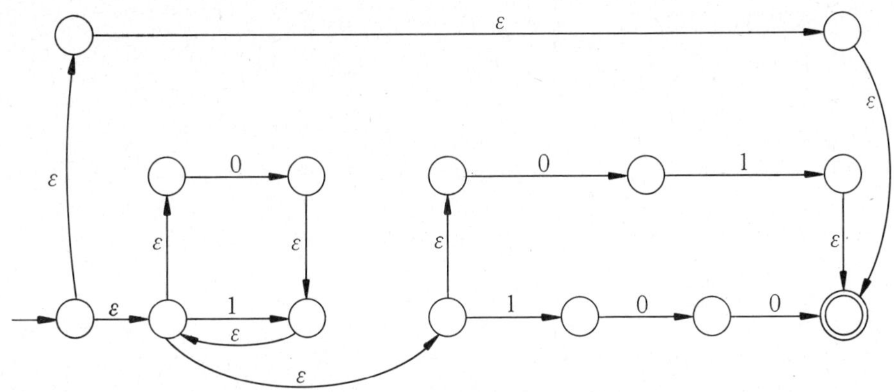

**Figure 3.6** The finite automaton $M(\varepsilon \cup (0 \cup 1)^*(01 \cup 100))$

We shall show by induction on the length of $E$ that

$$L(M(E)) = L(E) \ .$$

In the base case, $E$ takes one of the forms $\varnothing$, $\varepsilon$, or $a \in T$. Then the claim is immediately seen to hold because by construction

$$L(M(\varnothing)) = \varnothing \ ,$$
$$L(M(\varepsilon)) = \{\varepsilon\} \ ,$$
$$L(M(a)) = \{a\} \ .$$

In the induction step, $E$ takes one of the forms $(E_1)$, $E_1^*$, $E_1 E_2$, or $E_1 \cup E_2$, and we can assume as an induction hypothesis that $L(M(E_1)) = L(E_1)$ and $L(M(E_2)) = L(E_2)$. But then the claim also holds for $E$, because by construction we have

$$L(M((E_1))) = L(M(E_1)) \ ,$$
$$L(M(E_1^*)) = L(M(E_1))^* \ ,$$
$$L(M(E_1 E_2)) = L(M(E_1))L(M(E_2)) \ ,$$
$$L(M(E_1 \cup E_2)) = L(M(E_1)) \cup L(M(E_2)) \ .$$

Hence we may conclude that the claim holds for all regular expressions $E$.

We now outline a similar inductive proof for the claim that $M(E)$ is unambiguous if and only if $E$ is. The base case is again clear because, by definition, $\varnothing$, $\varepsilon$, and $a \in T$ are all unambiguous regular expressions, and because the corresponding automata $M(\varnothing)$, $M(\varepsilon)$, and $M(a)$ have no more than one accepting computation in all.

In the induction step, $E$ takes one of the forms $(E_1)$, $E_1^*$, $E_1 E_2$, or $E_1 \cup E_2$, and we can assume as an induction hypothesis that the claim holds for $E_1$ and $E_2$, i.e., $E_i$ is unambiguous if and only if $M(E_i)$ is, for $i = 1, 2$. If $E = (E_1)$, the claim holds immediately because by construction $M(E) = M(E_1)$ and by definition $E$ is unambiguous if and only if $E_1$ is. Next let $E = E_1^*$ and assume that $M(E)$ is ambiguous. We prove that $E$ is also. By definition, $M(E)$ has two accepting computations, $C, C'$, on some string $x \in T^*$. By the construction of $M(E_1^*)$, $C$ and $C'$ are made up of accepting computations of $M(E_1)$ on substrings of $x$. More specifically, for some $m, n \geqslant 0$, for $i = 1, \ldots, m$ there is an accepting computation $C_i$ of $M(E_1)$ on some string $x_i$, and for $j = 1, \ldots, n$ there is an accepting computation $C'_j$ of $M(E_1)$ on some string $x'_j$, such that $x_1 \ldots x_m = x'_1 \ldots x'_n = x$ and one of the following statements holds (1) $m \neq n$; (2) $m = n$, and for some $i$, $x_i \neq x'_i$; or (3) $m = n$, and for some $i$, $x_i = x'_i$ and $C_i \neq C'_i$. In cases (1) and (2) we use the facts that $L(M(E_1)) = L(E_1)$ and $L(M(E)) = L(E)$ to conclude that $E$ is ambiguous. In case (3) we use the induction hypothesis to conclude that $E_1$ is ambiguous and hence so is $E$. By similar reasoning we can show that $M(E)$ is ambiguous if $E$ is. We leave this as an exercise, together with the proof of the claim for $E = E_1 E_2$ and $E = E_1 \cup E_2$.

The inductive definition of $M(E)$ suggests an algorithm for constructing $M(E)$ from $E$. The difficult step in the algorithm is how to decompose $E$ into the smaller components (regular expressions, regular terms, regular factors, regular primaries) from which it is made up. This decomposition can be done using a parser for a context-free grammar (or, more specifically, an LL(1) grammar) that generates the language of all regular expressions over $T$ (see Chapter 5 for a discussion of parsers). This parser is then easily augmented by "semantic actions" so as to construct $M(E)$ from the smaller automata corresponding to the components of $E$. It is shown in Chapter 5 that an LL(1) parser for an LL(1) grammar is deterministic and runs in time linear in the length of the input string to be parsed. Thus we may conclude that $E$ can be transformed into $M(E)$ in time $O(|E|)$.   $\square$

Theorem 3.16 says that any regular language is accepted by some finite automaton. This result can be used to prove that certain languages are nonregular.

As an example, we prove that the language

$$L_{\text{match}} = \{0^n 1^n \mid n \geqslant 0\}$$

is nonregular. The proof technique we use is known in the literature as *pumping*.

Suppose for the sake of contradiction that $L_{\text{match}}$ were regular. By Theorem 3.16, it would then be the language accepted by some finite automaton $M$ with input alphabet $\{0, 1\}$. By Theorem 3.15, we may assume that $M$ is $\varepsilon$-free and normal-form.

Now let $n = |Q| + 1$, where $|Q|$ is the number of states in $M$. As the string $0^n 1^n$ belongs to $L_{\text{match}}$, $M$ must accept it. Thus $M$ must have a state $q$ and a final state $q_f$ such that $q$ is reachable from the initial state $q_s$ upon reading $0^n$, and $q_f$ is reachable from $q$ upon reading $1^n$ (see Figure 3.7a).

Since $n$ is greater than the number of states in $M$, some state must appear twice in the path from $q_s$ to $q$. More specifically, $M$ must have a state $q'$ such that, for some

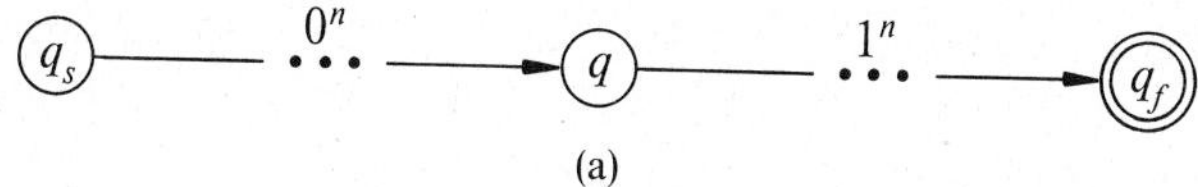

(a)

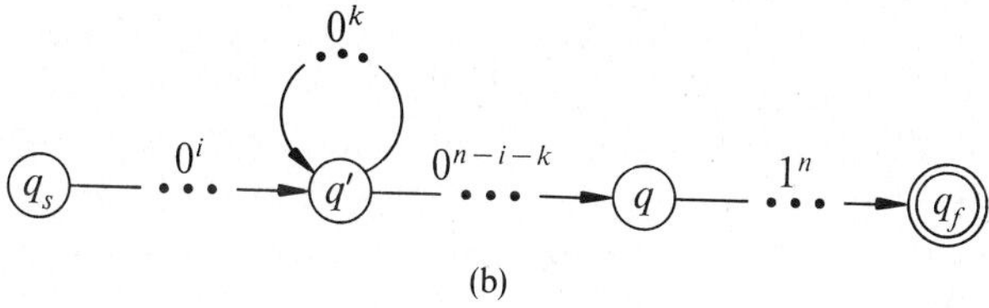

(b)

**Figure 3.7** Portions of a hypothetical finite automaton supposed to accept the nonregular language $\{0^n 1^n \mid n \geq 0\}$

$i \geq 0$ and $k > 0$, $q'$ is reachable from $q_s$ upon reading $0^i$, $q'$ is reachable from itself upon reading $0^k$, and $q$ is reachable from $q'$ upon reading $0^{n-i-k}$ (see Figure 3.7b). But then we see that $M$ also accepts strings of the form

$$0^i 0^{jk} 0^{n-i-k} 1^n, \quad j > 1 ,$$

which do not belong to $L_{\text{match}}$. This contradicts our assumption that $L(M) = L_{\text{match}}$, and we conclude that $L_{\text{match}}$ cannot be regular.

The following theorem says that finite automata are not more descriptive than regular expressions. Together with Theorem 3.16 this means that finite automata and regular expressions are equivalent in descriptional power.

**Theorem 3.17** *Any finite automaton $M$ with state alphabet $Q$ and input alphabet $T$ can be transformed in time $O(|Q| \cdot |M| \cdot 4^{|Q|})$ into an equivalent regular expression $E(M)$ over $T$. Moreover, $E(M)$ is unambiguous if and only if $M$ is.*

*Proof.* Let $Q = \{q_1, \ldots, q_n\}$. The idea is to construct, for $i, j = 1, \ldots, n$ and $k = 0, \ldots, n$, a regular expression $E_{ijk}$ that denotes the set of input strings $x$ for which state $q_j$ is reachable from state $q_i$ upon reading $x$ in one or more derivation steps without going through any state $q_m$, $m > k$. Specifically, we will arrange for

$$L(E_{ijk}) = \{x \in T^* \mid \text{there is a derivation } (q_{i_0} x_0, \ldots, q_{i_m} x_m) \text{ in } M \text{ of length}$$
$$m \geq 1 \quad \text{such that} \quad i_0 = i, \quad x_0 = x, \quad i_m = j, \quad x_m = \varepsilon, \quad \text{and}$$
$$\{i_1, \ldots, i_{m-1}\} \subseteq \{1, \ldots, k\}\} .$$

The expressions $E_{ijk}$ are defined using induction on $k$. For $k = 0$ we set

$$E_{ij0} = (x_1 \cup \ldots \cup x_m) ,$$

where $x_1, \ldots, x_m$ are distinct strings in $T^*$ satisfying

$$\{x_1, \ldots, x_m\} = \{x \in T^* \mid q_i x \to q_j \text{ is a rule of } M\} \ .$$

(If this set is empty, $E_{ij0}$ is defined to be $\varnothing$.) For $k > 0$ we set:

   (1) $E_{ijk} = E_{ij(k-1)}^+$, when $i = j = k$.

   (2) $E_{ijk} = (E_{ij(k-1)} E_{jk(k-1)}^*)$, when $i \neq j = k$.

   (3) $E_{ijk} = (E_{ik(k-1)}^* E_{kj(k-1)})$, when $i = k \neq j$.

   (4) $E_{ijk} = (E_{ij(k-1)} \cup E_{ik(k-1)} E_{kk(k-1)}^* E_{kj(k-1)})$, when $i \neq k \neq j$.

We leave it as an exercise to prove that each $E_{ijk}$ does indeed denote the desired language, and that $L(M)$ is denoted by the regular expression

$$E(M) = E_{sf_1 n} \cup \ldots \cup E_{sf_m n} \cup E_\varepsilon \ ,$$

where $q_s$ is the initial state of $M$, $\{q_{f_1}, \ldots, q_{f_m}\}$ is the set of final states of $M$, and $E_\varepsilon = \varepsilon$ if $q_s$ is a final state of $M$ and $\varnothing$ otherwise.

    That $E(M)$ is unambiguous if and only if $M$ is follows from the fact that $E_{ijk}$ is unambiguous if and only if for all strings $x$ there is at most one positive-length derivation of $q_j$ from $q_i x$ in $M$ that does not go through any state $q_m, m > k$. This fact can be proved by a straightforward but tedious induction on $k$. We leave the details for the exercises and only note here that in the definition of $E_{ijk}$ we have taken care not to create any extra ambiguities not present in $M$. A slightly simpler construction would have been possible had we not paid attention to the preservation of unambiguity.

    It remains for us to establish the time complexity of the transformation. Obviously, the inductive definition implies that each $E_{ijk}$ can be constructed in time linear in its size. Now the length of each $E_{ij0}$ is $O(|M|)$, whereas the length of $E_{ijk}$ for $k > 0$ is $O(4 \cdot l_{k-1})$, where $l_{k-1}$ is the length of the longest $E_{ij(k-1)}$. Thus the length of each $E_{ijk}$ is $O(|M| \cdot 4^n)$. Since the length of $E(M)$ is $O(n \cdot l_n)$, we may conclude that $E(M)$ can be constructed from $M$ in time $O(|Q| \cdot |M| \cdot 4^{|Q|})$.   $\square$

    From Theorems 3.16 and 3.17, we obtain the following characterization of regular languages.

**Theorem 3.18** *A language over an alphabet $T$ is regular if and only if it is the language accepted by some finite automaton with input alphabet $T$.*   $\square$

    The exponential time bound in Theorem 3.17 is in contrast to the linear time bound in Theorem 3.16. This suggests that finite automata can be exponentially more succinct than regular expressions. Indeed, it can be shown that there is an infinite sequence of regular languages $L_1, L_2, \ldots$ such that each $L_n$ is accepted by an $\varepsilon$-free normal-form finite automaton of size $O(n^2)$, but any regular expression denoting $L_n$ must have length at least $2^n$ (see the exercises).

## 3.3 Regular Grammars

In this section we shall give another mechanism for regular language description, namely regular grammars, which are equivalent in descriptional power to regular expressions. The regular grammars form a subclass of the context-free grammars (see Chapter 4).

Let $G=(V, P)$ be a rewriting system and $T$ a proper subset of $V$. Further, let $N$ denote the set difference $V \setminus T$ and let $S$ be an element of $N$. We say that $G$ is a *right-linear grammar with nonterminal alphabet N, terminal alphabet T* and *start symbol S*, denoted by

$$G=(V, T, P, S) ,$$

if each rule in $P$ has one of the forms

(rl)     $A \rightarrow x, \quad A \rightarrow xB$ ,

where $A$ and $B$ are nonterminals, i.e., elements of $N$, and $x$ is a terminal string, i.e., an element of $T^*$.

A *left-linear grammar* is defined similarly, except that each rule has one of the forms

(ll)     $A \rightarrow x, \quad A \rightarrow Bx$ .

A rewriting system is a *regular grammar* if it is either a right-linear grammar or a left-linear grammar. In a regular grammar, then, either all rules are of the form (rl) or all rules are of the form (ll).

The language *generated* (or *described*) by a regular grammar $G=(V, T, P, S)$, denoted by $L(G)$, is the set of terminal strings derived by the start symbol. In other words,

$$L(G)=\{w \in T^* \mid S \Rightarrow^* w \quad \text{in} \quad G\} .$$

Regular grammars differ from general context-free grammars in that the right-hand sides of rules can contain only one nonterminal and that this nonterminal, when present, must be located either at the extreme right end of the right-hand side in all rules (right-linear grammars) or at the extreme left end of the right-hand side in all rules (left-linear grammars). The grammar $G_{\text{match}}$ (see Section 1.6), for example, is not a regular grammar. The presence of the "nonregular" rule $S \rightarrow 0S1$ has the effect that the grammar generates a nonregular language, $L_{\text{match}}$.

A regular grammar $G$ is *ambiguous* if some sentence in $L(G)$ has two distinct derivations in $G$ from the start symbol $S$; otherwise $G$ is *unambiguous*.

The following theorem states that right-linear grammars are at least as descriptive and succinct as finite automata.

**Theorem 3.19** *Any finite automaton M with input alphabet T can be transformed in time $O(|M|)$ into an equivalent right-linear grammar G(M) with terminal alphabet T. Moreover, G(M) is unambiguous if and only if M is.*

*Proof.* The nonterminal alphabet of $G(M)$ is the state alphabet of $M$, and its start symbol is the initial state of $M$. The set of rules of $G(M)$ is

$$\{q_1 \rightarrow xq_2 \mid q_1 x \rightarrow q_2 \text{ is a rule of } M\} \cup \{q \rightarrow \varepsilon \mid q \text{ is a final state of } M\} \ .$$

It can be shown by a simple induction on derivation length that, for all states $q_1$ and $q_2$ and input strings $w$, $q_1 w \Rightarrow^* q_2$ in $M$ if and only if $q_1 \Rightarrow^* wq_2$ in $G(M)$. Choosing $q_1$ here to be the initial state and $q_2$ some final state, since each final state $q$ has the rule $q \rightarrow \varepsilon$ in $G(M)$, we deduce that $L(M) = L(G(M))$.

It is also obvious that a sentence $w$ has two derivations in $G(M)$ from the initial state of $M$ if and only if $M$ has two accepting computations on $w$. Moreover, $G(M)$ is of size $O(|M|)$ and can obviously be constructed from $M$ in time $O(|M|)$.  $\square$

For example, the right-linear grammar $G(M_{\text{end}})$ corresponding to the finite automaton $M_{\text{end}}$ (see Section 3.2) is

$$G(M_{\text{end}}) = (\{q_0, q_1, q_2, 0, 1\}, \{0, 1\}, P, q_0) \ ,$$

where $P$ consists of the rules

$$q_0 \rightarrow q_1, \qquad q_1 \rightarrow 0q_1, \qquad q_1 \rightarrow 1q_1, \qquad q_1 \rightarrow 01q_2,$$
$$q_1 \rightarrow 100q_2, \qquad q_0 \rightarrow \varepsilon, \qquad q_2 \rightarrow \varepsilon \ .$$

The following theorem states the converse of Theorem 3.19. As a corollary, right-linear grammars are equivalent in descriptional power as well as in succinctness to finite automata.

**Theorem 3.20** *Any right-linear grammar $G$ with terminal alphabet $T$ can be transformed in time $O(|G|)$ into an equivalent finite automaton $M(G)$ with input alphabet $T$. Moreover, $M(G)$ is unambiguous if and only if $G$ is.*

*Proof.* We may assume that the rules of $G$ are of the forms $A \rightarrow \varepsilon$, $A \rightarrow xB$, since any rule $A \rightarrow x$, where $x$ is a nonempty terminal string, can be replaced by the pair of rules

$$A \rightarrow x[Ax], \quad [Ax] \rightarrow \varepsilon \ ,$$

where $[Ax]$ is a new nonterminal. This transformation can obviously be carried out in time linear in the size of the grammar and yields a grammar that, besides being equivalent to the original grammar, is unambiguous if and only if the original grammar is.

The set of states of the automaton $M(G)$ is the nonterminal alphabet of $G$, and its initial state is the start symbol of $G$. The set of rules of $M(G)$ is

$$\{Ax \rightarrow B \mid A \rightarrow xB \text{ is a rule of } G\} \ .$$

The set of final states of $M(G)$ is

$$\{A \mid A \to \varepsilon \text{ is a rule of } G\} \ .$$

By reasoning completely analogous to that in the proof of Theorem 3.19, we deduce that $L(M(G)) = L(G)$ and that $M(G)$ is unambiguous if and only if $G$ is. Moreover, $M(G)$ is of size $O(|G|)$ and can obviously be constructed from $G$ in time $O(|G|)$.  $\square$

By Theorems 3.18, 3.19 and 3.20 we have

**Theorem 3.21** *A language over an alphabet $T$ is regular if and only if it is the language generated by some right-linear grammar with terminal alphabet $T$.*  $\square$

In what follows, we shall show that in Theorem 3.21 "right-linear grammar" can be replaced by "left-linear grammar" and hence by "regular grammar".

**Theorem 3.22** *Any left-linear grammar $G$ with terminal alphabet $T$ can be transformed in time $O(|G|)$ into an equivalent right-linear grammar $G'$ with terminal alphabet $T$. Moreover, $G'$ is unambiguous if and only if $G$ is.*  $\square$

*Proof.* The nonterminal alphabet of the transformed grammar $G'$ is $N \cup \{S'\}$, where $N$ is the nonterminal alphabet of $G$ and $S'$ is a new nonterminal, the start symbol of $G'$. The set of rules of $G'$ is

$$\{B \to xA \mid A \to Bx \text{ is a rule of } G\} \cup \{S' \to xA \mid A \to x \text{ is a rule of } G\}$$
$$\cup \{S \to \varepsilon\} \ ,$$

where $A$, $B$ denote nonterminals of $G$, $x$ denotes any terminal string, and $S$ is the start symbol of $G$.

By definition, any derivation in $G$ of a terminal string $w$ from the start symbol $S$ is of the form

$$(1) \qquad (A_0, \ A_1 x_1, \ A_2 x_2 x_1, \ \ldots,$$
$$A_{n-1} x_{n-1} \cdots x_1, \ A_n x_n x_{n-1} \cdots x_1, \ x_{n+1} \cdots x_1) \ ,$$

where $n \geqslant 0$, $A_0 = S$, $x_{n+1} \cdots x_1 = w$, and $A_i \to A_{i+1} x_{i+1}$ and $A_n \to x_{n+1}$ are rules of $G$, for $i = 0, \ldots, n-1$. By construction, any derivation in $G'$ of $w$ from the start symbol $S'$ is of the form

$$(2) \qquad (A_{n+1}, \ x_{n+1} A_n, \ x_{n+1} x_n A_{n-1}, \ \ldots, \ x_{n+1} \cdots x_2 A_1,$$
$$x_{n+1} \cdots x_2 x_1 A_0, \ x_{n+1} \cdots x_1) \ ,$$

where $n \geqslant 0$, $A_{n+1} = S'$, $A_0 = S$, $x_{n+1} \cdots x_1 = w$, and $A_n \to x_{n+1}$ and $A_i \to A_{i+1} x_{i+1}$ are rules of $G$, for $i = 0, \ldots, n-1$. In fact, there is a bijective correspondence between derivations of form (1) in $G$ and derivations of form (2) in $G'$. This means that $L(G') = L(G)$, and that $G'$ is unambiguous if and only if $G$ is. Moreover, $G'$ is of size $O(|G|)$ and can obviously be constructed from $G$ in time $O(|G|)$.  $\square$

Using a completely analogous construction we can prove

**Theorem 3.23** *Any right-linear grammar $G$ with terminal alphabet $T$ can be transformed in time $O(|G|)$ into an equivalent left-linear grammar $G'$ with terminal alphabet $T$. Moreover, $G'$ is unambiguous if and only if $G$ is.*  $\square$

Theorems 3.22 and 3.23 imply that left-linear grammars are equivalent to right-linear grammars both in descriptional power and in succinctness. By Theorem 3.21 we therefore have

**Theorem 3.24** *A language over an alphabet $T$ is regular if and only if it is the language generated by some regular grammar with terminal alphabet $T$.*  $\square$

We conclude this section with another application of Theorems 3.22 and 3.23, showing that the family of regular languages is effectively closed under reversal. Recall that the reversal of a language $L$, denoted by $L^R$, is the language whose sentences are exactly the reversals, or mirror images, of the sentences in $L$.

Let $G$ be any rewriting system. The *reversal* of a rule $r = \omega_1 \rightarrow \omega_2$ in $P$ is the rule $r^R = \omega_1^R \rightarrow \omega_2^R$. The *reversal* of $G$, denoted by $G^R$, is the rewriting system that is obtained from $G$ by replacing each rule in $P$ by its reversal.

**Lemma 3.25** *Let $G = (V, P)$ be a rewriting system, $r_1, \ldots, r_n$ rules in $P$, and $\gamma_1$ and $\gamma_2$ strings over $V$. Then $\gamma_1$ derives $\gamma_2$ in $G$ using rule string $r_1 \ldots r_n$ if and only if $\gamma_1^R$ derives $\gamma_2^R$ in $G^R$ using rule string $r_1^R \ldots r_n^R$.*

*Proof.* First we note that the "if" part follows immediately from the "only if" part, because $(\gamma^R)^R = \gamma$, $(r^R)^R = r$, and $(G^R)^R = G$ for all strings $\gamma$, rules $r$, and rewriting systems $G$. The "only if" part is proved by induction on $n$. The base case $n = 0$ is trivial because then $r_1 \ldots r_n = \varepsilon = r_1^R \ldots r_n^R$. In the induction step we have

$$\gamma_1 \xrightarrow{r_1 \ldots r_{n-1}} \alpha\omega_1\beta \xrightarrow{r_n} \alpha\omega_2\beta = \gamma_2$$

in $G$, where $r_n = \omega_1 \rightarrow \omega_2$. By the induction hypothesis we have

$$\gamma_1^R \xrightarrow{r_1^R \ldots r_{n-1}^R} (\alpha\omega_1\beta)^R = \beta^R\omega_1^R\alpha^R$$

in $G^R$. Since $r_n^R = \omega_1^R \rightarrow \omega_2^R$ is a rule of $G^R$, we therefore have

$$\beta^R\omega_1^R\alpha^R \xrightarrow{r_n^R} \beta^R\omega_2^R\alpha^R = (\alpha\omega_2\beta)^R = \gamma_2^R$$

in $G^R$. In other words, $\gamma_1^R$ derives $\gamma_2^R$ in $G^R$ using rule string $r_1^R \ldots r_n^R$, as required.  $\square$

**Theorem 3.26** *Any regular grammar $G$ with terminal alphabet $T$ can be transformed in time $O(|G|)$ into a regular grammar $G'$ with terminal alphabet $T$ such that $L(G') = L(G)^R$.*

*Proof.* $G'$ is the reversal $G^R$ of $G$. Observe that $G^R$ is left-linear if $G$ is right-linear, and right-linear if $G$ is left-linear. Lemma 3.25 implies that $L(G^R)=L(G)^R$. Moreover, $|G^R|=|G|$ and $G^R$ can obviously be constructed from $G$ in time $O(|G|)$.  $\square$

We therefore have

**Theorem 3.27** *The family of regular languages over any alphabet $T$ is effectively closed under reversal.*  $\square$

## 3.4 Deterministic Finite Automata

A finite automaton $M$ is *nondeterministic* if it has a configuration to which two rules are applicable, i.e., if the statements

$$qw \overset{r_1}{\Longrightarrow} q_1 w_1 \ ,$$

$$qw \overset{r_2}{\Longrightarrow} q_2 w_2 \ ,$$

hold for some configurations $qw$, $q_1 w_1$ and $q_2 w_2$, and distinct rules $r_1$ and $r_2$. $M$ is *deterministic* if it is not nondeterministic.

**Fact 3.28** A finite automaton is nondeterministic if and only if it has distinct rules

$$qx \to q_1, \qquad qy \to q_2 \ ,$$

where $y$ is a prefix of $x$.  $\square$

The finite automaton $M_{\text{end}}$ given in Section 3.2 is nondeterministic. It has in fact two pairs of rules that cause nondeterminism: rules $q_1 0 \to q_1$ and $q_1 01 \to q_2$ are both applicable to any configuration of the form $q_1 01w$, and rules $q_1 1 \to q_1$ and $q_1 100 \to q_2$ to any configuration of the form $q_1 100w$, where $w$ is an arbitrary string in $\{0, 1\}^*$.

**Fact 3.29** Any deterministic finite automaton is unambiguous, provided it has no $\varepsilon$-transitions from final states.  $\square$

The converse of Fact 3.29 does not hold: $M_{\text{end}}$ is unambiguous although it is nondeterministic.

The following theorem states that any finite automaton can be *made deterministic*, i.e., transformed into an equivalent deterministic one. Thus deterministic finite automata are equivalent in descriptional power to unrestricted finite automata, and hence to all the other classes of regular language descriptions already presented.

**Theorem 3.30** *Any finite automaton $M$ with input alphabet $T$ can be transformed in time $O(2^{|M|+\log|M|+\log|T|})$ into an equivalent deterministic ε-free normal-form finite automaton $\hat{M}$ of size $O(2^{|M|+\log|T|})$.*

*Proof.* By Theorem 3.13, we may assume that $M$ is normal-form. Let $M = (Q, T, P, q_s, F)$. The set of states of $\hat{M}$ is

$$\hat{Q} = 2^Q \ ,$$

and its initial state is

$$\hat{q}_s = \{q \in Q \mid q_s \Rightarrow^* q \text{ in } M\} \ ,$$

the set of states of $M$ that are reachable from its initial state upon reading the empty string. The set of final states of $\hat{M}$ is

$$\hat{F} = \{\hat{q} \in \hat{Q} \mid \hat{q} \cap F \neq \varnothing\} \ ,$$

i.e., the states of $\hat{M}$ that contain some final state of $M$. The set of rules of $\hat{M}$ is

$$\hat{P} = \{\hat{q}_1 a \rightarrow \hat{q}_2 \mid \hat{q}_1 \in \hat{Q}, a \in T, \text{ and } \hat{q}_2 = \text{GOTO}(\hat{q}_1, a)\} \ ,$$

where

$$\text{GOTO}(\hat{q}_1, a) = \{q_2 \in Q \mid q_1 a \Rightarrow^* q_2 \text{ in } M \text{ for some } q_1 \in \hat{q}_1\} \ .$$

Thus $\hat{P}$ contains all rules of the form $\hat{q}_1 a \rightarrow \hat{q}_2$, where $\hat{q}_2$ is the set of states of $M$ that are reachable from some state in $\hat{q}_1$ upon reading input symbol $a$.

The automaton obtained in this way from the nondeterministic automaton of Figure 3.3 is shown in Figure 3.8. We have included only those states that are accessible.

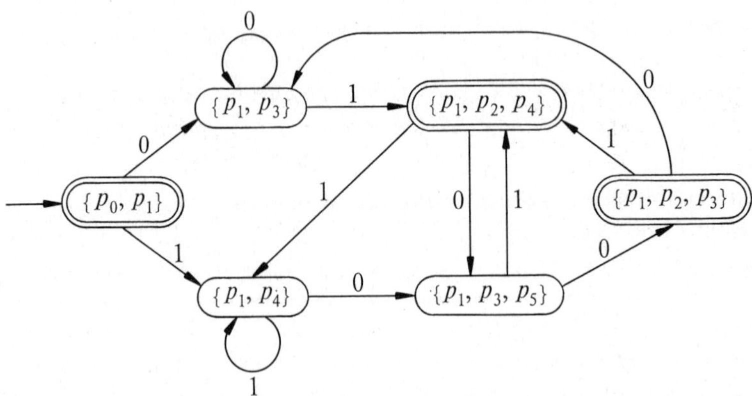


**Figure 3.8** The deterministic automaton produced from the nondeterministic finite automaton of Figure 3.3

$\hat{M}$ is deterministic because by definition it has transitions on single input symbols only, and because for all states $\hat{q}_1$ and input symbols $a$ there is exactly one state, namely $\text{GOTO}(\hat{q}_1, a)$, to which there is a transition from $\hat{q}_1$ on $a$.

It can be shown by induction that, for all states $\hat{q}_1$ and $\hat{q}_2$ in $\hat{Q}$ and strings $w \in T^*$,

$$\hat{q}_1 w \Rightarrow^* \hat{q}_2 \text{ in } \hat{M}$$

if and only if

$$\hat{q}_2 = \text{GOTO}(\hat{q}_1, w) ,$$

where $\text{GOTO}(\hat{q}_1, w)$ denotes the set $\underset{M}{\Longrightarrow}^*(\hat{q}_1 w) \cap Q$. Thus in particular

$$\begin{aligned}
L(\hat{M}) &= \{w \in T^* \mid \hat{q}_s w \Rightarrow^* \hat{q} \text{ for some } \hat{q} \text{ in } \hat{F}\} \\
&= \{w \in T^* \mid \text{GOTO}(\hat{q}_s, w) \in \hat{F}\} \\
&= \{w \in T^* \mid \text{GOTO}(\hat{q}_s, w) \cap F \neq \varnothing\} \\
&= \{w \in T^* \mid q_1 w \Rightarrow^* q_2 \text{ for some } q_1 \text{ in } \hat{q}_s \text{ and } q_2 \text{ in } F\} \\
&= \{w \in T^* \mid q_s w \Rightarrow^* q_2 \text{ for some } q_2 \text{ in } F\} \\
&= L(M) .
\end{aligned}$$

Now let **empty-trans** and $a$-**trans**, for $a \in T$, be relations on $Q$ defined by

$$\begin{aligned}
q_1 \text{ \textbf{empty-trans} } q_2, &\quad \text{if } q_1 \to q_2 \text{ is a rule of } M , \\
q_1 \text{ } a\text{-\textbf{trans} } q_2, &\quad \text{if } q_1 a \to q_2 \text{ is a rule of } M .
\end{aligned}$$

Further, let **reads-empty** and **reads-**$a$, for $a \in T$, denote the relations

$$\begin{aligned}
\textbf{reads-empty} &= \textbf{empty-trans}^* , \\
\textbf{reads-}a &= \textbf{reads-empty } a\text{-\textbf{trans} reads-empty} .
\end{aligned}$$

Then we have, for all $q_1, q_2 \in Q$ and $a \in T$,

$$\begin{aligned}
q_1 &\Rightarrow^* q_2 \text{ in } M \text{ if and only if } q_1 \text{ \textbf{reads-empty} } q_2 , \\
q_1 a &\Rightarrow^* q_2 \text{ in } M \text{ if and only if } q_1 \text{ \textbf{reads-}}a \text{ } q_2 .
\end{aligned}$$

The relations **empty-trans** and $a$-**trans** are of size $O(|M|)$ and can be constructed from $M$ in time $O(|M|)$. Thus, by Theorem 2.29, the relations **reads-empty** and **reads-**$a$ can be constructed in time $O(|Q| \cdot |M|)$.

Using the relations **reads-empty** and **reads-**$a$ we can write an algorithm for constructing $\hat{M}$, as shown in Figure 3.9. Actually this algorithm does not construct the whole of $\hat{M}$ (as defined above), but a reduced automaton equivalent to $\hat{M}$.

It remains for us to evaluate the complexity of the algorithm. First we note that the space complexity is proportional to the size of $\hat{M}$. Since $\hat{M}$ has one transition for each pair $(\hat{q}, a) \in \hat{Q} \times T$, we have

$$\begin{aligned}
|\hat{M}| &= 3 \cdot |\hat{P}| = 3 \cdot |\hat{Q}| \cdot |T| = 3 \cdot |2^Q| \cdot |T| = 3 \cdot |T| \cdot 2^{|Q|} \\
&= 3 \cdot 2^{|Q| + \log |T|} .
\end{aligned}$$

**Theorem 3.32** *Given any deterministic ε-free normal-form finite automaton M with input alphabet T, and any string $w \in T^*$, it is decidable simultaneously in deterministic time $O(|M| + |w| \cdot \log|T|)$ and workspace $O(|M|)$ whether or not w belongs to L(M).*

*Proof.* The algorithm shown in Figure 3.10 provides a total solution to the decision problem in question. The algorithm takes as input any string $\text{rep}(M)\#w$, where $\text{rep}(M)$ is the string representation of a deterministic ε-free normal-form finite automaton M, and w is a string over T. Since M only has transitions on single symbols in T, and since for any given state q and symbol $a \in T$ there is at most one transition on a from q, it is obvious that the algorithm produces output "yes" whenever M accepts w, and output "no" otherwise. Moreover, the algorithm runs in time $O(|M| + |w| \cdot \log|T|)$, because the statements inside the **while** loop are executed at most $|w|$ times, and because it can be decided in time $O(\log|T|)$ whether or not M has a rule $qa \to q'$, for given q and a (provided that M is stored using a suitable data structure). The workspace required by the algorithm is essentially just the space needed to store M.  □

```
Read rep(M)#;
q := q_s;
while true do
      if end-of-input then
          if q is a final state then
              write "yes" and halt
          else
              write "no" and halt
      else begin
          Read the next symbol a of w;
          if M has a transition qa → q' for some q' then q := q'
              else
                  write "no" and halt
      end.
```

**Figure 3.10** An $O(|M| + |w| \cdot \log|T|)$ time-bounded and $O(|M|)$ workspace-bounded total solution to the membership problem for deterministic ε-free normal-form finite automata. The algorithm produces output "yes" for input $\text{rep}(M)\#w$ if w belongs to L(M), and output "no" otherwise

**Corollary 3.33** *The membership problem for deterministic ε-free normal-form finite automata is solvable simultaneously in deterministic time $O(n \log n)$ and workspace $O(n)$.*  □

We leave it as an exercise to prove that Theorem 3.32 and Corollary 3.33 in fact hold for any deterministic finite automaton M, so that M need not be ε-free normal-form.

If we regard the automaton M in Theorem 3.32 as fixed, then Theorem 3.31 yields

**Theorem 3.34** *For any regular language L, the membership problem for L is solvable simultaneously in deterministic time $O(n)$ and workspace $O(1)$.*  □

For arbitrary normal-form finite automata we have

**Theorem 3.35** *Given any normal-form finite automaton M with state alphabet Q and input alphabet T, and any string $w \in T^*$, it is decidable simultaneously in non-deterministic time $O(|M| + |Q| \cdot |w|)$ and workspace $O(|M|)$ whether or not w belongs to $L(M)$.*

*Proof.* The nondeterministic algorithm shown in Figure 3.11 provides a partial solution to the decision problem in question. The algorithm takes as input any string $\text{rep}(M)\#w$, where $\text{rep}(M)$ is the string representation of a normal-form finite automaton $M$, and $w$ is a string over $T$. The algorithm produces output "yes" if and only if $M$ accepts $w$. The space complexity of the algorithm is obviously $O(|M|)$. The time complexity in turn is proportional to $|M|$ plus the number of iterations of the **while** loop needed to accept the sentence $w$. Note that the number of iterations can be greater than $|w|$ when $M$ has $\varepsilon$-transitions. However, if $w \in L(M)$ then we need never apply more than $|Q| - 1$ $\varepsilon$-transitions from any state before reaching some state from which there is a transition on the next input symbol. Thus only $|Q| \cdot |w|$ iterations are needed to accept any $w \in L(M)$, and we conclude that, for all $w \in L(M)$, $M$ has an accepting computation on input $\text{rep}(M)\#w$ of length $O(|M| + |Q| \cdot |w|)$.   $\square$

```
Read rep(M)#;
q := q_s;
while true do begin
    if end-of-input and q is a final state then
        write "yes" and halt;
    Guess a transition qx → q' of M;
    if x ∈ T then
        if not end-of-input then begin
            Read the next symbol a of w;
            if a ≠ x then halt
        end else
            halt;
    q := q'
end.
```

**Figure 3.11** An $O(|M| + |Q| \cdot |w|)$ time-bounded and $O(|M|)$ workspace-bounded nondeterministic partial solution to the membership problem for normal-form finite automata. The algorithm produces output "yes" for input $\text{rep}(M)\#w$ if and only if $M$ accepts $w$. The algorithm runs in time $O(|M| + |w|)$ if $M$ is $\varepsilon$-free

For $\varepsilon$-free finite automata, we have a slightly better time bound:

**Theorem 3.36** *Given any $\varepsilon$-free finite automaton M with input alphabet T, and any string $w \in T^*$, it is decidable simultaneously in nondeterministic time $O(|M| + |w|)$ and workspace $O(|M|)$ whether or not w belongs to $L(M)$.*

*Proof.* We may assume that $M$ is normal-form because, by Theorem 3.13, $M$ can be transformed in time $O(|M|)$ into an equivalent $\varepsilon$-free normal-form finite automaton. But for $\varepsilon$-free normal-form automata the algorithm in Figure 3.11 runs in time $O(|M|+|w|)$.    $\square$

**Corollary 3.37** *The membership problem for $\varepsilon$-free finite automata is solvable in nondeterministic time $O(n)$.*    $\square$

Theorem 3.35 says that the membership problem for normal-form finite automata is solvable simultaneously in nondeterministic time $O(n^2)$ and workspace $O(n)$. By Theorems 3.13, 3.16, 3.20 and 3.22, the membership problems for finite automata, regular expressions and regular grammars all reduce in linear time to the membership problem for normal-form finite automata. We therefore conclude, in view of Lemma 1.42, that the membership problems for all these four classes of regular language descriptions are solvable simultaneously in nondeterministic time $O(n^2)$ and workspace $O(n)$.

On the other hand, Theorem 3.30 implies that the membership problem for finite automata reduces in time $O(2^{n+2\log n})$ to the membership problem for deterministic $\varepsilon$-free normal-form finite automata. Hence, by Corollary 3.33, the membership problems for finite automata, regular expressions and regular grammars are all solvable in deterministic time $O(2^{n+4\log n})$.

However, we can establish considerably tighter complexity bounds by making use of the results in Chapter 2. In fact, we can show that the above membership problems are all solvable simultaneously in deterministic time $O(n^2)$ and workspace $O(n)$.

**Theorem 3.38** *Given any finite automaton M with input alphabet T, and any string $w \in T^*$, it is decidable simultaneously in deterministic time $O(|M|\cdot|w|)$ and workspace $O(|M|)$ whether or not w belongs to $L(M)$.*

*Proof.* As in Theorem 3.36, we may assume that $M$ is normal-form. We use the algorithm shown in Figure 3.12. The relations **reads-empty** and **reads-**$a$, for $a \in T$, are as in the proof of Theorem 3.30. The idea of the algorithm is to keep track of the set of states reachable from the initial state $q_s$ upon reading the already consumed

```
Read rep (M) #;
S := reads-empty(q_s);
while true do
    if end-of-input then
            if S contains a final state then
                write "yes" and halt
            else
                write "no" and halt
    else begin
            Read the next symbol a of w;
            S := reads-a(S)
    end.
```

**Figure 3.12** An $O(|M|\cdot|w|)$ time-bounded and $O(|M|)$ workspace-bounded total solution to the membership problem for normal-form finite automata. The algorithm produces output "yes" for input $rep(M) \# w$ if $w$ belongs to $L(M)$, and output "no" otherwise

prefix of $w$. This set of states is stored in the variable $S$. Initially, all states that are reachable from $q_s$ upon reading the empty string $\varepsilon$ are inserted into $S$. After reading each input symbol, the current contents of $S$ are replaced by the set of all states reachable from some state in $S$ upon reading this symbol. Clearly, $M$ accepts $w$ if and only if $S$ contains some final state at the conclusion of this process.

By Theorem 2.28, the time taken by the assignments $S := \textbf{reads-empty}(q_s)$ and $S := \textbf{reads-}a\,(S)$ is $O(|M|)$. As the statements inside the **while** loop are executed at most $|w|$ times, we conclude that the time complexity of the algorithm is $O(|M| + |M| \cdot |w|)$. The workspace complexity of the algorithm is $O(|M|)$ because only one of the relational expressions **reads-**$a$, $a \in T$, need be accessible at any given time.    $\square$

In the following theorem, we summarize the implications of Theorem 3.38.

**Theorem 3.39** *The membership problems for finite automata, regular expressions and regular grammars are all solvable simultaneously in deterministic time $O(n^2)$ and workspace $O(n)$.*

*Proof.* For regular expressions the claim follows from Theorem 3.16, for right-linear grammars from Theorem 3.20, and for left-linear grammars from Theorems 3.22 and 3.20.    $\square$

Next we consider the containment and noncontainment problems for regular language descriptions.

**Theorem 3.40** *Given any finite automata $M_1$ and $M_2$ with input alphabet $T$, it is decidable in nondeterministic space $O(|M_1| + |M_2|)$ whether or not $L(M_1)$ is not contained in $L(M_2)$.*

*Proof.* Again we may assume that $M_1$ and $M_2$ are normal-form. We use the algorithm shown in Figure 3.13, which takes as input any string $\mathrm{rep}(M_1)\,\#\,\mathrm{rep}(M_2)$, where $\mathrm{rep}(M_1)$ and $\mathrm{rep}(M_2)$ are the string representations of $M_1$ and $M_2$. The

```
Read rep(M₁) # rep(M₂);
S₁ := reads-empty(initial state of M₁);
S₂ := reads-empty(initial state of M₂);
while true do
    if S₁ contains some final state of M₁ and
    S₂ does not contain any final state of M₂ then
        write "yes" and halt
    else begin
        Guess an input symbol a∈T;
        S₁ := reads-a(S₁);
        S₂ := reads-a(S₂)
    end.
```

**Figure 3.13** An $O(|M_1| + |M_2|)$ space-bounded nondeterministic partial solution to the noncontainment problem for normal-form finite automata. The algorithm produces output "yes" for input $\mathrm{rep}(M_1)\,\#\,\mathrm{rep}(M_2)$ if and only if $L(M_1) \nsubseteq L(M_2)$

relations **reads-empty** and **reads-**$a$, for $a \in T$, are as in the proof of Theorem 3.30. The idea of the algorithm is to guess a string $w \in T^*$ and check whether or not $w$ belongs to $L(M_1) \setminus L(M_2)$. This guessing is done one input symbol at a time. The algorithm keeps track of the sets of states reachable from the initial states of $M_1$ and $M_2$ upon reading the already guessed prefix of $w$. These two sets of states are stored in the variables $S_1$ and $S_2$ respectively. Initially, $S_1$ and $S_2$ contain all states of $M_1$ and $M_2$ reachable from their respective initial states upon reading the empty string $\varepsilon$. After guessing the next input symbol, the current contents of $S_i$ are replaced by the set of all states of $M_i$ reachable from some state in $S_i$ upon reading the guessed input symbol, for $i = 1, 2$. It is obvious that the algorithm produces output "yes" if and only if it guesses a string in $L(M_1) \setminus L(M_2)$.

By Theorem 2.28, the workspace needed to compute the image of a set under the relations **reads-empty** and **reads-**$a$ is $O(|M_1| + |M_2|)$. Since the already-guessed prefix of $w$ need never be stored in memory, we conclude that the algorithm runs in space $O(|M_1| + |M_2|)$.  $\square$

**Corollary 3.41** *The noncontainment problem for finite automata is solvable in nondeterministic space $O(n)$.*  $\square$

Since $L(M_1) \neq L(M_2)$ if and only if either $L(M_1) \nsubseteq L(M_2)$ or $L(M_2) \nsubseteq L(M_1)$, we have

**Corollary 3.42** *Given any finite automata $M_1$ and $M_2$ with input alphabet $T$, it is decidable in nondeterministic space $O(|M_1| + |M_2|)$ whether or not $L(M_1)$ differs from $L(M_2)$.*  $\square$

**Corollary 3.43** *The inequivalence problem for finite automata is solvable in nondeterministic space $O(n)$.*  $\square$

By Savitch's Theorem (Proposition 1.38) and Fact 1.36 we have

**Theorem 3.44** *The noncontainment and inequivalence problems for finite automata are solvable in deterministic space $O(n^2)$.*  $\square$

But then we also have immediately

**Theorem 3.45** *The containment and equivalence problems for finite automata are solvable in deterministic space $O(n^2)$.*  $\square$

In the following theorem, we summarize the implications of Corollaries 3.41 and 3.43 and Theorem 3.45.

**Theorem 3.46** *The noncontainment and inequivalence problems for finite automata, regular expressions and regular grammars are all solvable in nondeterministic space $O(n)$. The corresponding containment and equivalence problems are all solvable in deterministic space $O(n^2)$.*

*Proof.* For regular expressions the claim follows from Theorem 3.16, for right-linear grammars from Theorem 3.20, and for left-linear grammars from Theorems 3.22 and 3.20.  □

For deterministic finite automata, the containment and equivalence problems are solvable in deterministic time $O(n^3)$ (see the exercises). This in turn implies, by Theorem 3.30, that the containment and equivalence problems for arbitrary finite automata (and hence for arbitrary regular expressions and regular grammars) are solvable in deterministic time $O(2^{3n+6\log n})$. In Chapter 10 we shall prove a lower bound result stating that the inequivalence problem for finite automata is hard for the class of decision problems solvable in polynomial space. This result strongly suggests that the containment and equivalence problems for arbitrary finite automata, regular expressions and regular grammars are not solvable in deterministic polynomial time.

As we shall see, the proof of the lower bound result is highly dependent on the use of ambiguous regular expressions. This dependence is inherent because for unambiguous regular language descriptions the containment and equivalence problems turn out to be solvable in deterministic polynomial time, as is stated in the following proposition.

**Proposition 3.47** (*Stearns and Hunt*) *There exists a natural number k such that, given any pair $D_1$ and $D_2$ of unambiguous finite automata, regular expressions, or regular grammars, it is decidable in deterministic time $O((|D_1|+|D_2|)^k)$ whether or not $L(D_1)$ is contained in $L(D_2)$ and whether or not $L(D_1)$ equals $L(D_2)$.*  □

Finally, we point out that the question of ambiguity itself is easy to solve. More precisely, the decision problem

$$P_{\mathrm{namb}}(\mathbb{D}): \text{``Given a language description } D \in \mathbb{D}, \text{ is } D \text{ unambiguous?''},$$

known as the *unambiguity problem for* $\mathbb{D}$, can be shown to be solvable in deterministic polynomial time when $\mathbb{D}$ denotes the class of finite automata, regular expressions, or regular grammars. It can in fact be shown that this problem reduces in linear time to the problem of testing a regular grammar for the LR(0) property. As this latter problem turns out to be solvable in deterministic time $O(n^2)$ (see Chapter 10), we have

**Theorem 3.48** *The unambiguity problems for finite automata, regular expressions and regular grammars are all solvable in deterministic time $O(n^2)$.*  □

## 3.6 Applications to Lexical Analysis

The theory of regular languages has applications in various text processing systems. For example, in advanced text editors the user is allowed to specify a regular-expression-like pattern $E$ over $T$, the underlying character alphabet, and to search a file for substrings belonging to the language $L(E)$. The search is implemented by transforming the pattern $E$ into a finite automaton that accepts the language $T^*L(E)$, and then repeatedly simulating this automaton on characters read from the file until an accepting state is entered (or the end of file is encountered). This application, then, makes direct use of the results of Theorems 3.16 and 3.38.

In this section we shall demonstrate how the theory of regular languages can be applied to compiler design. More specifically, we shall show how to derive a scanner, or lexical analyzer, for a programming language whose lexical structure is described by a regular expression. The scanner is a subroutine (sometimes a coroutine) of the compiler whose task is to read the program text to be compiled and to pass it in analyzed form to the next phase of the compilation, the parsing phase.

We assume that the regular expression used to describe the lexical structure is of the form

$$E = (E_1 \cup \ldots \cup E_n)^* ,$$

where $E_1, \ldots, E_n$ are regular terms over $T$, the character alphabet used. Each regular term $E_i$ denotes a particular "token class" of the language. $E$ is called a *lexical description over* $T$. A text is *lexically correct* if it belongs to $L(E)$.

As an example, consider the lexical description

$$P\text{-}text \;=\; (identifier \cup integer \cup comment \cup leftpar \cup rightpar \cup$$
$$spaces \cup semicolon \cup equals \cup colon \cup becomes)^* ,$$

where the regular terms describing the token classes are:

$$identifier = letter(letter \cup digit)^* ,$$
$$integer = digit\ digit^* ,$$
$$comment = {}`\,(\,{}^{*\prime}\,(notstar \cup {}`{}^{*\prime}\ notrightpar)^*\ {}`{}^{*\prime}\,)\prime ,$$
$$leftpar = {}`(\prime ,$$
$$rightpar = {}`)\prime ,$$
$$spaces = {}`\ \prime\ {}`\ \prime^* ,$$
$$semicolon = {}`;\prime ,$$
$$colon = {}`:\prime ,$$
$$equals = {}`=\prime ,$$
$$becomes = {}`:=\prime .$$

To distinguish the operator and parenthesis symbols used in regular expressions from the characters in the underlying alphabet $T$, we have enclosed in single quotes all strings in $T^*$. The regular factors *letter* and *digit* are defined by

$$letter = ({}`A\prime \cup {}`B\prime \cup {}`C\prime \cup {}`D\prime \cup {}`E\prime \cup {}`F\prime \cup {}`G\prime \cup {}`H\prime \cup {}`I\prime$$
$$\cup {}`J\prime \cup {}`K\prime \cup {}`L\prime \cup {}`M\prime \cup {}`N\prime \cup {}`O\prime \cup {}`P\prime \cup {}`Q\prime \cup$$
$${}`R\prime \cup {}`S\prime \cup {}`T\prime \cup {}`U\prime \cup {}`V\prime \cup {}`W\prime \cup {}`X\prime \cup {}`Y\prime \cup {}`Z\prime) ,$$
$$digit = ({}`0\prime \cup {}`1\prime \cup {}`2\prime \cup {}`3\prime \cup {}`4\prime \cup {}`5\prime \cup {}`6\prime \cup {}`7\prime \cup$$
$${}`8\prime \cup {}`9\prime).$$

The regular factors *notstar* and *notrightpar* denote the following character sets:

$$L(notstar) = T \setminus \{`*`\} \ ,$$
$$L(notrightpar) = T \setminus \{`)`\} \ .$$

Let $E = (E_1 \cup \ldots \cup E_n)^*$ be a lexical description over alphabet $T$. An *interpretation* of a sentence $w \in L(E)$ is a string over $T^* \times \{1, \ldots, n\}$ of the form

$$(x_1, m_1) \ldots (x_k, m_k) \ ,$$

where $k \geq 1$, $x_1 \ldots x_k = w$, and $x_i \in L(E_{m_i})$ for $i = 1, \ldots, k$.

**Fact 3.49** If $E = (E_1 \cup \ldots \cup E_n)^*$ is an unambiguous lexical description, then any sentence in $L(E)$ has exactly one interpretation.   $\square$

Unfortunately, lexical descriptions are seldom unambiguous. This can be seen by considering the lexical description *P-text*, which is highly ambiguous. The sentence 'XYZ', for example, has four interpretations:

('XYZ', *identifier*) ,
('XY', *identifier*) ('Z', *identifier*) ,
('X', *identifier*) ('YZ', *identifier*) ,
('X', *identifier*) ('Y', *identifier*) ('Z', *identifier*) .

(Here we have for clarity used token class names in place of their numbers.) Intuitively, the first interpretation, in which the whole letter string is regarded as a single *identifier*, is the desirable one. This gives rise to the following definition.

An interpretation $(x_1, m_1) \ldots (x_k, m_k)$ is *right-biased* if for $i = 1, \ldots, k$, $x_i$ is the longest string in $L(E_1 \cup \ldots \cup E_n) \cap \text{PREFIX} (x_i \ldots x_k)$.

For example, the only right-biased interpretation of the text

'VAR X2: INTEGER;   BEGIN X2 := 125 END (*BLOCK*)'

in the lexical description *P-text* is

('VAR', *identifier*) (' ', *spaces*) ('X2', *identifier*)
(':', *colon*) (' ', *spaces*) ('INTEGER', *identifier*)
(';', *semicolon*) ('  ', *spaces*) ('BEGIN', *identifier*)
(' ', *spaces*) ('X2', *identifier*) (':=', *becomes*)
(' ', *spaces*) ('125', *integer*) (' ', *spaces*) ('END', *identifier*)
(' ', *spaces*) ('(*BLOCK*)', *comment*) .

Unfortunately, some sentences may not have right-biased interpretations. Consider for example the lexical description

$$(a \cup ab \cup bc)^* \ ,$$

in which the only interpretation of *abc* is $(a, 1) (bc, 2)$, which is not right-biased.

We say that the lexical description $E = (E_1 \cup \ldots \cup E_n)^*$ is *well-formed* if every sentence in $L(E)$ has exactly one right-biased interpretation. It should be clear that *P-text* is well-formed.

We leave it as an exercise to prove the following:

**Theorem 3.50** *Given any lexical description E, it is decidable whether or not E is well-formed.*   $\square$

A *scanner* (or *lexical analyzer*) for a well-formed lexical description $E = (E_1 \cup \ldots \cup E_n)^*$ is a program that recognizes the language $L(E)$ and produces for every sentence in $L(E)$ its right-biased interpretation.

Let $E = (E_1 \cup \ldots \cup E_n)^*$ be a well-formed lexical description over alphabet $T$. We recall that a recognizer for $L(E)$ can be constructed as follows. First, apply the algorithm given in the proof of Theorem 3.16 to obtain an equivalent nondeterministic finite automaton. Then apply the algorithm in Figure 3.9 (proof of Theorem 3.30) to obtain an equivalent deterministic $\varepsilon$-free normal-form automaton. If desired, this automaton can be further *minimized* so that it has as few states as possible. (Minimization of deterministic $\varepsilon$-free normal-form finite automata is discussed in a series of exercises at the end of this chapter.) Finally, write a program that simulates this automaton.

To make possible the generation of the right-biased interpretation for a given sentence $w$, we modify the construction algorithm as follows. To guarantee that the distinction between the different token classes is carried over in the construction process, we pad each token class description $E_i$ with a new symbol $\#_i$, and rewrite $E$ as the regular expression $E_\#$ over the extended alphabet $T \cup \{\#_1, \ldots, \#_n\}$ defined by

$$E_\# = (E_1 \#_1 \cup \ldots \cup E_n \#_n)^* \ .$$

This expression of course no longer denotes the language $L(E)$. The resulting finite automaton for $E_\#$ has transitions on the symbols $\#_i$. However, as we shall see, the simulating program can handle the $\#_i$-transitions in a special way so that the language recognized remains $L(E)$. Moreover, whenever a $\#_i$-transition is encountered, the simulating program knows that it has recognized a token $x$ belonging to $L(E_i)$ and can therefore output the corresponding pair $(x, i)$. The program uses a character buffer to store the token currently being recognized. The buffer is empty initially, and is emptied whenever a token has been recognized.

The minimal deterministic $\varepsilon$-free normal-form finite automaton for the padded lexical description *P-text*$_\#$ is shown in Figure 3.14. Arrows labeled *letter*, *digit*, *notstar* or *notrightpar* mean that there are transitions on all characters in the sets denoted by these regular expressions.

The scanner program for $E$ can be written from the deterministic automaton for $E_\#$ as follows. For each state $q$ of the automaton the program has a segment that handles the transitions from $q$. We call this segment the *state program for q*.

Let the transitions from $q$ on symbols in $T$ be

$$q a_1 \rightarrow q_1, \ldots, q a_m \rightarrow q_m \ ,$$

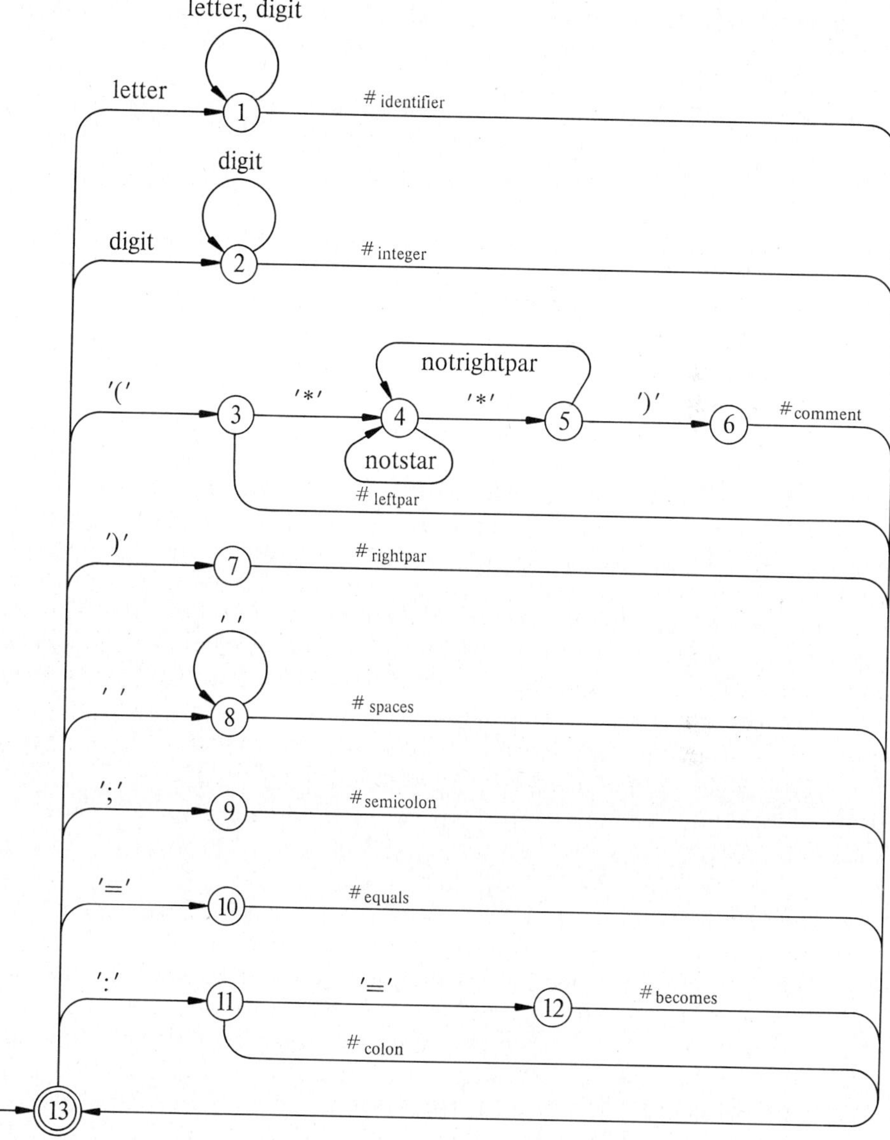


**Figure 3.14** The minimal deterministic $\varepsilon$-free normal-form finite automaton for $P\text{-text}_{\#}$

and let there be a $\#$-transition

$$q\#_i \rightarrow p \ .$$

Note that, since $E$ is assumed to be well-formed, there cannot be more than one $\#$-transition from $q$. (Otherwise some sentence would have two right-biased interpretations.) The state program for $q$ is shown in Figure 3.15.

```
 7: begin
        write(buffer, rightpar); empty(buffer); go to 13
    end;
 8: if ch=' ' then begin
        store(ch); getnext(ch); go to 8
    end else begin
        write(buffer, spaces); empty(buffer); go to 13
    end;
 9: begin
        write(buffer, semicolon); empty(buffer); go to 13
    end;
10: begin
        write(buffer, equals); empty(buffer); go to 13
    end;
11: if ch='=' then begin
        store(ch); getnext(ch); go to 12
    end else begin
        write(buffer, colon); empty(buffer); go to 13
    end;
12: begin
        write(buffer, becomes); empty(buffer); go to 13
    end;
13: if ch in letter then begin
        store(ch); getnext(ch); go to 1
    end else
    if ch in digit then begin
        store(ch); getnext(ch); go to 2
    end else
    if ch='(' then begin
        store(ch); getnext(ch); go to 3
    end else
    if ch =')' then begin
        store(ch); getnext(ch); go to 7
    end else
    if ch=' ' then begin
        store(ch); getnext(ch); go to 8
    end else
    if ch=';' then begin
        store(ch); getnext(ch); go to 9
    end else
    if ch= '=' then begin
        store(ch); getnext(ch); go to 10
    end else
    if ch= ':' then begin
        store(ch); getnext(ch); go to 11
    end else
    if end-of-input then begin
        write(ε, eof); halt
    end else begin
        write(buffer, error); empty(buffer);
        getnext(ch); go to 13
    end;
```

**Figure 3.16** (cont.)

implemented as single **if** statements, using membership queries for the corresponding character sets.

Finally we note that in practice some of the tokens denoted by a lexical description are of no interest to the further phases of the compilation. For example, in a compiler for the programming language Pascal, tokens belonging to the classes *spaces* and *comments* play no role in the context-free parsing of the language, nor in the object code generation, and can therefore be omitted from the scanner output. Furthermore, the actual representations of some interesting tokens may be irrelevant. This is often the case with token classes containing only one member, such as the delimiter classes *leftpar, rightpar, semicolon, colon, equals* and *becomes* in *P-text*. In the case of a token of this kind, the scanner need only produce the number (or name) of the token class to which it belongs.

The scanner for *P-text* can easily be modified so that uninteresting tokens and representations of delimiters are ignored. The output produced for the text

'VAR X2: INTEGER; BEGIN X2: = 125 END (* BLOCK *)'

then looks like the following:

('VAR', *identifier*) ('X2', *identifier*) (,*colon*)

('INTEGER', *identifier*) (,*semicolon*) ('BEGIN', *identifier*)

('X2', *identifier*) (,*becomes*) ('125', *integer*)

('END', *identifier*) .

Depending on the environment, the scanner can be augmented so as to analyze the text even further. Often it is convenient to discover in the lexical analysis phase whether or not a token recognized as an identifier is actually a keyword or an identifier having a predefined meaning. This separation of special strings from other members in a token class is known in the literature as *screening*. If the scanner for *P-text* were augmented with screening, the output might look like the following:

(,*var-keyword*) ('X2', *identifier*) (,*colon*)

('INTEGER', *type-identifier*) (,*semicolon*)

(,*begin-keyword*) ('X2', *identifier*) (,*becomes*)

('125', *integer*) (,*end-keyword*) .

The scanner of a one-pass compiler usually has access to the symbol table of the compiler, and can therefore produce an even more elaborate output. However, as these additional features are highly dependent on the environment in which the lexical analysis is to be performed, we forego further consideration of them. It should be clear that the generation of the final scanner program can easily be modified so as to take into account the additional features.

## Exercises

3.1   Write regular expressions over $\{0, 1\}$ that denote the following languages:

   a) Strings with a number of zeros divisible by three.
   b) Strings with exactly one occurrence of the substring 000.
   c) Strings that do not contain the substring 101.

3.2   Show that any regular language over an alphabet $V$ is denoted by a countably infinite number of unambiguous regular expressions over $V$.

3.3   A regular expression is in *disjunctive normal-form* if it is of the form $(E_1 \cup \ldots \cup E_n)$ for some $n \geqslant 1$, where each $E_i$ is a regular term that does not contain the operator $\cup$. Show that any regular expression can be transformed into an equivalent regular expression in disjunctive normal-form. Evaluate the relative succinctness of arbitrary regular expressions and those in disjunctive normal-form.

3.4   Write regular expressions that denote the languages accepted by the following finite automata:

   a) $(\{q_1, q_2\}, \{0, 1\}, \{q_1 0 \to q_2, q_1 01 \to q_2, q_2 11 \to q_2\}, q_1, \{q_1\})$.

   b) $(\{q_1, q_2, q_3, q_4\}, \{0, 1\}, \{q_1 0 \to q_2, q_2 1 \to q_3, q_2 1 \to q_4, q_3 0 \to q_2, q_4 0 \to q_3\}, q_1, \{q_1, q_3\})$.

   c) $(\{q_1, q_2, q_3, q_4, q_5, q_6\}, \{0, 1\}, \{q_1 \to q_2, q_2 0 \to q_3, q_3 0 \to q_4, q_4 0 \to q_2, q_1 0 \to q_5, q_5 0 \to q_6, q_6 0 \to q_5\}, q_1, \{q_2, q_6\})$.

3.5   Are the automata given in the previous exercise unambiguous?

3.6   Show that any finite automaton $M$ can be transformed in time $O(|M|)$ into a finite automaton $M_p$ that accepts the language PREFIX($L(M)$), and into a finite automaton $M_s$ that accepts the language SUFFIX($L(M)$).

3.7   Let $n \geqslant 1$ and let $\{a_1, \ldots, a_n\}$ be an alphabet of $n$ symbols. Further, let $L_n$ be the language over $\{a_1, \ldots, a_n\}$ defined by

$$L_n = \{\varepsilon, a_1\} \{\varepsilon, a_2\} \ldots \{\varepsilon, a_n\} .$$

   a) Show that $L_n$ is accepted by an unambiguous normal-form finite automaton of size $O(n)$.
   b) Show that any $\varepsilon$-free normal-form finite automaton accepting $L_n$ must have size at least $3n(n+1)/2$.

3.8   Give the finite automaton $M(E)$ corresponding to the regular expression $E$, when $E$ is

a) $(01)^*(10)^* \cup 00^*$
b) $((01 \cup 001)^*0^*)^*$
c) $((0^*1^*0^*)^*1)^*$

**3.9** Complete the proof of Theorem 3.16 (i.e., prove that $M(E)$ is unambiguous if and only if $E$ is).

**3.10** Show that, for any regular language $L$, there is a constant $c$ such that the following is true: Given any $z$ in $L$, $|z| \geq c$, we may write $z = uvw$ in such a way that $|uv| \leq c$, $|v| \geq 1$, and for all $n \geq 0$, $uv^n w$ is in $L$. Moreover, $c$ is no greater than the number of states of the smallest $\varepsilon$-free normal-form finite automaton accepting $L$. This result is known as the *pumping lemma* (for regular languages).

**3.11** Use the pumping lemma to show that the following languages are not regular.

a) $\{0^{n^2} \mid n \geq 1\}$, the language of all strings of 0's whose length is a perfect square.
b) $\{0^n \mid n \text{ is a prime}\}$.
c) $\{x \in \{0,1\}^* \mid x^R = x\}$, the set of palindromes over $\{0,1\}$.

**3.12** Show that any finite automaton $M$ *runs in linear time*, i.e., there is a constant $c$ depending only on $M$ such that, on any sentence $w \in L(M)$, there is an accepting computation of length at most $c|w|$. Also show that, if $M$ is $\varepsilon$-free, then it *runs in real time*, i.e., in time $|w|$.

**3.13** Give the regular expression $E(M)$ corresponding to the finite automaton $M = (\{q_0, q_1, q_2\}, \{0,1\}, \{q_0 0 \to q_1, q_1 1 \to q_0, q_1 1 \to q_2, q_2 0 \to q_0\}, q_0, \{q_0\})$.

**3.14** Complete the proof of Theorem 3.17 (i.e., show that $E(M)$ denotes $L(M)$ and that $E(M)$ is unambiguous if and only if $M$ is).

**3.15** If the unambiguity of the finite automaton $M$ need not be preserved, the construction of the equivalent regular expression $E(M)$ can be simplified slightly. How is this done? (*Hint*: Let $E_{ijk}$ denote the set of input strings $x$ for which state $q_j$ is reachable from state $q_i$ upon reading $x$ in *zero* or more derivation steps and without going through any state $q_m$, $m > k$.)

**3.16** For $n \geq 1$ let $A_n$ denote the set $\{1, \ldots, n\}$, and for all pairs $a, b \in A_n$ define

$$L_n(a, b) = \{(k_1, k_2)(k_2, k_3) \ldots (k_m, k_{m+1}) \in (A_n \times A_n)^m \mid m \geq 1,\ k_1 = a,\ k_m = b\}.$$

Thus $L_n(a, b)$ is the language of all paths in the directed graph $(A_n, A_n \times A_n)$ from node $a$ to node $b$, where paths are represented by sequences of edges.

a) Show that $L_n(a, b)$ is accepted by an $\varepsilon$-free normal-form finite automaton of size $O(n^2)$.

b) (Hard) Show that any regular expression denoting the language $L_n(a, b)$ is of length at least $2^n$.

3.17 Show that finite automata and regular grammars can be encoded uniquely as binary strings of length linear in their norms.

3.18 Design an efficient data structure for storing a normal-form finite automaton. The number of bits needed by the data structure should be linear in the norm of the automaton. Moreover, it should be possible to retrieve the set of all transitions from a given state in time linear in the number of such transitions. Given a state $q$ and a string $x \in T \cup \{\varepsilon\}$, it should also be possible to retrieve the set of all transitions on $x$ from $q$ in time $O(n \log |T|)$, where $n$ is the number of these transitions.

3.19 Show that any right-linear grammar $G$ with terminal alphabet $T$ can be transformed in time $O(|G|)$ into a right-linear grammar $G'$ with terminal alphabet $T \cup \{\$\}$ such that $L(G') = L(G)\$$. (Here $\$$ is a new symbol not found in the alphabet of $G$.) Moreover, $G'$ is unambiguous if and only if $G$ is.

3.20 A language $L$ is *prefix-free* if no proper prefix of any sentence in $L$ belongs to $L$, i.e., the conditions $x \in L$ and $xy \in L$ always imply $y = \varepsilon$. Show that, given any right-linear grammar $G$, it is decidable in deterministic time $O(|G|^2)$ whether or not $L(G)$ is prefix-free.

3.21 Let $L_1$ and $L_2$ be languages over an alphabet $T$. Define

$$L_1 L_2^{-1} = \{x \in T^* \mid xy \in L_1 \text{ for some } y \in L_2\} \, ,$$

$$L_1^{-1} L_2 = \{y \in T^* \mid xy \in L_2 \text{ for some } x \in L_1\} \, .$$

$L_1 L_2^{-1}$ is called the *right quotient of $L_1$ by $L_2$* and $L_1^{-1} L_2$ the *left quotient of $L_2$ by $L_1$*. Show that the family of regular languages over $T$ is closed under right and left quotient with any languages over $T$, i.e., if $L_1$ is a regular language and $L_2$ any language over $T$, then the languages $L_1 L_2^{-1}$ and $L_2^{-1} L_1$ are regular. (*Hints*: Use finite automata to show that the family of regular languages is closed under right quotient. Express $L_2^{-1} L_1$ in terms of the operators right quotient and reversal.)

3.22 Give a grammar that generates the language $L_{\text{match}}$. The grammar should contain only rules of the forms $A \to xB$, $A \to Bx$, $A \to x$, where $A$ and $B$ are nonterminals and $x$ is a terminal string.

3.23 Show that any regular expression $E$ can be transformed in time $O(|E|)$ into a regular expression denoting $L(E)^R$.

**3.24**  Prove Fact 3.29.

**3.25**  Give the deterministic $\varepsilon$-free normal-form finite automaton $\hat{M}$ corresponding to the finite automaton $M$ of Exercise 3.13.

**3.26**  An $\varepsilon$-free normal-form finite automaton is *completely specified* if from each state there is a transition on all input symbols. Note that the algorithm of Figure 3.9 always produces a completely specified automaton. Show that any $\varepsilon$-free normal-form finite automaton $M$ with state alphabet $Q$ and input alphabet $T$ can be transformed in time $O(|Q| \cdot |T|)$ into an equivalent completely specified finite automaton which is unambiguous if and only if $M$ is.

**3.27**  Show that any deterministic finite automaton $M$ can be transformed in time $O(|M|)$ into an equivalent deterministic $\varepsilon$-free normal-form finite automaton.

**3.28**  Show that any completely specified deterministic $\varepsilon$-free normal-form finite automaton $M$ with input alphabet $T$ can be transformed in time $O(|M|)$ into a deterministic finite automaton that accepts the language $T^* \setminus L(M)$.

**3.29**  Show that the family of regular languages over any alphabet $T$ is effectively closed under complement and finite intersection. That is, given any regular expressions $E_1$ and $E_2$ over $T$, $E_1$ can be transformed into a regular expression denoting $T^* \setminus L(E_1)$, and $E_1$ and $E_2$ can be transformed into a regular expression denoting $L(E_1) \cap L(E_2)$.

**3.30**  Show that the family of regular languages over any alphabet $T$ is the smallest family of languages over $T$ that contains all finite languages over $T$ and is closed under closure, concatenation, complement, finite intersection and finite union.

**3.31**  Show that any pair $M_1$, $M_2$ of unambiguous finite automata can be transformed in time $O(|M_1| \cdot |M_2|)$ into an unambiguous finite automaton accepting $L(M_1) \cap L(M_2)$.

**3.32**  Let $M$ be a finite automaton with state alphabet $Q$, input alphabet $T$, and initial state $q_s$, and let $R_M$ be the relation on $T^*$ defined by

$$x R_M y \text{ if } \Rightarrow^*(q_s x) \cap Q = \Rightarrow^*(q_s y) \cap Q \ .$$

Thus $x$ is $R_M$-related to $y$ if and only if the sets of states accessible upon reading $x$ and $y$ are equal. Prove the following:

a) $R_M$ is an equivalence.
b) There are at most $2^{|Q|}$ distinct equivalence classes under $R_M$. Moreover, if $M$ is completely specified deterministic $\varepsilon$-free normal-form, then there are at most $|Q|$ distinct equivalence classes under $R_M$.

   c) $R_M$ is *right-invariant* (with respect to concatenation), i.e., $x R_M y$ always implies $xz\, R_M\, yz$.

   d) $L(M) = \bigcup\limits_{x \in L(M)} [x]_{R_M}$.

We call $R_M$ the *equivalence induced by M on* $T^*$.

3.33 Let $L$ be a language over alphabet $T$, and let $R_L$ be the relation on $T^*$ defined by

$$x R_L y \quad \text{if for all} \quad z \in T^*, \quad xz \in L \quad \text{exactly when} \quad yz \in L.$$

Prove the following:
a) $R_L$ is an equivalence.
b) $R_L$ is right-invariant.

   c) $L = \bigcup\limits_{x \in L} [x]_{R_L}$.

We call $R_L$ the *equivalence induced by L on* $T^*$.

3.34 Let $M$ be a finite automaton with input alphabet $T$. Show that the relation $R_M$ is a refinement of the relation $R_{L(M)}$, i.e., $x\, R_M\, y$ always implies $x\, R_{L(M)}\, y$.

3.35 Let $T$ be an alphabet and $R$ a right-invariant equivalence relation on $T^*$. Further, assume that $R$ is *of finite index*, i.e., there are only a finite number of distinct equivalence classes under $R$. Show that, for any language $L$ over $T$, there is a completely specified deterministic $\varepsilon$-free normal-form finite automaton $M(R, L)$ with input alphabet $T$ such that:

a) The states of $M(R, L)$ are exactly the equivalence classes under $R$.

b) $L(M(R, L)) = \bigcup\limits_{x \in L} [x]_R$.

3.36 Show that the following three statements are logically equivalent for all languages $L$ over $T$.

a) $L$ is accepted by some completely specified deterministic $\varepsilon$-free normal-form finite automaton.

b) $L$ is the union of some of the equivalence classes under a right-invariant equivalence relation of finite index.

c) The equivalence $R_L$ induced by $L$ is of finite index.

This result is known as the *Myhill-Nerode theorem*.

3.37 Show that for any regular language $L$ there is a completely specified deterministic $\varepsilon$-free normal-form finite automaton $M$ accepting $L$ which is *minimal*, in the sense that any completely specified deterministic $\varepsilon$-free normal-form finite automaton accepting $L$ must have size at least $|M|$.

3.38  Let $M=(Q, T, P, q_s, F)$ be a finite automaton. The *language accepted* by a state $q \in Q$, denoted by $L_M(q)$, is defined to be

$$L_M(q) = \{w \in T^* \mid qw \Rightarrow^* p \text{ in } M \text{ for some } p \in F\} \ .$$

In other words, $L_M(q)$ is the language accepted by the automaton $(Q, T, P, q, F)$, and we have $L_M(q_s) = L(M)$. States $q_1$ and $q_2$ are *equivalent* if $L_M(q_1) = L_M(q_2)$. Show that if a completely specified deterministic $\varepsilon$-free normal-form finite automaton $M$ has two equivalent states, one can be eliminated; but if all pairs of distinct states are inequivalent, then the automaton is of minimal size.

3.39  Let $M=(Q, T, P, q_s, F)$ be a deterministic $\varepsilon$-free normal-form finite automaton. Let **ineq** be the relation on $Q \times Q$ defined by $(q_1, q_2)$ **ineq** $(q'_1, q'_2)$ if for some $a \in T$, $M$ has rules $q'_1 a \rightarrow q_1$ and $q'_2 a \rightarrow q_2$. Show that the set of pairs of inequivalent states is given by the closure

**ineq**$^*((Q \backslash F) \times F \cup F \times (Q \backslash F))$ .

3.40  Show that any deterministic normal-form finite automaton with state alphabet $Q$ and input alphabet $T$ can be transformed in time $O(|T| \cdot |Q|^2)$ into an equivalent completely specified deterministic $\varepsilon$-free normal-form finite automaton of minimal size.

3.41  Let $n \geqslant 1$ and let $M_n$ be a finite automaton with state alphabet $\{q_0, \ldots, q_{n-1}\}$, input alphabet $\{0, 1\}$, initial state $q_0$, set of final states $\{q_0\}$ and set of rules

$$\{q_i 1 \rightarrow q_{i+1} \mid i = 0, \ldots, n-2\} \cup \{q_{n-1} 1 \rightarrow q_0\}$$
$$\cup \{q_i 0 \rightarrow q_i \mid i = 1, \ldots, n-1\} \cup \{q_i 0 \rightarrow q_0 \mid i = 1, \ldots, n-1\} \ .$$

Show that the states of the equivalent deterministic automaton $\hat{M}_n$ for $M_n$ are all accessible and inequivalent. Thus, by the result of Exercise 3.38, $\hat{M}_n$ is the smallest completely specified deterministic $\varepsilon$-free normal-form finite automaton that accepts $L(M_n)$. Also observe that $\hat{M}_n$ is of size greater than $2^n$, whereas $M_n$ is only of size $O(n)$.

3.42  Let $n \geqslant 0$ and define

$$L_n = \{0, 1\}^* 1 \{0, 1\}^n \ .$$

a)  Show that $L_n$ is accepted by an unambiguous finite automaton of size $O(n)$.
b)  Show that any deterministic $\varepsilon$-free normal-form finite automaton accepting $L_n$ must have at least $2^n$ states.

3.43  Show that the membership problem for arbitrary deterministic finite automata is solvable simultaneously in deterministic time $O(n \log n)$ and workspace $O(n)$.

**3.44** Show that the containment and equivalence problems for deterministic finite automata are solvable in deterministic time $O(n^3)$. (*Hint*: Use the result of Exercise 3.40.)

**3.45** Show that the noncontainment and inequivalence problems for regular expressions that do not contain occurrences of the closure operator are solvable in nondeterministic time $O(n)$.

**3.46** Show that, given any finite automaton, regular expression, or regular grammar $D$, it is decidable in deterministic time $O(|D|)$ whether or not $L(D)$ is nonempty and whether or not $L(D)$ is infinite.

**3.47** Show that, given any finite automaton, regular expression, or regular grammar $D$, it is decidable in nondeterministic space $O(|D|)$ whether or not $D$ is ambiguous.

**3.48** Show that the family of regular languages over any alphabet $T$ is effectively closed under right and left quotient with regular languages over $T$. That is, any pair of regular expressions $E_1, E_2$ over $T$ can be transformed into regular expressions denoting $L(E_1)L(E_2)^{-1}$ and $L(E_1)^{-1}L(E_2)$.

**3.49** Show that the following decision problems are solvable:

a) "Is $L(M_1) \cap L(M_2) = \emptyset$, for finite automata $M_1$ and $M_2$?"
b) "Is $L(M_1) = T^* \setminus L(M_2)$, for finite automata $M_1$ and $M_2$ with input alphabet $T$?"
c) "Is $L(M_1)^* = L(M_2)$, for finite automata $M_1$ and $M_2$?"

Evaluate the complexity of the solutions.

**3.50** Consider the lexical description

$$number\text{-}text = (unsigned\text{-}integer \cup unsigned\text{-}real \cup spaces)^* \, ,$$

where *unsigned-integer* and *unsigned-real* are regular terms denoting the corresponding token classes of the programming language Pascal, and *spaces* is a regular term denoting the set of all nonempty strings of spaces.

a) Give the nondeterministic finite automaton corresponding to the padded lexical description $number\text{-}text_{\#}$. (You may simplify the construction by regarding all digits as a single symbol. When does this simplification work (in general)?)
b) Give the deterministic $\varepsilon$-free normal-form finite automaton corresponding to that obtained in (a).
c) Minimize the automaton obtained in (b) using the algorithm suggested in Exercise 3.40.
d) Give the state programs for the automaton obtained in (c).

3.51  Consider ways of reducing the size and time complexity of scanners constructed by the algorithm given in Section 3.6. Modify the construction of the state programs so that the resulting scanners run in time $O(|w| \cdot \log|T|)$.

3.52  Prove Theorem 3.50.


## Bibliographic Notes

The basic theory of regular languages (or "regular sets" or "regular events", as they were originally called) was developed by Kleene (1956), Rabin and Scott (1959), and McNaughton and Yamada (1960). Theorem 3.4 comes from Kleene (1956), who also introduced regular expressions and proved their equivalence to finite automata (or, more specifically, to completely specified deterministic $\varepsilon$-free normal-form finite automata in our terminology). Our proof of Theorem 3.16 is based on Aho, Hopcroft and Ullman (1974), and that of Theorem 3.17 on McNaughton and Yamada (1960). Rabin and Scott (1959) introduced nondeterministic (normal-form) finite automata and proved their equivalence to deterministic finite automata (Theorem 3.30). Regular grammars are due to Chomsky (1956, 1959), and their equivalence to deterministic finite automata was shown by Chomsky and Miller (1958). The pumping lemma (Exercise 3.10) is from Bar-Hillel, Perles and Shamir (1961). The Myhill-Nerode theorem (Exercise 3.36) comes from Nerode (1958); a similar result was proved by Myhill (1957). The basic algorithm for minimizing deterministic finite automata (Exercise 3.40) was discovered by Huffman (1954) and independently by Moore (1956). A more efficient algorithm is given by Hopcroft (1971).

The complexity of the equivalence and containment problems for different classes of regular language descriptions has been studied by Meyer and Stockmeyer (1972), Stockmeyer and Meyer (1973), Hunt, Rosenkrantz and Szymanski (1976), Hunt (1979), and Stearns and Hunt (1981). The deterministic polynomial time solvability of the equivalence and containment problems for unambiguous regular language descriptions (Proposition 3.47) was established by Stearns and Hunt (1981). Efficient solutions to the membership problem for finite automata can be found in Aho, Hopcroft and Ullman (1974).

The relative succinctness of different classes of regular language descriptions has been studied by Meyer and Fischer (1971), Ehrenfeucht and Zeiger (1976), Schmidt (1978), and Stearns and Hunt (1981). Meyer and Fischer (1971) proved the fact that nondeterministic finite automata can be exponentially more succinct than deterministic ones (Exercise 3.41). The sequence of languages given in Exercise 3.42 (for obtaining a slightly stronger result) is from Stearns and Hunt (1981). A sequence of languages serving the same purpose is given in Schmidt (1978). Ehrenfeucht and Zeiger (1976) showed that nondeterministic finite automata can be exponentially more succinct than regular expressions (Exercise 3.16). That ambiguous regular language descriptions can be exponentially more succinct than unambiguous ones (Proposition 3.7) is due to Stearns and Hunt (1981).

The use of the theory of regular languages in the design of lexical analyzers is considered by Johnson, Porter, Ackley and Ross (1968) and Lesk (1975) (see also Aho and Ullman (1977)). Its use in the design of text editors and other text processing programs is discussed in Thompson (1968), Aho and Corasick (1975), Knuth, Morris and Pratt (1977), and Aho, Hopcroft and Ullman (1974).

The classical results of the theory of regular languages can be found in any general text on formal languages and automata, such as Aho and Ullman (1972), Harrison (1978), Lewis and Papadimitriou (1981), McNaughton (1982), Salomaa (1973), Savitch (1982) and Wood (1987). A more thorough treatment of the theory is given in Hopcroft and Ullmann (1979) and in Salomaa (1969), while an approach emphasizing efficient algorithms can be found in Aho, Hopcroft and Ullmann (1974).

# 4. Context-free Languages

In this chapter we shall define a class of rewriting systems called context-free grammars. The left-hand side of a rule in a context-free grammar consists of a single symbol, so that symbols are rewritten "context-freely". Context-free grammars are of central importance to us because they define the class of context-free languages, the parsing of which is the subject of this book. In this chapter we shall consider some structural properties of context-free grammars which are of importance in parsing. Also, a basic method for recognizing context-free languages will be given.

In Section 4.1 context-free grammars and languages are defined, and in Section 4.2 special kinds of derivations, called "leftmost" and "rightmost" derivations, are introduced. In Section 4.3 a bijective correspondence between leftmost and rightmost derivations is explicitly constructed, and it is shown that the "ambiguity" of context-free grammars can be defined equivalently using either of these kinds of derivation. In Section 4.4 algorithms are given for removing from a context-free grammar "useless" symbols and symbols that can derive the empty string. A useful normal form, "canonical two-form", for context-free grammars is considered in Section 4.5. Section 4.6 is devoted to a proof of the fact that any sentence in a context-free language can be derived in time linear in the length of the sentence. Finally, in Section 4.7 deterministic and nondeterministic algorithms are given for context-free language recognition.

## 4.1 Context-free Grammars

A context-free grammar is a rewriting system in which the left-hand side of each rule must be a single symbol, called a "nonterminal". Moreover, one nonterminal is chosen as a designated "start symbol". Context-free grammars are a generalization of regular grammars in that no restrictions are placed on the right-hand sides of rules.

Let $G = (V, P)$ be a rewriting system and $T$ a subset of $V$. Further, let $N$ denote the complement $V \setminus T$ and let $S$ be a symbol in $N$. We say that $G$ is a *context-free grammar* (or *grammar*, for short) *with nonterminal alphabet N, terminal alphabet T, and start symbol S*, denoted by

$$G = (V, T, P, S) \, ,$$

if the left-hand side of each rule in $P$ consists of a single nonterminal. In other words, $P \subseteq N \times V^*$.

For clarity, we use capital letters $A, B, C, \ldots, S$ to denote nonterminals, i.e., symbols in $N = V \backslash T$, and lower case letters $a, b, c, \ldots, t$ to denote terminals, i.e., symbols in $T$. General symbols in $V$ are denoted by $X, Y, Z$. The letters $u, v, w, x, y, z$ are used to denote terminal strings in $T^*$, while general strings in $V^*$ are denoted by Greek letters $\alpha, \beta, \gamma, \ldots, \omega$. Recall that $\varepsilon$ is reserved for the empty string.

A context-free grammar is often given by listing only its rules. Its nonterminals are then the set of symbols appearing on the left-hand sides of the rules. We also allow a group of rules

$$A \to \omega_1, \ldots, A \to \omega_n$$

with the same left-hand side to be written in the abbreviated form

$$A \to \omega_1 | \ldots | \omega_n .$$

The start symbol appears as the left-hand side of the first rule or group of rules. For example, the rewriting system $G_{\text{match}}$ (see Section 1.6), which is a context-free grammar with nonterminal alphabet $\{S\}$, terminal alphabet $\{0, 1\}$, and start symbol $S$, may be written as

$$S \to \varepsilon | 0S1 .$$

Because the left-hand sides of the rules in a context-free grammar are single nonterminals, derivations from a nonterminal can conveniently be described using tree structures known as "derivation trees". For example, consider the derivation

$$(S, 0S1, 00S11, 0011)$$

in the grammar $G_{\text{match}}$. The corresponding derivation tree is depicted in Figure 4.1.

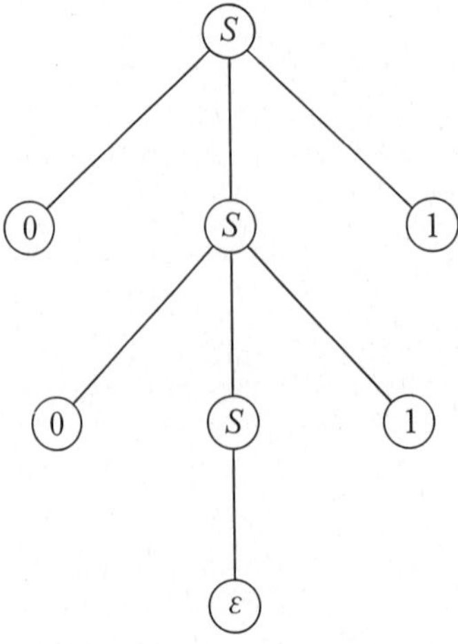

**Figure 4.1** A derivation tree

A *derivation tree* (also called a *parse tree* or *syntax tree*) with respect to a grammar is an *ordered* tree (i.e., the descendants of each node are totally ordered) whose nodes are labeled by nonterminals, terminals, or the empty string $\varepsilon$ in such a way that, if a node $u$ is labeled by a nonterminal $A$ and has sons $u_1, \ldots, u_n$ (in this order) labeled by $X_1, \ldots, X_n$ respectively, then $A \to X_1 \ldots X_n$ is a rule of the underlying grammar. (Nodes with labels other than nonterminals are leaves of the tree.)

Sentential forms of the start symbol $S$ of a grammar $G$, as defined for general rewriting systems, are called *sentential forms of $G$*. A derivation of a string $\gamma$ from the start symbol $S$ in $G$ is called a *derivation of $\gamma$ in $G$*.

Let $\gamma$ be a general string. Sentential forms of $\gamma$ which are terminal strings are called *sentences of $\gamma$*. In particular, sentences of the start symbol $S$ are called *sentences of $G$*.

The *language generated* by $\gamma$ in $G$, denoted by $L_G(\gamma)$ (or $L(\gamma)$ for short), is just the set of sentences of $\gamma$, i.e.,

$$L_G(\gamma) = \{ w \in T^* \mid \gamma \Rightarrow^* w \text{ in } G \} \ .$$

The language $L_G(S)$ generated by the start symbol $S$ of $G$ is called the *language generated* (or *described*) by $G$ and denoted by $L(G)$, so that

$$L(G) = \{ w \in T^* \mid S \Rightarrow^* w \text{ in } G \} \ .$$

Thus we have, for example, $L(G_{\text{match}}) = L_{\text{match}}$.

A language $L_1$ over alphabet $T$ is *context-free* if it is described by a context-free grammar with terminal alphabet $T$, i.e., if there exists a context-free grammar $G = (V, T, P, S)$ such that $L(G) = L_1$.

Not all languages are context-free. For example, it can be shown that the language

$$\{ wcw \mid w \in \{0, 1\}^* \}$$

over $\{0, 1, c\}$ is not context-free. On the other hand, all regular grammars are context-free, which means that regular languages form a subfamily of context-free languages. This inclusion is proper (for non-unary alphabets), because, for example, $L_{\text{match}}$ is not regular (see Section 3.2).

In Section 1.6 we discussed the question of how to represent a rewriting system as a string of symbols and the size of the representation. Just as for a general rewriting system, the *size* $|G|$ of a grammar $G = (V, T, P, S)$ is the sum of the lengths of the rules in $P$ (or $|V|$, whichever is greater). The *norm* $\|G\|$ of $G$ is $|G| \cdot \log|V|$.

In order to be able to derive efficient algorithms for handling grammars, we have to devise appropriate data structures for storing a grammar $G$ in space $O(|G|)$. The basic structure for storing a grammar consists of two linear lists. The first of these contains the left-hand sides of the rules, and the second contains all right-hand side symbols. Each left-hand side points to the first symbol in the corresponding right-hand side, which is followed in the second list by the rest of the right-hand side symbols for that rule. The structure is depicted in Figure 4.2. An identification of the

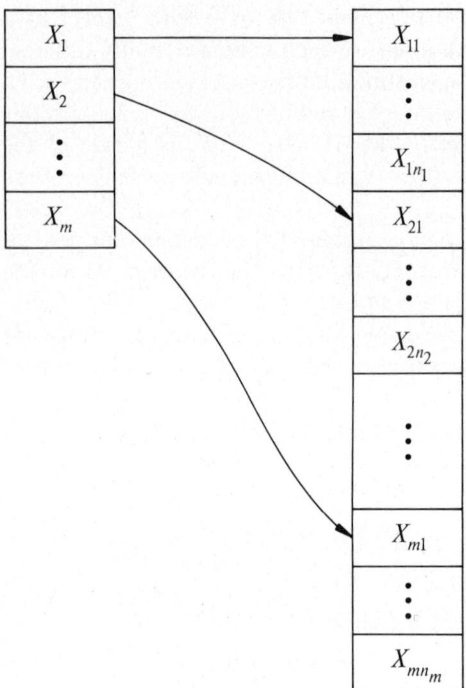

**Figure 4.2** Basic structure for representing a grammar $X_1 \rightarrow X_{11} \ldots X_{1n_1}, X_2 \rightarrow X_{21} \ldots X_{2n_2},$ $\ldots, X_m \rightarrow X_{m1} \ldots X_{mn_m}$

rule is attached to each symbol appearing in its right-hand side. This can be done by storing a link to the left-hand side of the rule. An empty right-hand side is denoted by a special symbol in the list containing the right-hand sides of the rules, and will thus be of length one in the internal representation.

## 4.2 Leftmost and Rightmost Derivations

In context-free grammars one derivation step rewrites a single nonterminal by a string. It is natural to assume that the rewriting of nonterminals happens in some order, so that, say the leftmost nonterminal is rewritten first. In fact, besides the derives relation induced by a general rewriting system, we will need for grammars the subrelations "leftmost derives" and "rightmost derives".

Let $G = (V, T, P, S)$ be a grammar. If $r = A \rightarrow \omega$ is a rule in $P$, we define relations denoted by $\xrightarrow[G,\text{lm}]{r}$ and $\xrightarrow[G,\text{rm}]{r}$ (or $\xrightarrow[\text{lm}]{r}$ and $\xrightarrow[\text{rm}]{r}$ for short) by

$$\xrightarrow[G,\text{lm}]{r} = \{(xA\beta, x\omega\beta) \mid x \in T^*, \beta \in V^*\} ,$$

$$\xrightarrow[G,\text{rm}]{r} = \{(\alpha Ay, \alpha\omega y) \mid \alpha \in V^*, y \in T^*\} .$$

If for strings $\gamma_1$ and $\gamma_2$ in $V^*$, $\gamma_1 \xrightarrow[G,\,\mathrm{lm}]{r} \gamma_2$ (resp. $\gamma_1 \xrightarrow[G,\,\mathrm{rm}]{r} \gamma_2$), we say that $\gamma_1$ *leftmost derives* (resp. *rightmost derives*) $\gamma_2$ in $G$ using rule $r$.

Let $\pi$ be a rule string of $G$. The relations denoted by

$$\xrightarrow[G,\,\mathrm{lm}]{\pi} \quad \text{and} \quad \xrightarrow[G,\,\mathrm{rm}]{\pi} \left( \text{or} \xrightarrow[\mathrm{lm}]{\pi} \text{and} \xrightarrow[\mathrm{rm}]{\pi} \text{ for short} \right)$$

on $V^*$ are defined in an analogous manner to the relation $\xrightarrow[G]{\pi}$. If for strings $\gamma_1$ and $\gamma_2$ in $V^*$

$$\gamma_1 \xrightarrow[G,\,\mathrm{lm}]{\pi} \gamma_2 \left( \text{resp. } \gamma_1 \xrightarrow[G,\,\mathrm{rm}]{\pi} \gamma_2 \right),$$

we say that $\gamma_1$ *leftmost derives* (resp. *rightmost derives*) $\gamma_2$ in $G$ using rule string $\pi$. We introduce the following notational conventions:

$$\xrightarrow[G,\,\mathrm{lm}]{} = \bigcup_{r \in P} \xrightarrow[G,\,\mathrm{lm}]{r} ,$$

$$\xrightarrow[G,\,\mathrm{rm}]{} = \bigcup_{r \in P} \xrightarrow[G,\,\mathrm{rm}]{r} .$$

Furthermore, $\xrightarrow[G,\,\mathrm{lm}]{}$ and $\xrightarrow[G,\,\mathrm{rm}]{}$ may be denoted by $\xrightarrow[\mathrm{lm}]{}$ and $\xrightarrow[\mathrm{rm}]{}$, respectively.

If for strings $\gamma_1$ and $\gamma_2$ in $V^*$,

$$\gamma_1 \xrightarrow[G,\,\mathrm{lm}]{} \gamma_2 \left( \text{resp. } \gamma_1 \xrightarrow[G,\,\mathrm{rm}]{} \gamma_2 \right),$$

we say that $\gamma_1$ *directly leftmost derives* (resp. *directly rightmost derives*) $\gamma_2$ in $G$. If for strings $\gamma_1$ and $\gamma_2$ in $V^*$,

$$\gamma_1 \xrightarrow[G,\,\mathrm{lm}]{}{}^{*} \gamma_2 \left( \text{resp. } \gamma_1 \xrightarrow[G,\,\mathrm{rm}]{}{}^{*} \gamma_2 \right),$$

we say that $\gamma_1$ *leftmost derives* (resp. *rightmost derives*) $\gamma_2$ in $G$, and that $\gamma_2$ is a *left sentential form* (resp. *right sentential form*) of $\gamma_1$. A left sentential form (resp. right sentential form) of the start symbol $S$ of $G$ is called a *left sentential form* (resp. *right sentential form*) *of* $G$.

A string sequence $(\gamma_0, \ldots, \gamma_n)$, $n \geq 0$, is a *leftmost derivation* (resp. *rightmost derivation*) *of length* $n$ *of* $\gamma_n$ *from* $\gamma_0$ *in* $G$ if it is a path of length $n$ from node $\gamma_0$ to node $\gamma_n$ in the directed graph $(V^*, \xrightarrow[G,\,\mathrm{lm}]{})$ (resp. $(V^*, \xrightarrow[G,\,\mathrm{rm}]{})$). That is, if $n > 0$ then $\gamma_i$ directly leftmost derives (resp. directly rightmost derives) $\gamma_{i+1}$ in $G$, for $i = 0, \ldots, n-1$.

As in Fact 1.43, we conclude that for strings $\gamma$ and $\gamma'$ in $V^*$, and rule string $\pi = r_1 \ldots r_n$, $n \geq 0$,

$$\gamma \xrightarrow[\mathrm{lm}]{\pi} \gamma' \left( \text{resp. } \gamma \xrightarrow[\mathrm{rm}]{\pi} \gamma' \right)$$

if and only if there is a leftmost derivation (resp. rightmost derivation) $(\gamma_0, \ldots, \gamma_n)$ in $G$, where $\gamma_0 = \gamma$, $\gamma_n = \gamma'$, and $\gamma_{i-1} \overset{r_i}{\Rightarrow} \gamma_i$ for $i = 1, \ldots, n$.

A leftmost derivation (resp. a rightmost derivation) of a string $\gamma$ from the start symbol $S$ in grammar $G$ is called a *leftmost derivation* (resp. a *rightmost derivation*) of $\gamma$ in $G$.

*Left sentences* (resp. *right sentences*) *of* $G$ are left sentential forms (resp. right sentential forms) that are terminal strings. The set of left sentences and the set of right sentences of $G$ both coincide with the set of sentences of $G$. To prove this fact we need the following technical lemma.

**Lemma 4.1** *Let* $\alpha_1, \ldots, \alpha_m$, $m \geq 1$, *and* $\beta$ *be general strings such that for some* $n \geq 0$

$$\alpha_1 \ldots \alpha_m \Rightarrow^n \beta$$

*in a grammar* $G$. *Then there exist natural numbers* $n_1, \ldots, n_m$ *and strings* $\beta_1, \ldots, \beta_m$ *such that*

$$n_1 + \ldots + n_m = n, \ \alpha_i \Rightarrow^{n_i} \beta_i \quad \text{for } i = 1, \ldots, m, \text{ and } \beta_1 \ldots \beta_m = \beta \ .$$

*Proof.* We use induction on $n$. If $n = 0$ then $\beta = \alpha_1 \ldots \alpha_m$, and the lemma holds if we choose $n_i = 0$ and $\beta_i = \alpha_i$ for all $i$.

Assume then that $n > 0$ and, as an induction hypothesis, that the lemma holds for derivations of length less than $n$. Since $n > 0$, there are strings $\gamma$, $\delta$ and $\psi$, and a rule $A \to \omega$ such that

$$\alpha_1 \ldots \alpha_m = \delta A \psi \Rightarrow \delta \omega \psi = \gamma \Rightarrow^{n-1} \beta \ .$$

Here $A$ is contained in some $\alpha_i$. Thus there exist natural numbers $n'_1, \ldots, n'_m$ and strings $\gamma_1, \ldots, \gamma_m$ such that

$$n'_1 + \ldots + n'_m = 1, \alpha_i \Rightarrow^{n'_i} \gamma_i \text{ for } i = 1, \ldots, m, \text{ and } \gamma_1 \ldots \gamma_m = \gamma,$$

and we have

$$\alpha_1 \ldots \alpha_m \Rightarrow \gamma_1 \ldots \gamma_m \Rightarrow^{n-1} \beta \ .$$

The induction hypothesis implies that there exist natural numbers $n''_1, \ldots, n''_m$ and strings $\beta_1, \ldots, \beta_m$ such that

$$n''_1 + \ldots + n''_m = n - 1, \gamma_i \Rightarrow^{n''_i} \beta_i \quad \text{for } i = 1, \ldots, m, \text{ and } \beta_1 \ldots \beta_m = \beta \ .$$

By choosing $n_i = n'_i + n''_i$ for $i = 1, \ldots, m$, we obtain the desired result. $\quad \square$

We are now in a position to prove that all sentences are also left and right sentences.

**Theorem 4.2** *Let $G=(V, T, P, S)$ be a grammar. For all strings $\gamma$ in $V^*$ and natural numbers $n$,*

$$\{w\in T^*\mid \gamma \underset{\text{lm}}{\Rightarrow}^n w\} = \{w\in T^*\mid \gamma \Rightarrow^n w\} = \{w\in T^*\mid \gamma \underset{\text{rm}}{\Rightarrow}^n w\} \ .$$

*Proof.* We prove the first equality: the second follows in a completely analogous way. Since $\underset{\text{lm}}{\Rightarrow}$ is a subset of $\Rightarrow$,

$$\{w\in T^*\mid \gamma \underset{\text{lm}}{\Rightarrow}^n w\} \subseteq \{w\in T^*\mid \gamma \Rightarrow^n w\} \ .$$

To prove the converse inclusion, we shall first show by induction on $n$ that

$$X\Rightarrow^n w \text{ implies } X \underset{\text{lm}}{\Rightarrow}^n w \tag{4.1}$$

whenever $X$ is a symbol in $V$ and $w$ is a terminal string. The case $n=0$ is trivial. Assume then that $n>0$ and, as an induction hypothesis, that $X'\Rightarrow^k w'$ implies $X' \underset{\text{lm}}{\Rightarrow}^k w'$ whenever $k<n$. Since $n>0$, there is a rule $X\rightarrow X_1 \ldots X_m$, $m\geq 0$, in $P$ such that

$$X\Rightarrow X_1 \ldots X_m \Rightarrow^{n-1} w \ .$$

If $m=0$ then $X_1 \ldots X_m=\varepsilon=w$ and we obtain immediately the desired result. If $m>0$ then, by Lemma 4.1, there exist natural numbers $n_1, \ldots, n_m$ and terminal strings $w_1, \ldots, w_m$ such that

$$n_1 + \ldots + n_m = n-1, \ X_i \Rightarrow^{n_i} w_i \text{ for } i=1, \ldots, m, \text{ and } w_1 \ldots w_m = w \ .$$

Thus, by the induction hypothesis,

$$X_i \underset{\text{lm}}{\Rightarrow}^{n_i} w_i$$

for $i=1, \ldots, m$, which implies that

$$X \underset{\text{lm}}{\Rightarrow} X_1 \ldots X_m \underset{\text{lm}}{\Rightarrow}^{n_1 + \ldots + n_m} w \ ,$$

where $1+n_1 + \ldots + n_m = n$, as desired.

If $Y_1 \ldots Y_p, p\geq 0$, is a string in $V^*$ and $w$ a terminal string such that $Y_1 \ldots Y_p \Rightarrow^n w$, then, by Lemma 4.1,

$$Y_i \Rightarrow^{n_i} w_i \quad \text{for } i=1, \ldots, p \ ,$$

where $n_1 + \ldots + n_p = n$ and $w_1 \ldots w_p = w$. By condition (4.1),

$$Y_i \underset{\text{lm}}{\Rightarrow}^{n_i} w_i \ ,$$

and thus

$$Y_1 \ldots Y_p \underset{\text{lm}}{\Rightarrow}{}^n w \ .$$

Hence we deduce the inclusion

$$\{w \in T^* \mid \gamma \Rightarrow^n w\} \subseteq \{w \in T^* \mid \gamma \underset{\text{lm}}{\Rightarrow}{}^n w\} \ .$$

$\square$

**Corollary 4.3** *For any grammar $G$, $L(G)$ coincides with the set of left sentences of $G$ and the set of right sentences of $G$.*  $\square$

## 4.3 Ambiguity of Grammars

In this section we shall discuss the ambiguity of grammars, which is defined as follows. A grammar $G$ is *ambiguous* if some sentence in $L(G)$ has more than one leftmost derivation in $G$. Otherwise, $G$ is *unambiguous*. We shall show that there exists a bijective correspondence between the leftmost and the rightmost derivations of sentences of $G$. Thus $G$ is ambiguous if and only if some sentence in $L(G)$ has more than one rightmost derivation.

As an example of ambiguity consider the grammar

$$S \to a \mid \textbf{ifcl } S \mid \textbf{ifcl } S \textbf{ else } S \ .$$

This grammar is ambiguous because, for example, the sentence

> **ifcl ifcl** $a$ **else** $a$

has two leftmost derivations:

$$S \underset{\text{lm}}{\Rightarrow} \textbf{ifcl } S \underset{\text{lm}}{\Rightarrow} \textbf{ifcl ifcl } S \textbf{ else } S$$

$$\underset{\text{lm}}{\Rightarrow} \textbf{ifcl ifcl } a \textbf{ else } S \underset{\text{lm}}{\Rightarrow} \textbf{ifcl ifcl } a \textbf{ else } a \ ,$$

$$S \underset{\text{lm}}{\Rightarrow} \textbf{ifcl } S \textbf{ else } S \underset{\text{lm}}{\Rightarrow} \textbf{ifcl ifcl } S \textbf{ else } S$$

$$\underset{\text{lm}}{\Rightarrow} \textbf{ifcl ifcl } a \textbf{ else } S \underset{\text{lm}}{\Rightarrow} \textbf{ifcl ifcl } a \textbf{ else } a \ .$$

It is easy to see by intuitive arguments that different leftmost derivations (or rightmost derivations) of sentence $w$ in the grammar correspond to different derivation trees of $w$, and vice versa. Thus a grammar is ambiguous if and only if a sentence has at least two different derivation trees. Figure 4.3 shows the derivation trees corresponding to the above two leftmost derivations of **ifcl ifcl** $a$ **else** $a$.

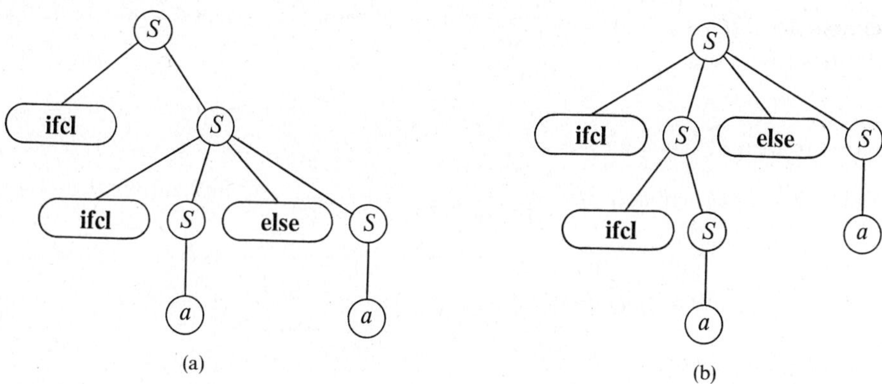

**Figure 4.3** Two derivation trees of the sentence **ifcl ifcl** $a$ **else** $a$ in the grammar $S \rightarrow a\,|\,$**ifcl** $S\,|\,$**ifcl** $S$ **else** $S$

Another example of an ambiguous grammar is

$$S \rightarrow a\,|\,S+S\,|\,S*S \ .$$

For instance, the sentence $a+a*a$ has two leftmost derivations:

$$S \underset{\text{lm}}{\Rightarrow} S+S \underset{\text{lm}}{\Rightarrow} a+S \underset{\text{lm}}{\Rightarrow} a+S*S \underset{\text{lm}}{\Rightarrow} a+a*S \underset{\text{lm}}{\Rightarrow} a+a*a \ ,$$

$$S \underset{\text{lm}}{\Rightarrow} S*S \underset{\text{lm}}{\Rightarrow} S+S*S \underset{\text{lm}}{\Rightarrow} a+S*S \underset{\text{lm}}{\Rightarrow} a+a*S \underset{\text{lm}}{\Rightarrow} a+a*a \ .$$

The grammar

$$S \rightarrow a\,|\,S$$

is highly ambiguous: its only sentence $a$ has infinitely many derivations.

A context-free language $L$ is *inherently* *ambiguous* if every grammar that generates $L$ is ambiguous.

**Proposition 4.4** (*Parikh (1966)*) *There exist inherently ambiguous context-free languages: one example is the language* $\{a^i b^j c^k \,|\, i=j \text{ or } j=k\}$. $\square$

In what follows we shall prove formally that ambiguity of grammars can also be defined by means of rightmost derivations. First we need some technical lemmas and facts.

**Fact 4.5** The following statements hold for general strings $\alpha$, $\beta$, $\beta'$, and any rule string $\pi$:

(1) If $\alpha \underset{\text{lm}}{\overset{\pi}{\Rightarrow}} \beta$  and  $\alpha \underset{\text{lm}}{\overset{\pi}{\Rightarrow}} \beta'$,  then  $\beta = \beta'$.

(2) If $\alpha \underset{\text{rm}}{\overset{\pi}{\Rightarrow}} \beta$  and  $\alpha \underset{\text{rm}}{\overset{\pi}{\Rightarrow}} \beta'$,  then  $\beta = \beta'$. $\square$

**Lemma 4.6** *Let $\alpha_1, \ldots, \alpha_m$, $m \geq 1$, be general strings, $w$ a terminal string, and $\pi$ a rule string such that*

$$\alpha_1 \ldots \alpha_m \underset{\mathrm{lm}}{\overset{\pi}{\Longrightarrow}} w \ .$$

*Then there exist uniquely defined rule strings $\pi_1, \ldots, \pi_m$ and terminal strings $w_1, \ldots, w_m$ such that*

$$\pi_1 \ldots \pi_m = \pi, \quad \alpha_i \underset{\mathrm{lm}}{\overset{\pi_i}{\Longrightarrow}} w_i \quad \text{for} \quad i = 1, \ldots, m, \quad \text{and} \quad w_1 \ldots w_m = w \ .$$

*Proof.* The proof of the existence of the rule strings $\pi_1, \ldots, \pi_m$ and the terminal strings $w_1, \ldots, w_m$ as claimed in the lemma is very similar to the proof of Lemma 4.1 and is left as an exercise.

Let $\pi_1, \ldots, \pi_m, \pi'_1, \ldots, \pi'_m$ be rule strings and $w_1, \ldots, w_m, w'_1, \ldots, w'_m$ terminal strings such that

$$\pi_1 \ldots \pi_m = \pi'_1 \ldots \pi'_m = \pi \ ,$$
$$w_1 \ldots w_m = w'_1 \ldots w'_m = w \ ,$$

and for $i = 1, \ldots, m$

$$\alpha_i \underset{\mathrm{lm}}{\overset{\pi_i}{\Longrightarrow}} w_i \quad \text{and} \quad \alpha_i \underset{\mathrm{lm}}{\overset{\pi'_i}{\Longrightarrow}} w'_i \ .$$

We shall show by induction on $i$ that

$$\pi_i = \pi'_i \quad \text{and} \quad w_i = w'_i$$

for $i = 1, \ldots, m$. The base case of the induction follows from the proof of the inductive step below with $i = 1$.

Assume then that $i > 1$ and, as an induction hypothesis, that $\pi_1 \ldots \pi_{i-1} = \pi'_1 \ldots \pi'_{i-1}$. Since $\pi_1 \ldots \pi_m = \pi'_1 \ldots \pi'_m$, either $\pi_i$ is a prefix of $\pi'_i$ or vice versa. Assume w.l.o.g. that $\pi_i$ is a prefix of $\pi'_i$. Then the condition

$$\alpha_i \underset{\mathrm{lm}}{\overset{\pi'_i}{\Longrightarrow}} w'_i$$

implies that, for some $\beta$,

$$\alpha_i \underset{\mathrm{lm}}{\overset{\pi_i}{\Longrightarrow}} \beta \underset{\mathrm{lm}}{\overset{\pi''_i}{\Longrightarrow}} w'_i \ ,$$

where $\pi_i \pi''_i = \pi'_i$. By Fact 4.5, the condition $\alpha_i \underset{\mathrm{lm}}{\overset{\pi_i}{\Longrightarrow}} w_i$ implies that $\beta = w_i$. Thus $\pi''_i = \varepsilon$, $\pi_i = \pi'_i$, and $w_i = w'_i$, completing the proof. $\square$

The proof of the following lemma is analogous to that of Lemma 4.6.

**Lemma 4.7** *Let $\alpha_1, \ldots, \alpha_m$, $m \geqslant 1$, be general strings, $w$ a terminal string, and $\pi$ a rule string such that*

$$\alpha_1 \ldots \alpha_m \overset{\pi}{\underset{\mathrm{rm}}{\Longrightarrow}} w.$$

*Then there exist uniquely defined rule strings $\pi_1, \ldots, \pi_m$ and terminal strings $w_1, \ldots, w_m$ such that*

$$\pi_m \ldots \pi_1 = \pi, \quad \alpha_i \overset{\pi_i}{\underset{\mathrm{rm}}{\Longrightarrow}} w_i \quad \text{for} \quad i = 1, \ldots, m, \quad \text{and} \quad w_1 \ldots w_m = w \ .$$

$\square$

Let $G = (V, T, P, S)$ be a grammar. For any $\alpha \in V \cup \{\varepsilon\}$, we denote by $\Pi(\alpha)$ the set of rule strings by which a terminal string is leftmost derived from $\alpha$, i.e.,

$$\Pi(\alpha) = \{\pi \mid \alpha \overset{\pi}{\underset{\mathrm{lm}}{\Longrightarrow}} w \quad \text{for some} \quad w \in T^*\} \ .$$

Lemma 4.6 implies

**Lemma 4.8** *Let $A$ be a nonterminal, and let $\pi$ be a rule string in $\Pi(A)$. Then there is a rule $r = A \to X_1 \ldots X_m$, $m \geqslant 0$, and a terminal string $w$ such that*

$$A \overset{r}{\Longrightarrow} X_1 \ldots X_m \overset{\pi'}{\underset{\mathrm{lm}}{\Longrightarrow}} w,$$

*where $r\pi' = \pi$. Moreover, there exist uniquely defined rule strings $\pi'_1, \ldots, \pi'_m$ and terminal strings $w_1, \ldots, w_m$ such that*

$$\pi'_1 \ldots \pi'_m = \pi', \ X_i \overset{\pi_i}{\underset{\mathrm{lm}}{\Longrightarrow}} w_i \text{ for } i = 1, \ldots, m, \text{ and } w_1 \ldots w_m = w \ .$$

We are now able to define a function

$$f: \bigcup_{\alpha \in V \cup \{\varepsilon\}} \Pi(\alpha) \to P^*$$

that maps leftmost derivations to rightmost derivations. Lemma 4.8 implies that the following inductive definition is valid.

(1) $f(\varepsilon) = \varepsilon$.

(2) $f(\pi) = rf(\pi_m) \ldots f(\pi_1)$, if $\pi = r\pi_1 \ldots \pi_m$ for some rule $r = A \to X_1 \ldots X_m$, $m \geqslant 0$, and rule strings $\pi_i \in \Pi(X_i)$, $i = 1, \ldots, m$.

**Lemma 4.9** *Let $\alpha \in V \cup \{\varepsilon\}$. If $\alpha \overset{\pi}{\underset{\mathrm{lm}}{\Longrightarrow}} w$, for some rule string $\pi$ and terminal string $w$, then $\alpha \overset{f(\pi)}{\underset{\mathrm{rm}}{\Longrightarrow}} w$.*

*Proof.* If $\pi = \varepsilon$, the lemma holds trivially. Assume then that $|\pi| > 0$ and, as an induction hypothesis, that the lemma holds for rule strings of length less than $\pi$. The condition $|\pi| > 0$ implies that $\pi = r\pi'$ for some rule $r$ and rule string $\pi'$, i.e.,

$$\alpha \underset{\mathrm{lm}}{\overset{r}{\Longrightarrow}} X_1 \ldots X_m \underset{\mathrm{lm}}{\overset{\pi'}{\Longrightarrow}} w \; ,$$

where $m \geqslant 0$. If $\pi' = \varepsilon$, then $\alpha \underset{\mathrm{rm}}{\overset{f(r)}{\Longrightarrow}} w$ by definition. If $\pi' \neq \varepsilon$, we conclude from Lemma 4.6 that

$$X_i \underset{\mathrm{lm}}{\overset{\pi'_i}{\Longrightarrow}} w_i$$

for $i = 1, \ldots, m$, where $\pi'_1 \ldots \pi'_m = \pi'$ and $w_1 \ldots w_m = w$. The induction hypothesis implies that

$$X_i \underset{\mathrm{rm}}{\overset{f(\pi'_i)}{\Longrightarrow}} w_i$$

for $i = 1, \ldots, m$. Hence we deduce that

$$\alpha \underset{\mathrm{rm}}{\overset{r}{\Longrightarrow}} X_1 \ldots X_m \underset{\mathrm{rm}}{\overset{f(\pi'_m) \ldots f(\pi'_1)}{\Longrightarrow}} w \; ,$$

and from the definition of $f$ that

$$\alpha \underset{\mathrm{rm}}{\overset{f(\pi)}{\Longrightarrow}} w \; . \quad \square$$

Lemma 4.9 says that the function $f$ defines a correspondence between leftmost and rightmost derivations in the sense that, if $\pi$ is a leftmost derivation of some terminal string $w$, then $f(\pi)$ is a rightmost derivation of $w$. In the following lemma we show that, if $\pi$ is a rightmost derivation of $w$, then $w$ has a leftmost derivation $\pi'$ such that $f(\pi') = \pi$.

**Lemma 4.10** *Let* $\alpha \in V \cup \{\varepsilon\}$. *If* $\alpha \underset{\mathrm{rm}}{\overset{\pi}{\Longrightarrow}} w$, *for some rule string* $\pi$ *and terminal string* $w$, *then* $\alpha \underset{\mathrm{lm}}{\overset{\pi'}{\Longrightarrow}} w$, *where* $f(\pi') = \pi$.

*Proof.* If $|\pi| \leqslant 1$, the lemma holds by the definition of $f$. Assume then that $|\pi| > 1$ and, as an induction hypothesis, that the lemma holds for rule strings of length less than $\pi$. The condition $|\pi| > 1$ implies that $\pi = r\pi''$ for some rule $r$ and rule string $\pi'' \neq \varepsilon$. Thus

$$\alpha \underset{\mathrm{rm}}{\overset{r}{\Longrightarrow}} X_1 \ldots X_m \underset{\mathrm{rm}}{\overset{\pi''}{\Longrightarrow}} w \; ,$$

where $m \geqslant 1$. By Lemma 4.7,

$$X_i \underset{\text{rm}}{\overset{\pi_i''}{\Longrightarrow}} w_i$$

for $i = 1, \ldots, m$, where $\pi_m'' \ldots \pi_1'' = \pi''$ and $w_1 \ldots w_m = w$. The induction hypothesis implies that

$$X_i \underset{\text{lm}}{\overset{\pi_i'}{\Longrightarrow}} w_i$$

where $f(\pi_i') = \pi_i''$, for $i = 1, \ldots, m$. Hence

$$\alpha \underset{\text{lm}}{\overset{r\pi_1' \ldots \pi_m'}{\Longrightarrow}} w \ ,$$

and

$$
\begin{aligned}
f(r\pi_1' \ldots \pi_m') &= rf(\pi_m') \ldots f(\pi_1') \\
&= r\pi_m'' \ldots \pi_1'' \\
&= r\pi'' \\
&= \pi \ .
\end{aligned}
$$

$\square$

We shall show in the following lemma that $f$ is an injection, so that $f$ defines a one-to-one correspondence between leftmost and rightmost derivations of terminal strings.

**Lemma 4.11**  *Let $\alpha \in V \cup \{\varepsilon\}$. If $\alpha \underset{\text{rm}}{\overset{\pi}{\Longrightarrow}} w$, for some rule string $\pi$ and terminal string $w$, then the conditions*

$$\alpha \underset{\text{lm}}{\overset{\pi'}{\Longrightarrow}} w, \quad \alpha \underset{\text{lm}}{\overset{\pi''}{\Longrightarrow}} w, \quad \text{and } f(\pi') = f(\pi'') = \pi$$

*imply that $\pi' = \pi''$.*

*Proof.* If $|\pi| \leqslant 1$, we conclude the lemma directly from the definition of $f$. Assume then that $|\pi| > 1$ and, as an induction hypothesis, that the lemma holds for rule strings of length less than $\pi$.

Let $\pi'$ and $\pi''$ be rule strings as in the lemma. The conditions $|\pi| > 1$ and $f(\pi') = f(\pi'') = \pi$ imply that $\pi' = r\tau'$ and $\pi'' = r\tau''$ for some rule $r$ and rule strings $\tau' \neq \varepsilon$ and $\tau'' \neq \varepsilon$. Thus

$$\alpha \underset{\text{lm}}{\overset{r}{\Longrightarrow}} X_1 \ldots X_m \underset{\text{lm}}{\overset{\tau'}{\Longrightarrow}} w \ ,$$

$$\alpha \underset{\text{lm}}{\overset{r}{\Longrightarrow}} X_1 \ldots X_m \underset{\text{lm}}{\overset{\tau''}{\Longrightarrow}} w \ ,$$

where $m \geq 1$. Lemma 4.6 implies that

$$X_i \xrightarrow[\text{lm}]{\tau'_i} w'_i, \quad X_i \xrightarrow[\text{lm}]{\tau''_i} w''_i$$

for $i = 1, \ldots, m$, where $\tau'_1 \ldots \tau'_m = \tau'$, $\tau''_1 \ldots \tau''_m = \tau''$, and $w'_1 \ldots w'_m = w''_1 \ldots w''_m = w$. On the other hand,

$$
\begin{aligned}
rf(\tau'_m) \ldots f(\tau'_1) &= f(r\tau'_1 \ldots \tau'_m) \\
&= f(r\tau') \\
&= f(\pi') \\
&= f(\pi'') \\
&= f(r\tau'') \\
&= f(r\tau''_1 \ldots \tau''_m) \\
&= rf(\tau''_m) \ldots f(\tau''_1) \ .
\end{aligned}
$$

Thus

$$f(\tau'_m) \ldots f(\tau'_1) = f(\tau''_m) \ldots f(\tau''_1) \ . \tag{4.2}$$

Further, it follows from Lemma 4.9 that

$$X_i \xrightarrow[\text{rm}]{f(\tau'_i)} w'_i \quad \text{and} \quad X_i \xrightarrow[\text{rm}]{f(\tau''_i)} w''_i$$

for $i = 1, \ldots, m$. Thus

$$X_1 \ldots X_m \xrightarrow[\text{rm}]{f(\tau'_m) \ldots f(\tau'_1)} w$$

and

$$X_1 \ldots X_m \xrightarrow[\text{rm}]{f(\tau''_m) \ldots f(\tau''_1)} w \ .$$

Now condition (4.2) and Lemma 4.7 together imply that

$$f(\tau'_i) = f(\tau''_i)$$

for $i = 1, \ldots, m$. Thus by the induction hypothesis

$$\tau'_i = \tau''_i$$

for $i = 1, \ldots, m$, and hence

$$
\begin{aligned}
\pi' = r\tau'_1 \ldots \tau'_m \\
= r\tau''_1 \ldots \tau''_m \\
= \pi'' \ .
\end{aligned}
$$

$\square$

We are now in a position to prove the main result of this section.

**Theorem 4.12** *Let $G = (V, T, P, S)$ be a grammar. G is ambiguous if and only if some sentence in $L(G)$ has more than one rightmost derivation in G.*

*Proof.* Assume first that $G$ is ambiguous. Then some sentence $w \in L(G)$ has at least two leftmost derivations in $G$. This means that there exist two distinct rule strings $\pi$ and $\pi'$ such that

$$S \underset{\text{lm}}{\overset{\pi}{\Longrightarrow}} w \quad \text{and} \quad S \underset{\text{lm}}{\overset{\pi'}{\Longrightarrow}} w .$$

By Lemma 4.9,

$$S \underset{\text{rm}}{\overset{f(\pi)}{\Longrightarrow}} w \quad \text{and} \quad S \underset{\text{rm}}{\overset{f(\pi')}{\Longrightarrow}} w ,$$

and Lemma 4.11 implies that $f(\pi) \neq f(\pi')$ because $\pi \neq \pi'$. Thus $w$ has more than one rightmost derivation in $G$.

Conversely, assume that some sentence $w \in L(G)$ has more than one rightmost derivation in $G$. In other words, there exist two distinct rule strings $\pi$ and $\pi'$ such that

$$S \underset{\text{rm}}{\overset{\pi}{\Longrightarrow}} w \quad \text{and} \quad S \underset{\text{rm}}{\overset{\pi'}{\Longrightarrow}} w .$$

By Lemma 4.10,

$$S \underset{\text{lm}}{\overset{\tau}{\Longrightarrow}} w \quad \text{and} \quad S \underset{\text{lm}}{\overset{\tau'}{\Longrightarrow}} w ,$$

where $f(\tau) = \pi$ and $f(\tau') = \pi'$. As $f(\tau)$ and $f(\tau')$ are distinct, we conclude that $\tau$ and $\tau'$ are distinct, and thus that $G$ is ambiguous. $\square$

## 4.4 Useless and Nullable Symbols

Symbols in a grammar are used for deriving sentences. However, the formal definition of a grammar also allows the appearance of symbols that cannot be used to derive any sentence. As these symbols merely enlarge the grammar unnecessarily, they may safely be removed. In this section we shall derive a linear time algorithm for removing useless symbols from a grammar.

Another topic of this section is to determine those nonterminals that can derive the empty string, and to show that any context-free language not containing the empty string can be generated without rules of the form $A \to \varepsilon$.

Let $G = (V, T, P, S)$ be a grammar. A symbol $X \in V$ is said to be *useful* if either $X = S$ or

$$S \Rightarrow^* \alpha X \beta \Rightarrow^* w$$

for some $w \in T^*$ and $\alpha, \beta \in V^*$. Otherwise $X$ is *useless.* A grammar $G$ is said to be *reduced* if it contains no useless symbols.

A nonterminal $A$ of a grammar $G$ is *nullable,* if $A \Rightarrow^+ \varepsilon$ in $G$. A rule of the form $A \to \varepsilon$ is called an *$\varepsilon$-rule.* A grammar having no $\varepsilon$-rules is called *$\varepsilon$-free.*

We shall derive efficient algorithms for determining useless symbols and nullable nonterminals. We begin with nullable nonterminals.

For a given grammar $G$, we set

$$W = \{A \mid A \text{ is nullable}\},$$
$$W_1 = \{A \mid G \text{ contains the rule } A \to \varepsilon\} \ ,$$

and for each $k > 1$,

$$W_k = \left\{ A \,\middle|\, A \notin \bigcup_{i=1}^{k-1} W_i, G \text{ contains the rule } A \to A_1 \ldots A_m, \right.$$
$$\left. \text{where for } j = 1, \ldots, m, \quad A_j \in \bigcup_{i=1}^{k-1} W_i \right\} .$$

**Lemma 4.13**

$$W = \bigcup_{k=1}^{l} W_k \ ,$$

*where $l = |W|$, the number of nullable nonterminals of the grammar $G$.*

*Proof.* Clearly, each $W_k$ is included in $W$. On the other hand, it can be shown by a simple induction on $j$ that, if $A \Rightarrow^j \varepsilon$, then $A \in W_k$ for some $k$. Thus

$$W = \bigcup_{k=1}^{\infty} W_k \ .$$

If $k > 1$ and $A \in W_k$, then by definition, $A$ is not in $\bigcup_{i=1}^{k-1} W_i$, and there is a rule $A \to A_1 \ldots A_m$ such that $A_j \in \bigcup_{i=1}^{k-1} W_i$ for $j = 1, \ldots, m$. Some $A_j$ must be in $W_{k-1}$, because otherwise $A$ would be in $W_{k'}$ for some $k' \leq k-1$. Thus for all $k > 1$ the set $W_{k-1}$ is nonempty whenever $W_k$ is nonempty. Since the sets $W_k$ form a pairwise disjoint partition of $W$, we conclude that $W_k$ is empty for all $k > l$.   $\square$

The individual sets $W_k$ can be computed in linear time, and in fact the time required to compute the union

$$W = \bigcup_{k=1}^{l} W_k$$

is bounded by $O(|G|)$, as stated in the following theorem.

**Theorem 4.14** *The set $W$ of nullable nonterminals of a grammar $G$ can be computed in time $O(|G|)$.*

*Proof.* We associate with each nonterminal a list of positions in which all instances of the nonterminal in the right-hand sides of rules are given. These lists can be formed during a single scan of the rules. We shall mark symbols in the course of the computation: all symbols are initially unmarked.

It is clear that the algorithm given in Figure 4.4 correctly computes the sets $W_k$ until $W_{k+1} = \varnothing$. The algorithm also terminates because, for some $k$, $W_{k+1}$ necessarily becomes empty. Thus by Lemma 4.13 the algorithm correctly computes the nullable nonterminals. The assignment to $W_{k+1}$ in the algorithm is implemented in such a way that, whenever a whole right-hand side is found to be marked, the corresponding left-hand side is added to the initially empty set $W_{k+1}$, provided that the left-hand side itself has not been marked. A simple counter can be used for testing whether a whole right-hand side has been marked. Since the symbols to be marked are accessed directly through the position lists, we thus conclude that the time spent by the algorithm is $O(|G|)$.  $\square$

$W_1 := \{A \mid A \rightarrow \varepsilon \text{ is a rule of } G\}$;
$k := 1$;
**while** $W_k \neq \varnothing$ **do**
    **begin**
        mark all instances of all symbols
        in $W_k$ using the associated
        position lists;
        $W_{k+1} := \{A \mid A \rightarrow A_1 \ldots A_m \text{ is a rule of } G \text{ and for } i = 1, \ldots, m,$
                $A_i \text{ has been marked but } A \text{ has not}\}$;
        $k := k + 1$
    **end**

**Figure 4.4** Computation of nullable nonterminals

We can also use the above algorithm for determining the nonterminals that can derive terminal strings. The following lemma is easily proved.

**Lemma 4.15** *Let $G$ be a grammar and $G'$ the grammar obtained from $G$ by replacing all terminal strings appearing in the rules by the empty string $\varepsilon$. Then a nonterminal $A$ derives a terminal string in $G$ if and only if $A$ derives $\varepsilon$ in $G'$.*  $\square$

The symbols of a grammar $G = (V, T, P, S)$ that may appear in some sentential form of $G$ are determined as follows. Let **contains** be a relation on $V$ defined by:
    $A$ **contains** $X$ if $A \in N$, $X \in V$, and $A \rightarrow \alpha X \beta$ is a rule of $G$ for some $\alpha, \beta \in V^*$.

**Lemma 4.16** *A symbol $X$ is in* **contains**$^*(S)$ *if and only if $S \Rightarrow^* \alpha X \beta$ for some $\alpha, \beta \in V^*$.*

*Proof.* If $X \in$ **contains**$^n(S)$, $n \geq 0$, then $S \Rightarrow^n \alpha X \beta$ for some $\alpha$ and $\beta$, as can be seen by an easy induction on $n$. Similarly, if $S \Rightarrow^n \alpha X \beta$ then $X \in$ **contains**$^m(S)$ for some $m \leq n$. Hence we conclude the lemma.  $\square$

In order to remove useless symbols from a grammar $G$, we first determine all nonterminals that can derive a terminal string. By Theorem 4.14 and Lemma 4.15 this can be done in linear time. All other nonterminals are then removed, except that the start symbol $S$ is always retained and all rules containing nonterminals that cannot derive a terminal string are deleted. Of the symbols still present, those that can appear in some sentential form are determined, which by Lemma 4.16 can be done by computing the closure **contains***$(S)$. The relation **contains** is of size $O(|G|)$, and thus by Theorem 2.2 the removal of symbols not appearing in any sentential form can be done in time $O(|G|)$. We therefore have

**Theorem 4.17** *Any grammar $G$ can be transformed into an equivalent reduced grammar in time $O(|G|)$.*

*Proof.* It is enough to show that after applying the algorithm just described the grammar has no useless symbols. Let $X \neq S$ be any symbol still present after applying the algorithm. After the first step of the algorithm, it must be the case that $X \Rightarrow^* x$ for some $x \in T^*$, and also that if $S \Rightarrow^* \alpha X \beta$ for some $\alpha, \beta \in V^*$, then $\alpha X \beta \Rightarrow^* w$ for some $w \in T^*$. The latter fact comes from the removal of rules that contain nonterminals not deriving any terminal string.

The second step of the algorithm implies that $X \in$ **contains***$(S)$. Hence

$$S \Rightarrow^* \alpha X \beta \Rightarrow^* w$$

for some $\alpha, \beta \in V^*$ and $w \in T^*$, as required.    $\square$

We turn now to the question of how to remove the nullable symbols from a grammar.

**Theorem 4.18** *Let $G=(V, T, P, S)$ be any grammar and $m \geq 1$ the length of the longest rule in $P$. Then $G$ can be transformed in time $O(2^m \cdot |G|)$ into a grammar $\hat{G}=(V, T, \hat{P}, S)$ satisfying*
*(1) $\hat{G}$ is $\varepsilon$-free.*
*(2) $L_{\hat{G}}(X)=L_G(X)\backslash\{\varepsilon\}$ for all $X \in V$.*

*Proof.* The $\varepsilon$-free grammar $\hat{G}$ is constructed from $G$ by replacing the rule set $P$ by the set

$$\hat{P}=\{A \rightarrow \alpha_1 \ldots \alpha_l \alpha_{l+1} | l \geq 0,\ \alpha_1 \ldots \alpha_{l+1} \neq \varepsilon,\ \text{and}$$
$$\text{for some nullable nonterminals } B_1, \ldots, B_l$$
$$\text{of } G,\ A \rightarrow \alpha_1 B_1 \alpha_2 B_2 \ldots \alpha_l B_l \alpha_{l+1} \text{ is in } P\}.$$

We shall show that $L_{\hat{G}}(X)=L_G(X)\backslash\{\varepsilon\}$ for all $X \in V$. Firstly, if $\alpha \underset{\hat{G}}{\Rightarrow} \beta$, then by construction $\alpha \underset{G}{\Rightarrow}^+ \beta$. Thus we conclude that $L_{\hat{G}}(X) \subseteq L_G(X)$ for all $X \in V$.

To prove the inclusion $L_G(X)\backslash\{\varepsilon\} \subseteq L_{\hat{G}}(X)$ we shall show by induction on $n$ that

$$X \underset{G}{\Rightarrow}^n w \text{ implies } X \underset{\hat{G}}{\Rightarrow}^* w$$

whenever $X$ is a symbol in $V$ and $w$ is a nonempty terminal string. The case $n=0$ is trivial.

Assume then that $n>0$ and, as an induction hypothesis, that

$$X \underset{G}{\Longrightarrow}{}^{n'} w \text{ implies } X \underset{\hat{G}}{\Longrightarrow}{}^* w$$

whenever $n'<n$ and $w \neq \varepsilon$. Since $n>0$ and $w \neq \varepsilon$,

$$X \underset{G}{\Longrightarrow} X_1 \ldots X_l \underset{G}{\Longrightarrow}{}^{n-1} w ,$$

for some rule $X \rightarrow X_1 \ldots X_l$ of $G$, $l>0$. Lemma 4.2 implies that there exist natural numbers $n_1, \ldots, n_l$ and terminal strings $w_1, \ldots, w_l$ such that

$$n_1 + \ldots + n_l = n-1, X_i \underset{G}{\Longrightarrow}{}^{n_i} w_i \quad \text{for } i=1, \ldots, l, \text{ and } w_1 \ldots w_l = w .$$

Let $\{i_1, \ldots, i_k\}$ be the set of indices in $\{1, \ldots, l\}$ such that $w_{i_1} \ldots w_{i_k} = w$ and $w_{i_j} \neq \varepsilon$ for $j=1, \ldots, k$. The induction hypothesis implies that

$$X_{i_j} \underset{\hat{G}}{\Longrightarrow}{}^* w_{i_j}$$

for $j=1, \ldots, k$, i.e.

$$X_{i_1} \ldots X_{i_k} \underset{\hat{G}}{\Longrightarrow}{}^* w_{i_1} \ldots w_{i_k} = w .$$

By construction, $\hat{G}$ has a rule $X \rightarrow X_{i_1} \ldots X_{i_k}$, which implies that $X \underset{\hat{G}}{\Longrightarrow}{}^* w$, as required.

The inclusions $L_{\hat{G}}(X) \subseteq L_G(X)$ and $L_G(X) \setminus \{\varepsilon\} \subseteq L_{\hat{G}}(X)$ imply that $L_{\hat{G}}(X) = L_G(X) \setminus \{\varepsilon\}$, for all $X \in V$.

As the nullable nonterminals can be found in time $O(|G|)$, we conclude that the time bound for constructing $\hat{G}$ is $O(2^m \cdot |G|)$. Note that the grammar $\hat{G}$ may have $2^l$ rules corresponding to the rule $A \rightarrow X_1 \ldots X_l$ of $G$, $l<m$.  $\square$

## 4.5 Canonical Two-form Grammars

In this section we shall consider a normal form for grammars called "canonical two-form". A grammar $G=(V, T, P, S)$ is in *canonical two-form* if its rules are of the forms

$$A \rightarrow BC, \quad A \rightarrow B, \quad A \rightarrow a, \quad S \rightarrow \varepsilon ,$$

where $B, C \in V \setminus T$ and $a \in T$. Furthermore, if $S \rightarrow \varepsilon$ is in $P$, then $S$ may not occur in the right-hand side of any rule. We shall show that any grammar can be transformed in linear time into an equivalent canonical two-form grammar. We begin with a preparatory lemma.

**Lemma 4.19** *Any grammar $G=(V, T, P, S)$ can be transformed in time $O(|G|)$ into a grammar $G'=(V', T, P', S)$ satisfying*

(1) *The rules in $P'$ are of the forms*

$$A \to BC, \quad A \to B, \quad A \to a, \quad A \to \varepsilon ,$$

*where $B$ and $C$ are nonterminals and $a$ is a terminal.*

(2) $V \subseteq V'$.

(3) $L_{G'}(X) = L_G(X)$ *for all $X \in V$.*

*Proof.* The idea of the proof is to construct for each rule $A \to X_1 \ldots X_m$, $m \geqslant 2$, of $G$ the rules

$$A \to [X_1][X_2 \ldots X_m] ,$$
$$[X_2 \ldots X_m] \to [X_2][X_3 \ldots X_m] ,$$
$$\vdots$$
$$[X_{m-1} X_m] \to [X_{m-1}][X_m] ,$$

and

$$[X_i] \to X_i$$

for $i = 1, \ldots, m$. Thus the set $V'$ of symbols of $G'$ is

$$V \cup \{[\beta] \mid \beta \in V^+ \text{ and } A \to \alpha\beta \text{ is in } P \text{ for some } A \text{ and } \alpha\}$$

$$\cup \{[X] \mid X \in V \text{ and } A \to \alpha X \beta \text{ is in } P \text{ for some } A, \alpha \text{ and } \beta\} ,$$

and the set $P'$ of rules of $G'$ is

$$\{A \to \alpha \mid A \to \alpha \text{ is in } P \text{ and } |\alpha| \leqslant 1\}$$

$$\cup \{A \to [X][\beta] \mid A \to X\beta \text{ is in } P, X \in V, \text{ and } \beta \in V^+\}$$

$$\cup \{[X\gamma] \to [X][\gamma] \mid [X\gamma] \in V', X \in V, \text{ and } \gamma \in V^+\}$$

$$\cup \{[X] \to X \mid [X] \in V' \text{ and } X \in V\} .$$

It is clear that statements (1) and (2) of the lemma are satisfied. It remains to show that $L_{G'}(X) = L_G(X)$ for all $X \in V$. Clearly, if $\alpha \underset{G}{\Longrightarrow} \beta$ then $\alpha \underset{G'}{\Longrightarrow}^+ \beta$, and thus $L_G(X) \subseteq L_{G'}(X)$ for all $X \in V$.

To prove the inclusion $L_{G'}(X) \subseteq L_G(X)$, we shall show by induction on $n$ that

$$X \underset{G'}{\Longrightarrow}^n w \quad \text{implies} \quad X \underset{G}{\Longrightarrow}^* w ,$$

and

$$[\alpha] \underset{G'}{\Longrightarrow}{}^n w \quad \text{implies} \quad \alpha \underset{G}{\Longrightarrow}{}^* w \;,$$

whenever $X \in V$, $w \in T^*$, and $[\alpha]$ is a nonterminal of $G'$ not in $V$. The case $n=0$ is trivial.

Assume then that $n>0$ and, as an induction hypothesis, that the above claim holds for derivations of length less than $n$.

*Case* 1. Let $X \underset{G'}{\Longrightarrow}{}^n w$. Since $n>0$, we have

$$X \underset{G'}{\Longrightarrow} \eta \underset{G'}{\Longrightarrow}{}^{n-1} w$$

for some $\eta \in V'^*$. If $\eta = \varepsilon$, then by the construction of $G'$, $X \underset{G}{\Longrightarrow}{}^* w$. If $|\eta| = 1$, $\eta \in V$, and $X \to \eta$ is a rule of $G$. Then by the induction hypothesis $\eta \underset{G}{\Longrightarrow}{}^* w$, and thus $X \underset{G}{\Longrightarrow}{}^* w$. If $|\eta| > 1$, then $\eta = [Y][\beta]$ where $[Y]$ and $[\beta]$ are in $V'$, and

$$X \underset{G'}{\Longrightarrow} [Y][\beta] \underset{G'}{\Longrightarrow}{}^{n-1} w \;.$$

In this case, Lemma 4.2 and the induction hypothesis imply that $Y\beta \underset{G}{\Longrightarrow}{}^* w$. By construction, $G$ contains the rule $X \to Y\beta$ and thus $X \underset{G}{\Longrightarrow}{}^* w$, as required.

*Case* 2. Let $[\alpha] \underset{G'}{\Longrightarrow}{}^n w$. Then

$$[\alpha] \underset{G'}{\Longrightarrow} \eta \underset{G'}{\Longrightarrow}{}^{n-1} w$$

for some $\eta \in V'^*$. If $|\alpha| = 1$, then $\eta = \alpha$ and by the induction hypothesis $\alpha \underset{G}{\Longrightarrow}{}^* w$. Assume then that $\alpha = X\gamma$ where $X \in V$ and $\gamma \in V^+$. By the construction of $G'$ we have

$$[X\gamma] \underset{G'}{\Longrightarrow} [X][\gamma] \underset{G'}{\Longrightarrow}{}^{n-1} w \;.$$

By Lemma 4.2 and the induction hypothesis

$$X \underset{G}{\Longrightarrow}{}^* w_1 \quad \text{and} \quad \gamma \underset{G}{\Longrightarrow}{}^* w_2 \;,$$

where $w_1 w_2 = w$. Thus $X\gamma \underset{G}{\Longrightarrow}{}^* w$, as required.

For each rule $A \rightarrow X_1 \ldots X_m$, $m \geqslant 2$, of $G$ of length $m+1$, the grammar $G'$ has a set of rules of total length $3(m-1)+m=4m-3$. It is clear that the transformation in the construction of $G'$ can be performed in time $O(|G|)$. $\quad\square$

Using Lemma 4.19 we can prove the following theorem.

**Theorem 4.20** *Any grammar* $G=(V, T, P, S)$ *can be transformed in time* $O(|G|)$ *into a grammar* $G'=(V', T, P', S')$ *satisfying*

(1) $G'$ *is in canonical two-form.*
(2) $V \subseteq V'$.
(3) $L_{G'}(X)=L_G(X)\backslash\{\varepsilon\}$ *for all* $X \in V$.
(4) $L_{G'}(S')=L_G(S)$.

*Proof.* We first transform $G$ in time $O(|G|)$ into a grammar $G_1=(V_1, T, P_1, S)$ satisfying the conditions of Lemma 4.19.

Secondly, we determine the nullable nonterminals of $G_1$. By Theorem 4.14 this can be done in time $O(|G_1|)=O(|G|)$. Thirdly, we transform $G_1$ into an $\varepsilon$-free grammar $G_2=(V_1, T, P_2, S)$ such that $L_{G_2}(X)=L_{G_1}(X)\backslash\{\varepsilon\}$ for all $X \in V_1$. By Theorem 4.18 this can be done in time $O(|G_1|)=O(|G|)$, because the right-hand sides of rules in $P_1$ are all of length at most two.

If $S$ is not nullable (in $G_1$) then $G'=G_2$ satisfies the conditions of the theorem; otherwise, set $G'=(V_1 \cup \{S'\}, T, P_2 \cup \{S' \rightarrow S, S' \rightarrow \varepsilon\}, S')$, where $S'$ is a new non-terminal not in $V_1$. $\quad\square$

A grammar $G=(V, T, P, S)$ is in *Chomsky normal-form* if the rules in $P$ are of the forms

$$A \rightarrow BC, \quad A \rightarrow a, \quad \text{and} \quad S \rightarrow \varepsilon ,$$

where $B, C \in V\backslash T$ and $a \in T$. Moreover, if $S \rightarrow \varepsilon$ is in $P$, then $S$ may not occur in the right-hand side of any rule. Thus a grammar in canonical two-form can be transformed into Chomsky normal-form by eliminating all rules of the form $A \rightarrow B$. These rules are called *unit rules* (or *single rules*). The standard way of eliminating unit rules is to add, for each rule $A \rightarrow BC$, all rules of the form $A \rightarrow B'C'$, where $B \Rightarrow^* B'$ and $C \Rightarrow^* C'$, and then delete all rules of the form $A \rightarrow B$. This construction, however, may result in a grammar of size $O(|G|^2)$, where $|G|$ is the size of the original grammar. No better algorithm is known for eliminating unit rules.


## 4.6 Derivational Complexity

In this section we shall consider the time and space complexities of deriving a sentence in a grammar. The concepts of time and space complexity of a derivation were defined in Section 1.6 for general rewriting systems. The *time complexity of deriving* a sentence $w$ *in* a grammar $G = (V, T, P, S)$, denoted by $\text{TIME}_G(w)$, is the time complexity of deriving $w$ from $S$ in $G$. The *space complexity of deriving $w$ in $G$*, denoted by $\text{SPACE}_G(w)$, is the space complexity of deriving $w$ from $S$ in $G$. In the notation of Section 1.6,

$$\text{TIME}_G(w) = \text{TIME}_G(S, w) \ ,$$
$$\text{SPACE}_G(w) = \text{SPACE}_G(S, w) \ .$$

We shall show that the time and space complexities of deriving a sentence in a context-free grammar are linear in the length of the sentence, so that the number of derivation steps needed to derive a sentence $w$ is bounded by $O(|w|)$. Actually we determine *minimal* grammar-dependent upper bounds of the form $c|w| + d$ on the time and space complexities of deriving a sentence $w$ in a context-free grammar. By minimality we mean that there exists a sequence of grammars for which the bounds are actually attained.

We consider first the case in which the grammars are $\varepsilon$-free. Let $G_n$, $n \geqslant 1$, be the grammar with rules

$$A_1 \rightarrow A_2 \ ,$$
$$A_2 \rightarrow A_3 \ ,$$
$$\vdots$$
$$A_n \rightarrow a \mid A_1 A_1 \ .$$

Thus $L(A_1) = a^+$, and $A_1$ derives the sentence $a^k$ simultaneously in time $2nk - n$ and space $k$, for all $k \geqslant 1$.

Note that the grammars $G_n$ are ambiguous: each sentence $a^k$, $k \geqslant 3$, has many derivation trees. However, the derivation trees are all of the same "size" and thus each of them represents the time and space complexity. Figure 4.5 shows one possible derivation tree of $aaaa$.

The following theorem states that the time and space complexities of derivations in $G_n$ are actually upper bounds on the complexities of derivations in any $\varepsilon$-free grammar.


**Theorem 4.21** *Let $G$ be an $\varepsilon$-free grammar with $n$ nonterminals. If $X$ is a symbol of $G$ and $w \in L(X)$, then $X$ derives $w$ simultaneously in time $2n|w| - n$ and space $|w|$. Moreover, these bounds are minimal.*


*Proof.* First we note that the space complexity of any derivation in $G$ is $|w|$, because in an $\varepsilon$-free grammar no derivation step can decrease the length of the sentential form.

We now prove, by induction on $|w|$, that whenever $w \in L(X)$, $X$ derives $w$ in time $2n|w| - n$. If $|w| = 1$ and $X \overset{\pi}{\Longrightarrow} w$, then the fact that $G$ is $\varepsilon$-free implies that $\pi$ can contain only unit rules of the form $A \rightarrow B$ or $B \rightarrow w$. Thus, if $\pi$ is the shortest possible rule string such that $X \overset{\pi}{\Longrightarrow} w$, then $|\pi| \leqslant n = 2n|w| - n$, because two rules with the same left-hand side in $\pi$ would constitute an unnecessary loop.

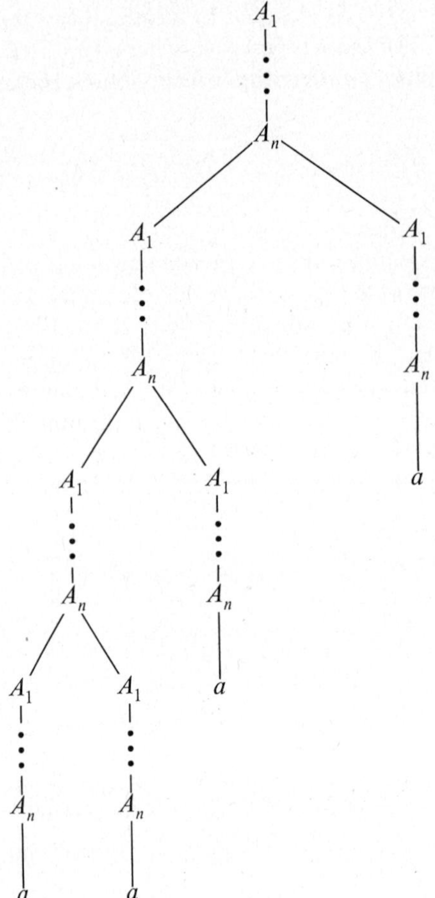

**Figure 4.5** Derivation tree of *aaaa* in the grammar $G_n$. The time complexity of deriving *aaaa* from $A_1$ is $7n = 2n \cdot 4 - n$

We may thus assume that $|w| > 1$ and, as an induction hypothesis, that whenever $w' \in L(X')$ and $|w'| < |w|$, $X'$ derives $w'$ in time $2n|w'| - n$. If $X \Rightarrow^* w$, then there is a rule $r = A \rightarrow X_1 \ldots X_m$, $m \geqslant 2$, and a rule string $\pi$ such that

$$X \xrightarrow{\pi} A \xrightarrow{r} X_1 \ldots X_m \Rightarrow^* w \ .$$

Moreover, by Lemma 4.2 there are rule strings $\pi_1, \ldots, \pi_m$ and terminal strings $w_1, \ldots, w_m$ such that

$$X_i \xrightarrow{\pi_i} w_i \quad \text{for} \quad i = 1, \ldots, m \ ,$$

$$\text{and } w_1 \ldots w_m = w \ .$$

Here $\pi$ can contain only unit rules of the form $B \to C$. Thus, if $\pi$ has minimal length, then $|\pi| \leqslant n-1$. On the other hand, $m \geqslant 2$ implies that $|w_i| < |w|$ for $i = 1, \ldots, m$, which means that we can apply the induction hypothesis and assume that $|\pi_i| \leqslant 2n|w_i| - n$ for $i = 1, \ldots, m$.

We then have

$$|\pi r \pi_1 \ldots \pi_m| = |\pi| + 1 + \sum_{i=1}^{m} |\pi_i|$$

$$\leqslant (n-1) + 1 + \sum_{i=1}^{m} (2n|w_i| - n)$$

$$= 2n|w| + (1-m)n$$

$$\leqslant 2n|w| - n \ ,$$

as required. The grammars $G_n$, $n \geqslant 1$, presented above show that this bound is also minimal.  $\square$

Our second task is to analyze the complexity of deriving the empty string. Let $G_{n', m}$, $n' \geqslant 1$, $m \geqslant 2$, be the grammar with rules

$$A_1 \to A_2^m \ ,$$
$$A_2 \to A_3^m \ ,$$
$$\vdots$$
$$A_{n'-1} \to A_{n'}^m \ ,$$
$$A_{n'} \to \varepsilon \ .$$

Then $L(A_i) = \{\varepsilon\}$ for $i = 1, \ldots, n'$. Moreover, $A_i$ derives $\varepsilon$ simultaneously in time

$$1 + m + \ldots + m^{k_i - 1} = (m^{k_i} - 1)/(m-1)$$

and space $(k_i - 1)(m-1) + 1$, where $k_i = n' - i + 1$.

Figure 4.6 shows the derivation tree of $\varepsilon$ in $G_{n', m}$ in the case $n' = 4$, $m = 2$. In Figure 4.7 some intermediate steps of the leftmost derivation of $\varepsilon$ in $G'_{4, 2}$ are given. Figure 4.6 confirms that $(m^{n'} - 1)/(m-1)$ is the time complexity of deriving $\varepsilon$ from $A_1$, and Figure 4.7 that $(n' - 1)(m-1) + 1$ is the space complexity of deriving $\varepsilon$ from $A_1$ when only leftmost derivations are allowed. It should be clear that $(n' - 1)(m-1) + 1$ is in fact the space complexity for any kind (general, leftmost, rightmost) of derivation.

We now prove that the time and space complexities of deriving $\varepsilon$ in $G_{n', m}$ are upper bounds on the complexities of deriving $\varepsilon$ in any grammar. Let $G$ be a grammar, and let $W$ and $W_k$, for $k \geqslant 1$, be sets as defined in Section 4.4. Thus the set $W$ contains all nullable symbols of $G$, and a nonterminal $A$ is in $W_k$ if and only if $\varepsilon$ has a derivation of length $k$ from $A$, but no derivation of length less than $k$ from $A$.

**Lemma 4.22** *Let $G$ be a grammar and $m \geqslant 2$ the length of the right-hand side of the longest rule in $G$. Then for all $k \geqslant 1$ and $A \in W_k$, $A$ derives $\varepsilon$ simultaneously in time*

$$(m^k - 1)/(m-1)$$

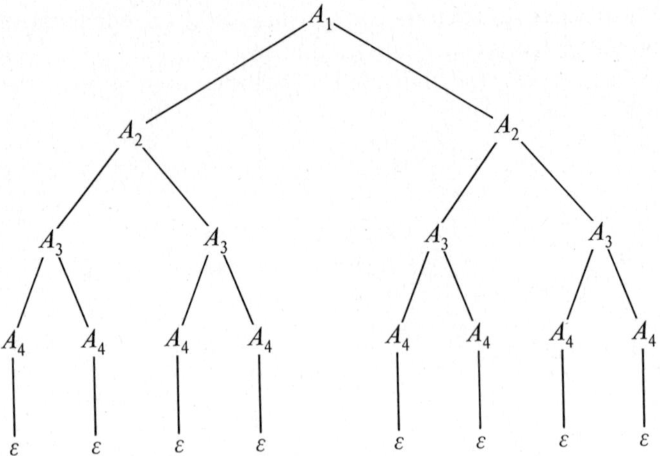

**Figure 4.6** Derivation tree of $\varepsilon$ in $G_{4,2}$. The time complexity ($=$ number of interior nodes) is 15, which equals $m^{n'}-1=(m^{n'}-1)/(m-1)$ for $m=2$ and $n'=4$

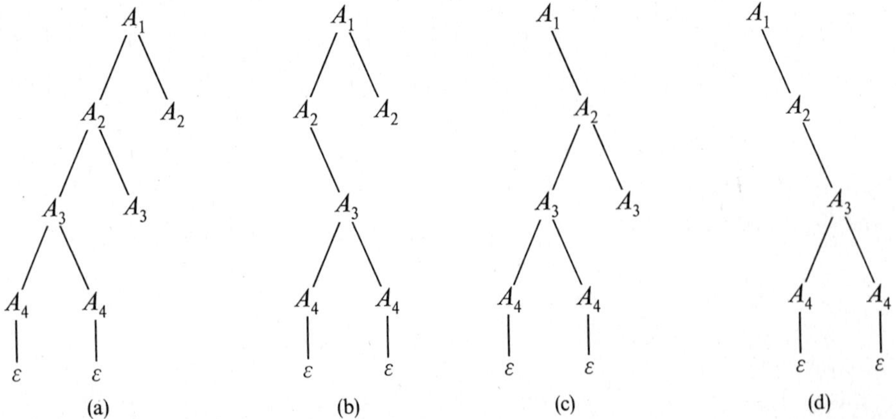

**Figure 4.7** Partial derivation trees in $G_{4,2}$ exhibiting the process of leftmost derivation. The space needed is at most 4, which equals $(n'-1)(m-1)+1$ for $n'=4$ and $m=2$

*and space*

$$(k-1)(m-1)+1.$$

*Moreover, these bounds are minimal.*

*Proof.* The proof is by induction on $k$. If $k=1$ and $A \in W_k$, then $A \to \varepsilon$ is a rule in $G$. Thus $A$ derives $\varepsilon$ simultaneously in time $1=(m^k-1)/(m-1)$ and space $1=(k-1)(m-1)+1$.

Assume then that $k>1$ and, as an induction hypothesis, that whenever $k'<k$ and $A' \in W_{k'}$, $A'$ derives $\varepsilon$ simultaneously in time $(m^{k'}-1)/(m-1)$ and space $(k'-1)$

$(m-1)+1$. If $A \in W_k$, then, by definition, $G$ has a rule $r = A \to A_1 \ldots A_l$ in which each $A_i \in W_{k_i}$ for some $k_i < k$. The induction hypothesis implies that there are rule strings $\pi_1, \ldots, \pi_l$ such that for $i = 1, \ldots, l$

$$A_i \overset{\pi_i}{\Longrightarrow} \varepsilon, \quad |\pi_i| \leqslant (m^{k_i} - 1)/(m-1),$$

and the space complexity $s_i$ of $A_i \overset{\pi_i}{\Longrightarrow} \varepsilon$ is at most $(k_i - 1)(m-1)+1$. The time complexity of the derivation $A \overset{r\pi_1 \ldots \pi_l}{\Longrightarrow} \varepsilon$ is

$$1 + \sum_{i=1}^{l} |\pi_i| \leqslant 1 + \sum_{i=1}^{l} (m^{k_i} - 1)/(m-1)$$

$$\leqslant 1 + l(m^{k-1} - 1)/(m-1)$$

$$\leqslant 1 + m(m^{k-1} - 1)/(m-1)$$

$$= (m^k - 1)/(m-1) \, ,$$

as required. The space complexity of this derivation is

$$\max\{s_i + (l-i) \mid i = 1, \ldots, l\}$$
$$\leqslant \max\{(k_i - 1)(m-1)+1+(l-i) \mid i = 1, \ldots, l\}$$
$$\leqslant \max\{((k-1)-1)(m-1)+1+(l-i) \mid i = 1, \ldots, l\}$$
$$\leqslant (k-2)(m-1)+1+(l-1)$$
$$\leqslant (k-2)(m-1)+1+(m-1)$$
$$= (k-1)(m-1)+1 \, ,$$

as required. The grammars $G_{n', m}$, $n' \geqslant 1$, $m \geqslant 2$, given above show that these bounds are also minimal. $\square$

From Lemmas 4.13 and 4.22 we get

**Theorem 4.23** *Let $G$ be a grammar, $n' \geqslant 1$ the number of nullable nonterminals in $G$, and $m \geqslant 2$ the length of the right-hand side of the longest rule in $G$. Then any nullable nonterminal $A$ derives $\varepsilon$ simultaneously in time*

$$(m^{n'} - 1)/(m-1)$$

*and space*

$$(n' - 1)(m-1)+1 \, .$$

*Moreover, these bounds are minimal.* $\square$

We consider next the derivation of an arbitrary sentence in a general context-free grammar. Let $G_{n,n',m}$, $n \geq 1$, $n' \geq 1$, $m \geq 2$, be the grammar with rules

$$A_1 \rightarrow A_2 B_1^{m-1} \ ,$$

$$A_2 \rightarrow A_3 B_1^{m-1} \ ,$$

$$\vdots$$

$$A_{n-1} \rightarrow A_n B_1^{m-1} \ ,$$

$$A_n \rightarrow A_1 A_1 B_1^{m-2} \mid a B_1^{m-1} \ ,$$

$$B_1 \rightarrow B_2^m \ ,$$

$$B_2 \rightarrow B_3^m \ ,$$

$$\vdots$$

$$B_{n'-1} \rightarrow B_{n'}^m \ ,$$

$$B_{n'} \rightarrow \varepsilon \ .$$

Thus $G_{n,n',m}$ is a combination of the grammars $G_n$ and $G_{n',m}$.

If $ck + d$ is the time complexity of deriving the string $a^k$ from $A_1$ in $G_n$, and if $t$ is the time complexity of deriving $\varepsilon$ from $B_1$, then the time complexity of deriving $a^k$ from $A_1$ in $G_{n,n',m}$ is

$$(ck+d)+((ck+d)(m-1)-(k-1))t$$
$$=(c+c(m-1)t-t)k+d+d(m-1)t+t.$$

Note that any application of an $A$-rule (a rule having $A$, possibly indexed, as the left-hand side) introduces into the current sentential form $m-1$ instances of $B_1$, except in the case of the rule $A_n \rightarrow A_1 A_1 B_1^{m-2}$, which introduces only $m-2$ instances. In deriving the sentence $a^k$ this rule is used $k-1$ times.

The most space-efficient way to derive $a^k$ is to erase the nonterminals $B_1$ from the sentential form as soon as they appear: after each application of an $A$-rule the $m-1$ (or $m-2$) instances of $B_1$ which are thereby introduced are each made to derive $\varepsilon$ in the most space-efficient way. Thus if $s$ is the space complexity of deriving $\varepsilon$ from $B_1$, then the space complexity of deriving $a^k$ from $A_1$ in $G_{n,n',m}$ is $k+(m-2)+s$.

The following theorem states that the time and space complexities of deriving a sentence in grammars $G_{n,n',m}$ are upper bounds on the complexities of derivations in any grammar.

**Theorem 4.24** *Let $G$ be a grammar in which the length of the right-hand side of the longest rule is $m \geq 2$, and in which each nullable nonterminal derives $\varepsilon$ simultaneously in time $t$ and space $s$. Let $\hat{G}$ be the corresponding $\varepsilon$-free grammar constructed as in the proof of Theorem 4.18, so that*

$$L(\hat{G}) = L(G) \backslash \{\varepsilon\} \ .$$

*If a nonterminal $A$ derives a terminal string $w$ in $\hat{G}$ in time $c|w|+d$, then $A$ derives $w$ in $G$ simultaneously in time*

$$(c+c(m-1)t-t)|w|+d+d(m-1)t+t$$

*and space*

$$|w|+(m-2)+s \ .$$

*Moreover, these bounds are minimal.*

*Proof.* For each nullable nonterminal $B$ in $G$, let $D(B)$ be a rule string such that

$$B \xRightarrow{D(B)} \varepsilon \ ,$$

and let the time and space complexities of this derivation be $t$ and $s$ respectively. Further, for each rule $A\rightarrow\omega$ in $\hat{G}$ we choose a rule $A\rightarrow\alpha_1 B_1 \ldots \alpha_l B_l \alpha_{l+1}$ in $G$ such that $\alpha_1 \ldots \alpha_{l+1}=\omega$ and $B_i$ is nullable for $i=1,\ldots,l$. The construction of $\hat{G}$ guarantees that such a choice is always possible. We then define homomorphisms $f$ and $g$ from $\hat{P}^*$ to $P^*$ as follows:

$$f(A\rightarrow\omega)=A\rightarrow\alpha_1 B_1 \ldots \alpha_l B_l \alpha_{l+1} \ ,$$
$$g(A\rightarrow\omega)=f(A\rightarrow\omega)D(B_1) \ldots D(B_l) \ .$$

We say that $A\rightarrow\omega$ has $l$ *$\varepsilon$-positions* and $|\omega|$ *non-$\varepsilon$-positions with respect to $f$.*

Now if $A \xRightarrow{\pi} w$ in $\hat{G}$, then it can be shown by a simple induction on $|\pi|$ that $A \xRightarrow{g(\pi)} w$ in $G$ (see the exercises). Note that this derivation is obviously the least space consuming because the nullable $B$'s are erased as soon as possible.

The time complexity of the derivation $A \xRightarrow{g(\pi)} w$ is at most $|\pi|+et$, where $e$ is the total number of $\varepsilon$-positions in the rules appearing in $\pi$. Since $\hat{G}$ is $\varepsilon$-free, and the length of the right-hand side of any rule in $G$ is at most $m$, each rule in $\pi$ has at least one non-$\varepsilon$-position and at most $m-1$ $\varepsilon$-positions. Hence we know that $e\leqslant|\pi|(m-1)$. However, if $|w|>1$, not all rules appearing in $\pi$ can be unit rules of the form $B\rightarrow X$. More precisely, there must be $|w|-1$ additional non-$\varepsilon$-positions in $\pi$. This means that in fact

$$e\leqslant|\pi|(m-1)-(|w|-1) \ .$$

If $|\pi|\leqslant c|w|+d$, we may conclude that the time complexity of the derivation $A \xRightarrow{g(\pi)} w$ is at most

$$c|w|+d+((c|w|+d)(m-1)-(|w|-1))t$$
$$=(c+c(m-1)t-t)|w|+d+d(m-1)t+t \ ,$$

as required.

After any application of a rule $f(A\to\omega)$, the nullable nonterminals that correspond to the $\varepsilon$-positions in $A\to\omega$ are immediately erased. Moreover, each of them is erased in space $s$. Thus no intermediate sentential form in the derivation $A \overset{g(\pi)}{\Longrightarrow} w$ can contain more than $(m-2)+s$ nullable nonterminals that arise from $\varepsilon$-positions. This means that the space complexity of the derivation is at most $|w|+(m-2)+s$, as required.

The minimality of the bounds can be seen by considering the grammars $G_{n,n',m}$.  $\square$

Combining Theorems 4.21, 4.23 and 4.24, we get

**Theorem 4.25** *Let $G$ be a grammar, $n\geqslant 1$ the number of nonterminals that derive a nonempty terminal string, $n'\geqslant 0$ the number of nullable nonterminals, and $m\geqslant 2$ the length of the right-hand side of the longest rule in $G$. If $A$ is a nonterminal and $w\in L(A)\setminus\{\varepsilon\}$, then $A$ derives $w$ simultaneously in time*

$$(2nm^{n'}-(m^{n'}-1)/(m-1))\,|w|-nm^{n'}+(m^{n'}-1)/(m-1)$$

*and space*

$$|w|+n'(m-1)\ .$$

*Moreover, these bounds are minimal.*  $\square$

**Corollary 4.26** *The time and space complexities of deriving any sentence in any grammar $G$ are linear in the length of the sentence.*  $\square$

## 4.7 Context-free Language Recognition

In this section we shall give nondeterministic and deterministic algorithms which decide whether a given terminal string is a member of the language generated by a given context-free grammar. That is, we consider the decision problem

$P_{\text{mem}}(\mathbb{G})$: "Given a context-free grammar $G$ in the class $\mathbb{G}$ of all such grammars, and a string $w$, is $w\in L(G)$?"

We first give a nondeterministic partial solution to the problem $P_{\text{mem}}(\mathbb{G})$. The idea of the algorithm is to guess a derivation $(\gamma_0,\ldots,\gamma_n)$, where $\gamma_0$ is the start symbol of the input grammar and $\gamma_n$ is a terminal string. The algorithm produces output "yes" if $\gamma_n$ equals the terminal string given as input.

**Theorem 4.27** *Given any context-free grammar $G=(V,\,T,\,P,\,S)$ and any string $w\in T^*$, it is decidable simultaneously in nondeterministic time $O(|G|\cdot|V|)$ and space $O(|G|+|w|)$ whether or not $w$ belongs to $L(G)$.*

*Proof.* First, it may be assumed by Theorem 4.20 that $G$ is in canonical two-form (see Section 4.5). The nondeterministic algorithm shown in Figure 4.8 provides a partial solution to the decision problem in question. The algorithm takes as input any string $\text{rep}(G)\#w$, where $\text{rep}(G)$ is the string representation of a grammar $G$ and $w$ is a string over $T$, and produces output "yes" if and only if $S$ derives $w$. By Theorem 4.25, the space complexity of deriving $w$ in $G$ is $O(|w|)$ when $G$ is in canonical two-form. Thus the space complexity of the algorithm is $O(|G|+|w|)$. Similarly, by Theorem 4.25, the time complexity of the algorithm is $O(|G|\cdot|w|)$.  $\square$

```
Read rep(G) # w;
γ := S;
while γ ∉ T* do
      begin
            guess a nonterminal A in γ, γ = αAβ,
                  and a rule A→ω in G;
            γ := αωβ
      end;
if γ = w then write "yes";
```

**Figure 4.8** A nondeterministic partial solution to the membership problem for context-free grammars. The algorithm runs in time $O(|G|\cdot|w|)$ and space $O(|G|+|w|)$ when $G$ is in canonical two-form

We consider next a deterministic solution to the decision problem $P_{\text{mem}}(G)$. By Theorem 4.20, we may assume that the given grammar $G=(V,\ T,\ P,\ S)$ is in canonical two-form. Then the question of whether $\varepsilon$ is in $L(G)$ is trivial because it is equivalent to deciding whether the rule $S\to\varepsilon$ is in $P$. Thus we may assume that the string $w$ in the problem instance differs from the empty string.

Let $w=a_1\ldots a_n$, where $n\geqslant 1$ and each $a_i\in T$. For all $i,j,\ 1\leqslant i\leqslant j\leqslant n$, we define

$$N(i,j)=\{A\mid A \text{ derives } a_i\ \ldots\ a_j\}\ .$$

The basic idea of the algorithm is to construct the sets $N(i,j)$ for all pairs $i,j$. To do this we first define the relation **unit-rule** on $V$ as follows:

$$B\ \textbf{unit-rule}\ X \text{ if } B\to X \text{ is a rule in } G\ .$$

**Fact 4.28** For $i=1,\ldots,n,$

$$N(i,i)=(\textbf{unit-rule}^{-1})^{+}(a_i)\ .$$

$\square$

Now consider how to determine the set $N(i,i+1)$, for $i=1,\ldots,n-1$. If $B\in N(i,i),\ C\in N(i+1,i+1)$, and $A\to BC$ is a rule, then $A\in N(i,i+1)$. In fact,

$$N(i,i+1)=(\textbf{unit-rule}^{-1})*(\{A\mid A\to BC\in P,\ B\in N(i,i),$$
$$\text{and } C\in N(i+1,i+1)\})\ ,$$

and more generally we have

**Lemma 4.29** *For all $i, j$, $1 \leqslant i < j \leqslant n$,*

$$N(i, j) = \bigcup_{k=0}^{j-i-1} (\textbf{unit-rule}^{-1})*(\{A \mid A \rightarrow BC \in P, \; B \in N(i, i+k),$$
$$C \in N(i+k+1, j)\}) .$$

*Proof.* A straightforward induction on $j - i$ (see the exercises).  $\square$

The equations for $N(i, i)$ and $N(i, j)$, $i < j$, suggest an algorithm for computing the set $N(1, n)$. The algorithm is given in Figure 4.9: we now proceed to analyze its complexity.

```
Read rep(G) # a₁ ... aₙ;
for i := 1 to n do
    N(i, i) := (unit-rule⁻¹)⁺(aᵢ);
for d := 1 to n−1 do
for i := 1 to n−d do
    begin
        j := i+d;
                    j−i−1
        N(i, j) :=  ⋃  (unit-rule⁻¹)*({A | A → BC ∈ P,
                    k=0
                            B ∈ N(i, i+k), and
                            C ∈ N(i+k+1, j)});
    end;
if S∈N(1, n) then write "yes" else write "no".
```

**Figure 4.9** An $O(|G| \cdot |w|^3)$ time-bounded and $O(|G| \cdot |w|^2)$ space-bounded deterministic solution to the membership problem for canonical two-form grammars. The trivial case $w = \varepsilon$ is not handled by the algorithm

First, the time needed to compute a set $N(i, i)$ is, by Theorem 2.28, bounded by $O(|G|)$ because the relation **unit-rule** is of size $O(|G|)$ and can be computed from $G$ in time $O(|G|)$. Each assignment to $N(i, j)$, $i < j$, performed in the algorithm requires time $O(|G| \cdot d)$, because each set

$$(\textbf{unit-rule}^{-1})*(\{A \mid A \rightarrow BC \in P, \; B \in N(i, i+k), \text{ and } C \in N(i+k+1, j)\})$$

is computed in time $O(|G|)$ (since $N(i, i+k)$ and $N(i+k+1, j)$ have already been computed) and there are $(j-i-1)+1 = d$ such sets to be unioned. According to the algorithm, for each $d = 1, \ldots, n-1$ there will be $n-d$ such assignments. Thus the time needed to compute all sets $N(i, j)$, $i < j$, is

$$O\!\left( |G| \cdot \sum_{d=1}^{n-1} (n-d)d \right)$$
$$= O(|G| \cdot n^3) .$$

The space required by the algorithm in Figure 4.9 is just that needed to store all sets $N(i, j)$, $i \leqslant j$, which is $O(|G| \cdot n^2)$.

Since $w \in L(G)$ if and only if $S \in N(1, n)$, and any grammar can be transformed into canonical two-form in linear time, we have

**Theorem 4.30** *Given any context-free grammar $G=(V, T, P, S)$ and any string $w \in T^*$, it is decidable simultaneously in deterministic time $O(|G| \cdot |w|^3)$ and space $O(|G| \cdot |w|^2)$ whether or not w belongs to $L(G)$.*   $\square$

## Exercises

4.1   Let $G$ be the grammar

$$E \to E + T \,|\, T \;,$$
$$T \to T * F \,|\, F \;,$$
$$F \to a \,|\, (E) \;.$$

Give the derivation trees corresponding to the derivations of the following sentential forms:

(a) $a + a * a + a$        (b) $a + T * (a + T)$        (c) $a * (a + a + a)$

How does the derivation tree reflect the usual order of evaluation of the arithmetic expression?

4.2   In a derivation tree the sons of any node are totally ordered. We extend this ordering to the following partial order on the set of all nodes of the tree: $u$ **left-of** $v$ if there are nodes $u'$, $v'$ in the tree such that $u'$ is an ancestor of $u$, $v'$ is an ancestor of $v$, $u'$ and $v'$ have the same father, and $u' < v'$. Show that, for any two nodes $u$ and $v$, precisely one of the following statements holds:
(a) $u$ **left-of** $v$, (b) $v$ **left-of** $u$, (c) there is a path from $u$ to $v$ or from $v$ to $u$.

4.3   By the *frontier* of a derivation tree we mean the string obtained by concatenating the labels of the leaves in order from the left as defined in the previous exercise. Show that, for any nonterminal $A$ and string $\alpha$ in a grammar $G$, $A \Rightarrow^* \alpha$ if and only if there is a derivation tree with frontier $\alpha$ and root labeled by $A$.

4.4   Let $D$ be a derivation tree with frontier $\alpha$ and root labeled by a nonterminal $A$. Show that there may exist many derivations of $\alpha$ from $A$ in a grammar $G$ even if $D$ is the only derivation tree with respect to $G$ that has frontier $\alpha$ and root labeled by $A$.

4.5   Show (using informal arguments) that, for each leftmost (rightmost) derivation of a sentence $w$ in a grammar $G=(V, T, P, S)$, there exists a uniquely defined derivation tree with frontier $w$ and root labeled by $S$. Also show the converse: for each derivation tree with frontier $w \in T^*$ and root labeled by $S$, there exists a uniquely defined leftmost (rightmost) derivation of $w$ in $G$.

4.6  Show that the latter statement in the previous exercise does not hold if the frontier of the derivation tree is allowed to be a general string.

4.7  Show that if in a grammar $A \overset{\pi}{\Longrightarrow} w$ for a terminal string $w$, then

$$A \overset{\pi'}{\underset{\text{lm}}{\Longrightarrow}} w \quad \text{and} \quad A \overset{\pi''}{\underset{\text{rm}}{\Longrightarrow}} w \ ,$$

for some permutations $\pi'$ and $\pi''$ of $\pi$. ($\pi'$ is a *permutation* of $\pi$ if there exist elements $r_1, \ldots, r_n$ and indices $i_1, \ldots, i_n$ such that $\{i_1, \ldots, i_n\} = \{1, \ldots, n\}$, $\pi = r_1 \ldots r_n$, and $\pi' = r_{i_1} \ldots r_{i_n}$.)

4.8  Show that if in a grammar $\alpha \overset{\pi}{\Longrightarrow} \beta$ and $\alpha \overset{\pi}{\Longrightarrow} \beta'$, where $\alpha$, $\beta$ and $\beta'$ are general strings, then $\beta$ and $\beta'$ are not necessarily equal but $\beta'$ is a permutation of $\beta$.

4.9  Prove the following variation of Lemma 4.1: Let $\alpha_1, \ldots, \alpha_m$, $m \geqslant 1$, and $\beta$ be strings such that, for some rule string $\pi$, $\alpha_1 \ldots \alpha_m \overset{\pi}{\Longrightarrow} \beta$. Then for some rule strings $\pi_1, \ldots, \pi_m$ such that $\pi_1 \ldots \pi_m$ is a permutation of $\pi$,

$$\alpha_i \overset{\pi_i}{\Longrightarrow} \beta_i \quad \text{for} \quad 1 \leqslant i \leqslant m \ ,$$

where $\beta_1 \ldots \beta_m = \beta$.

4.10  Show that the family of context-free languages over any alphabet $T$ is effectively closed under closure, concatenation, and finite union. That is, any pair of grammars $G_1 = (V_1, T, P_1, S_1)$, $G_2 = (V_2, T, P_2, S_2)$ can be transformed into grammars for $L(G_1)^*$, $L(G_1)L(G_2)$, and $L(G_1) \cup L(G_2)$.

4.11  A nonterminal $A$ in a grammar $G$ is *self-embedding* if $A \Rightarrow^+ \alpha A \beta$ for some general strings $\alpha \neq \varepsilon$ and $\beta \neq \varepsilon$. Show that, for any grammar $G$ not containing self-embedding nonterminals, the language $L(G)$ is a regular language.

4.12  Give an unambiguous grammar which generates the regular expressions over the alphabet $\{a_1, \ldots, a_n\}$. What is the size of the grammar? What is the time complexity of deriving the regular expression $a_1 \ldots a_n$ from the start symbol in this grammar?

4.13  Give an unambiguous grammar equivalent to the grammar

$$S \rightarrow a \,|\, \textbf{if} cl\ S \,|\, \textbf{if} cl\ S \ \textbf{else} \ S \ .$$

4.14  A nonterminal $A$ of a grammar is *left-recursive* if $A \Rightarrow^+ A\alpha$ for some general string $\alpha$. Similarly, $A$ is *right-recursive* if $A \Rightarrow^+ \alpha A$ for some $\alpha$. Show that any reduced grammar is ambiguous if it contains a nonterminal which is both left-recursive and right-recursive.

**4.15**  Prove Fact 4.5.

**4.16**  Show that there exist rule strings $\pi_1, \ldots, \pi_m$ and terminal strings $w_1, \ldots, w_m$ satisfying the requirements of Lemma 4.6.

**4.17**  Prove Lemma 4.7.

**4.18**  Prove Lemma 4.15.

**4.19**  Complete the proof of Lemma 4.16: Show that for all $n \geqslant 0$ the condition $S \Rightarrow^n \alpha X \beta$ implies that $X \in \mathbf{contains}^*(S)$.

**4.20**  Remove the useless symbols from the grammar

$$S \to AB \mid D ,$$
$$A \to BD \mid EF \mid a ,$$
$$B \to ED \mid b ,$$
$$C \to AB ,$$
$$E \to B ,$$
$$D \to F .$$

**4.21**  Remove the nullable symbols (without altering the language generated) from the grammar

$$P \to \mathbf{begin}\, B \,\mathbf{end} ,$$
$$B \to L \mid D; L ,$$
$$D \to d \mid D; d ,$$
$$L \to S \mid L; S ,$$
$$S \to \varepsilon \mid a \mid P .$$

**4.22**  Give a grammar $G$ such that the grammar $\hat{G}$ as defined in the proof of Theorem 4.18 is of size exponential in the size of $G$.

**4.23**  Give an algorithm that transforms any grammar into a grammar which has no unit rules, i.e., rules of the form $A \to B$. What is the time complexity of your algorithm?

**4.24**  Does the transformation into canonical two-form given in the proof of Theorem 4.20 preserve unambiguity?

**4.25**  A grammar is *left-recursive* if it contains left-recursive nonterminals. Let $G = (V, T, P, S)$ be any $\varepsilon$-free grammar which is not left-recursive. Show that for any $X \in V$ and $w \in L(X)$ the time complexity of deriving $w$ from $X$ is at most $m|w|$, where $m$ is the number of nonterminals in $G$.

**4.26** Show that the time complexity bound given in the previous exercise is minimal.

**4.27** Let $G$ be any grammar, and let the grammar $\hat{G}$ and the homomorphism $g$ be as in the proof of Theorem 4.24. Show that if, for any nonterminal $A$ and terminal string $w$, $A \overset{\pi}{\underset{\hat{G}}{\Rightarrow}} w$, then $A \overset{g(\pi)}{\underset{G}{\Rightarrow}} w$ .

**4.28** What are the minimal time and space complexity bounds corresponding to the bounds given in Theorem 4.25, if the grammar $G$ is assumed to contain no left-recursive nonterminals?

**4.29** The *time complexity of leftmost deriving* $\gamma_2$ *from* $\gamma_1$ *in a grammar* $G$ is

$$\min\{\text{TIME}(D) \mid D \text{ is a leftmost derivation of } \gamma_2 \text{ from } \gamma_1 \text{ in } G\} \ .$$

The *time complexity of rightmost deriving* $\gamma_2$ *from* $\gamma_1$ *in* $G$ is defined analogously. Show that the bound on the time complexity of derivations given in Theorem 4.25 is also minimal for the time complexity of leftmost and rightmost derivations.

**4.30** We say that $\gamma_1$ *leftmost* (resp. *rightmost*) *derives* $\gamma_2$ *in space s* if

$$\min\{\text{SPACE}(D) \mid D \text{ is a leftmost (resp. rightmost) derivation of } \gamma_2$$
$$\text{from } \gamma_1 \text{ in } G\} \leqslant s \ .$$

Let $G$ be a non-left-recursive grammar, $n \geqslant 1$ the number of nonterminals that derive a nonempty terminal string, $n' \geqslant 0$ the number of nullable nonterminals, and $m \geqslant 2$ the length of the right-hand side of the longest rule in $G$. Show that, for any nonterminal $A$ and $w \in L(A)\backslash\{\varepsilon\}$, $A$ leftmost derives $w$ in space

$$n(m-1)|w| + (n'-1)(m-1) + 1 \ .$$

Show also that this bound is minimal.

**4.31** Prove Fact 4.28.

**4.32** Prove Lemma 4.29.

**4.33** A grammar is said to be *linear* if its rules are of the forms

$$A \to xBy, \quad A \to x \ ,$$

where $B$ is a nonterminal and $x$, $y$ are terminal strings. Show that any linear grammar $G$ can be transformed in time $O(|G|)$ into a grammar in which the rules are of the forms

$$A \to aB, \ A \to Ba, \ A \to B, \ A \to a, \ S \to \varepsilon \ .$$

Here $S$ is the start symbol, and it does not occur in the right-hand side of any rule if $S \to \varepsilon$ is in the grammar.

4.34  Given any linear grammar $G = (V, T, P, S)$ and any string $w \in T^*$, show that it is decidable in deterministic time $O(|G| \cdot |w|^2)$ whether or not $w \in L(G)$. *Hint:* Use the normal form given in the previous exercise.


## Bibliographic Notes

Context-free grammars were first introduced and studied by Chomsky (1956, 1959, 1963). Another notation similar to the context-free grammar formalism in Backus-Naur form (BNF), which was used to describe the programming language ALGOL (Backus, 1959; Naur *et al.*, 1960). Many books and monographs have appeared covering a variety of topics related to context-free grammars and languages, e.g., Ginsburg (1966), Salomaa (1969, 1973), Hopcroft and Ullman (1969, 1979), Aho and Ullman (1972, 1973), Harrison (1978), and Wood (1987). The application of context-free grammars to parsing and compiling is emphasized in Aho and Ullman (1972, 1973, 1977), Lewis, Rosenkrantz and Stearns (1976), Waite and Goos (1984), and Aho, Sethi and Ullman (1986).

The method for determining the nullable nonterminals of a context-free grammar in time proportional to its size is from Harrison (1978). Canonical two-form for grammars first appeared in Gray and Harrison (1969, 1972), and Chomsky normal form in Chomsky (1959). Blum (1982) has shown that grammars with unit rules can be more succinct language descriptions than grammars without unit rules.

The linear time complexity of deriving a sentence in a grammar is well-known. Proofs of this fact are published in Harrison (1978), Heilbrunner (1981), and Sippu (1982). The minimal bounds on the time and space complexities of derivations are from Sippu (1982). Solutions to the exercises concerning derivational complexity may be found in Sippu (1982).

The deterministic recognition algorithm for context-free languages given in Section 4.7 is a modification of the well-known Cocke-Kasami-Younger algorithm (Kasami, 1965; Younger, 1967). Another general recognition algorithm is given by Earley (1968, 1970). The time bound for this algorithm is $O(n^3)$ in general, where $n$ is the length of the input string, but $O(n^2)$ for unambiguous grammars. Graham, Harrison and Ruzzo (1980) have improved Earley's algorithm so that it works in time $O(n^3/\log n)$. The asymptotically best deterministic time bound $O(n^{2.81})$ for context-free language recognition is due to Valiant (1975).

# 5. Parsing

In this chapter we shall introduce the central concept of this monograph, namely the parsing of context-free languages. The theory of parsing plays an important role in the design of compilers for programming languages. Every compiler includes a module called the parser, which has a twofold task in the compilation process. First, the parser checks that the program text to be compiled is syntactically correct, i.e., derivable by the context-free grammar of the programming language. In doing this the parser acts as a language recognizer. Secondly, if the program text proves to be syntactically correct, the parser goes on to produce some intermediate represent-ation of the text for use as input to the module responsible for object code generation. In doing this the parser acts as a text transformer.

The form of the intermediate representation produced for the program text depends on how the entire compilation process is organized and, in particular, on how many "passes" there are. In a multi-pass compilation, where the program text is parsed in its entirety before any semantic analysis is performed, an explicit representation such as a tree-like data structure or a postfix-form expression is produced. In a one-pass compilation, where the lexical analysis, parsing and semantic analysis and code generation phases are all interleaved, the intermediate representation is usually not constructed explicitly. Instead, it is present implicitly in the form of the current configuration, or state, of the parsing module.

In any case the intermediate representation, be it explicit or implicit, should contain enough information about the structure of the program text for semantic analysis and code generation to be possible. Since the semantics of any program-ming language is defined with respect to the syntactic entities of the language, knowledge of the syntactic and lexical structure of the program text should be sufficient. But, as we have seen in Chapter 4, the syntactic structure of any sentence in a context-free language is defined completely by the derivation tree of the sentence. This means that, for theoretical purposes, we may always think of a parser for a context-free grammar $G$ as a program that recognizes the language $L(G)$ and produces for each sentence in $L(G)$ its derivation tree. In fact, we shall go even further in idealizing the compilation process: in place of derivation trees we shall use certain rule strings, called parses, which are equivalent to derivation trees but are better suited to a theoretical treatment.

As a formal model of a parser we shall use a device called a "pushdown transducer". This consists of a rewriting system called a "pushdown automaton", augmented with an output effect. Pushdown automata, discussed in Section 5.1, are language recognizers that accept exactly the context-free languages. The output effect of a parser will be a homomorphism that maps rule strings of the underlying pushdown automaton to parses of sentences in the grammar. The parsers for a grammar are classified according to the kind of parses they produce. In this monograph we are only interested in two major classes of parsers, namely "left parsers" and "right parsers". These are defined in Section 5.2, where we also show that any context-free grammar has (nondeterministic) left and right parsers. In Section 5.3 we consider a class of left parsers called "strong LL(k) parsers", and in Section 5.4 we investigate the class of grammars for which these parsers are deterministic. In Section 5.5 we use the results of Chapter 2 to derive an efficient algorithm for constructing strong LL(1) parsers, which are the practical variants of strong LL(k) parsers. In Section 5.6 we demonstrate how to implement strong LL(1) parsers as high-level language programs. Finally, Section 5.7 is devoted to a class of right parsers called "simple precedence parsers".

## 5.1 Pushdown Automata

In this section we shall discuss a subclass of rewriting systems called pushdown automata, which may be thought of as a generalization of finite automata. Recall that a finite automaton models a computer that runs in constant workspace. A pushdown automaton, in contrast, may use an unlimited quantity of workspace. This workspace cannot, however, be accessed in an arbitrary manner, but behaves like a stack, i.e., it can only be accessed in a last-in-first-out manner.

Let $M = (V, P)$ be a rewriting system such that

$$V = Q \cup T \cup \{\$, \mathsf{I}\} \ ,$$

where $Q$ and $T$ are (not necessarily disjoint) subsets of $V$, and $\$$ and $\mathsf{I}$ are distinct symbols not belonging to $Q \cup T$. Further, let $\gamma_s$ be a string in $Q^*$ and $F$ a finite subset of $Q^*$. We say that $M$ is a *pushdown automaton* (or *pushdown-machine program*) *with stack alphabet $Q$, input alphabet $T$, initial stack contents $\gamma_s$, set of final stack contents $F$, end marker $\$$, and delimiter* $\mathsf{I}$, denoted by

$$M = (Q, T, P, \gamma_s, F, \$, \mathsf{I}) \ ,$$

if each rule in $P$ is of the form

$$\alpha\mathsf{I}xy \to \beta\mathsf{I}y \ ,$$

where $\alpha, \beta$ are strings in $Q^* \cup \$Q^*$, $x$ is a string in $T^*$, and $y$ is a string in $T^* \cup T^*\$$. The rules of a pushdown automaton are often called *actions*.

A *configuration* (or an *instantaneous description*) of a pushdown automaton $M$ is a string of the form

$$\$\gamma\mathsf{I}w\$ \ ,$$

where $\gamma$, the *stack contents*, is a string in $Q^*$, and $w$, the *remaining input string*, is a string in $T^*$. The last symbol of the string $\$\gamma$ is called the *topmost stack symbol* and the first symbol of the string $w\$$ the *current input symbol*.

Note that the action $\alpha \mid xy \rightarrow \beta \mid y$ is applicable to the configuration $\$\gamma \mid w\$$ if and only if the top of the stack is $\alpha$ and the head of the remaining input string is $xy$, i.e., if and only if $\$\gamma : m = \alpha$ and $n : w\$ = xy$, where $m$ is the length of $\alpha$ and $n$ is the length of $xy$. The effect of the action is to replace $\alpha$ by $\beta$ and to remove $x$ from the input. The resulting string is clearly again a configuration of the automaton.

The configuration $\$\gamma \mid w\$$ is *initial for* $w$ if $\gamma$ is the initial stack contents $\gamma_s$, and *accepting* if $w = \varepsilon$ and $\gamma$ is one of the final stack contents in $F$. A nonaccepting configuration to which no action is applicable is called an *error configuration*.

A *computation* (or *process*) *of* a pushdown automaton $M$ *on* input string $w$ is any derivation in $M$ from the initial configuration for $w$. A computation is *accepting* if it ends with an accepting configuration. $M$ *accepts* $w$ if it has an accepting computation on $w$. $M$ *halts correctly on* $w$ if it accepts $w$, and *halts incorrectly on* $w$ if it has a computation on $w$ ending with an error configuration. $M$ *loops forever on* $w$ if it has arbitrarily long computations on $w$.

The *language accepted* (or *recognized* or *described*) by a pushdown automaton $M$, denoted by $L(M)$, is the set of input strings accepted by $M$. Thus

$$L(M) = \{ w \in T^* \mid \$\gamma_s \mid w\$ \Rightarrow^* \$\gamma \mid \$ \text{ in } M \text{ for some } \gamma \in F \} \ .$$

As an example, consider the pushdown automaton

$$M_{\text{match}} = (\{0, 1, c\}, \{0, 1\}, P, \varepsilon, \{c\}, \$, \mathsf{I}) \ ,$$

where $P$ consists of the actions

$$\$\mathsf{I}0 \rightarrow \$0\mathsf{I}, \quad 0\mathsf{I}0 \rightarrow 00\mathsf{I}, \quad 0\mathsf{I}1 \rightarrow 0c\mathsf{I}1, \quad 0c\mathsf{I}1 \rightarrow c\mathsf{I}, \quad \$\mathsf{I}\$ \rightarrow \$c\mathsf{I}\$ \ .$$

$M_{\text{match}}$ is a pushdown automaton with stack alphabet $\{0, 1, c\}$, input alphabet $\{0, 1\}$, initial stack contents $\varepsilon$, and set of final stack contents $\{c\}$.

The following is true in $M_{\text{match}}$ for all $n \geqslant 0$:

$$\$\mathsf{I}0^n 1^n \$ \Rightarrow^n \$0^n \mathsf{I} 1^n \$ \Rightarrow \$0^n c \mathsf{I} 1^n \$ \Rightarrow^n \$c\mathsf{I}\$ \ ;$$

in fact we have

$$L(M_{\text{match}}) = \{0^n 1^n \mid n \geqslant 0\} = L_{\text{match}} \ .$$

A pushdown automaton is *ambiguous* if there are two accepting computations on some sentence, and *unambiguous* otherwise.

A pushdown automaton $M$ is *nondeterministic* if it has some configuration to which two actions are applicable. $M$ is *deterministic* if it is not nondeterministic. The automaton $M_{\text{match}}$ is obviously deterministic.

**Fact 5.1** A pushdown automaton is nondeterministic if and only if it has distinct actions

$$\alpha \mid x \rightarrow \alpha' \mid x', \quad \beta \mid y \rightarrow \beta' \mid y' \ ,$$

where one of $x$, $y$ is a prefix of the other and one of $\alpha$, $\beta$ is a suffix of the other.    □

**Fact 5.2** Any deterministic pushdown automaton is unambiguous provided that no action is applicable to any of the accepting configurations.    □

The following fact states that pushdown automata are at least as descriptive and as succinct as finite automata.

**Fact 5.3** Any finite automaton $M$ with input alphabet $T$ can be transformed in time $O(|M|)$ into an equivalent pushdown automaton $M'$ with input alphabet $T$ which is unambiguous (respectively, deterministic) if and only if $M$ is. Also, $M'$ has a bounded stack: more specifically, the stack contents of every configuration in any computation of $M'$ consists of a single symbol only.

*Proof.* The stack alphabet of $M'$ is the state alphabet of $M$, and its set of actions is

$$\{q_1|x \to q_2| \mid q_1 x \to q_2 \text{ is a transition of } M\} \ .$$

The initial stack contents of $M'$ is the initial state of $M$, while the set of final stack contents of $M'$ is the set of final states of $M$.    □

The following proposition states that deterministic pushdown automata can be exponentially more succinct than nondeterministic finite automata.

**Proposition 5.4** *There exists a constant $c>0$ and an infinite sequence of regular languages $L_1, L_2, \ldots$, such that each $L_n$ is accepted by some deterministic pushdown automaton of size $O(n^3)$, but any finite automaton accepting $L_n$ must have size at least $2^n$.*    □

A pushdown automaton is *normal-form* if its actions are all of the form

$$\alpha|x \to \beta| \ ,$$

where $|\alpha| \leqslant 2$ and $|x| \leqslant 1$.

The following proposition states that normal-form pushdown automata are equivalent in descriptional power to unrestricted pushdown automata.

**Proposition 5.5** *Any pushdown automaton $M$ with input alphabet $T$ can be transformed into an equivalent normal-form pushdown automaton $M'$ with input alphabet $T$. Moreover, $M'$ is unambiguous (respectively, deterministic) if and only if $M$ is.*    □

Next we shall show that normal-form pushdown automata are at least as descriptive and succinct as context-free grammars.

Let $G = (V, T, P, S)$ be a context-free grammar. The *predictive machine* for $G$ is the pushdown automaton with stack alphabet $V$, input alphabet $T$, initial stack contents $S$, set of final stack contents $\{\varepsilon\}$, and actions of the forms

$$
\begin{array}{lll}
(pa) & A| \to \omega^R| & \text{``produce by } A \to \omega\text{''}, \\
(sa) & a|a \to | & \text{``shift } a\text{''}.
\end{array}
$$

Here $A \to \omega$ is a rule in $P$, $a$ is a terminal in $T$, and $\omega^R$ is the reversal of the right-hand side $\omega$. The machine has a *produce action (pa)* for each rule $A \to \omega$ in $P$, and a *shift action (sa)* for each terminal $a \in T$.

As an example, consider the grammar

$$G_{\text{match}} = (\{0, 1, S\}, \{0, 1\}, \{S \to \varepsilon \mid 0S1\}, S) .$$

The predictive machine for $G_{\text{match}}$ has stack alphabet $\{0, 1, S\}$, input alphabet $\{0, 1\}$, initial stack contents $S$, set of final stack contents $\{\varepsilon\}$, and actions

$$r_1 = S| \to | \ ,$$
$$r_2 = S| \to 1S0| \ ,$$
$$r_3 = 0|0 \to | \ ,$$
$$r_4 = 1|1 \to | \ .$$

The following statements are true for the machine:

$$\$S|\$ \ \overset{r_1}{\Longrightarrow} \ \$|\$ \ ,$$

$$\$S|0011\$ \ \overset{r_2}{\Longrightarrow} \ \$1S0|0011\$ \ \overset{r_3}{\Longrightarrow} \ \$1S|011\$ \ \overset{r_2}{\Longrightarrow} \ \$11S0|011\$$$

$$\overset{r_3}{\Longrightarrow} \ \$11S|11\$ \ \overset{r_1}{\Longrightarrow} \ \$11|11\$ \ \overset{r_4}{\Longrightarrow} \ \$1|1\$ \ \overset{r_4}{\Longrightarrow} \ \$|\$ \ ,$$

$$\$S|0^n1^n\$ \ \overset{(r_2r_3)^n}{\Longrightarrow} \ \$1^nS|1^n\$ \ \overset{r_1}{\Longrightarrow} \ \$1^n|1^n\$ \ \overset{r_4^n}{\Longrightarrow} \ \$|\$ \ \text{for all } n \geqslant 0 .$$

In fact, the language accepted by the machine is $L(G_{\text{match}}) = L_{\text{match}}$.

Note that the stack contents in any configuration of the predictive machine can be thought of as a *prediction* of the remaining input. If the prediction is correct in configuration $\$\gamma|w\$$, then the reversal of the stack contents can derive the remaining input, i.e., $\gamma^R \Rightarrow^* w$ holds in the grammar. An application of the action $A| \to \omega^R|$ means that the prediction is made more precise by *guessing* that $A$ will occur in the form $\omega$. Conversely, an application of the action $a|a \to |$ means *verifying* that the prediction is correct at least as regards the current input symbol $a$. Initially the prediction is $S$: we predict that the input string is derived by $S$. The final prediction is $\varepsilon$: the remaining input should be empty.

A wrong prediction is bound to lead to a blind alley, a configuration from which no accepting configuration is reachable. For example, if the action $r_1$ is applied to the configuration $\$1S|011\$$, then the error configuration $\$1|011\$$ is entered immediately.

In general we have

**Lemma 5.6** *For any grammar $G$, the language accepted by the predictive machine $M$ for $G$ is the language generated by $G$. Moreover, for any sentence $w \in L(G)$, there is a bijective correspondence between leftmost derivations of $w$ in $G$ and accepting computations of $M$ on $w$.*

*Proof.* The claim follows immediately from Theorem 5.16 of Section 5.2.   $\square$

The predictive machine for $G$ is always normal-form, has size $O(|G|)$, and can be constructed from $G$ in time $O(|G|)$. Thus Lemma 5.6 yields

**Theorem 5.7** *Any grammar $G$ with terminal alphabet $T$ can be transformed in time $O(|G|)$ into an equivalent normal-form pushdown automaton $M$ with input alphabet $T$. Moreover, $M$ is unambiguous if and only if $G$ is.*   $\square$

The following proposition states that normal-form pushdown automata are no more descriptive than context-free grammars.

**Proposition 5.8** *Any normal-form pushdown automaton $M$ with alphabet $V$ and input alphabet $T$ can be transformed in time $O(|M| \cdot |V|^3)$ into an equivalent context-free grammar $G$ with terminal alphabet $T$. Moreover, $G$ is unambiguous if and only if $M$ is.*   $\square$

By Theorem 5.7 and Propositions 5.5 and 5.8, we get the following characterization of context-free languages.

**Theorem 5.9** *A language over an alphabet $T$ is context-free if and only if it is the language accepted by some pushdown automaton with input alphabet $T$.*   $\square$

As there exist inherently ambiguous context-free languages (see Chapter 4), we can also conclude from the above that there cannot exist any algorithm for transforming an arbitrary pushdown automaton into an equivalent unambiguous one. This is in contrast to the fact that any finite automaton can be so transformed.

The predictive machine for $G$ is in practice almost always nondeterministic. Obviously, it is nondeterministic just when it has a "produce-produce conflict", that is, a pair of distinct produce actions of the form

$$A\mathsf{I} \to \omega_1^R\mathsf{I}, \quad A\mathsf{I} \to \omega_2^R\mathsf{I} \ .$$

This happens exactly when $G$ has a pair of distinct rules with the same left-hand side.

We say that a language is *deterministic* if it is accepted by some deterministic pushdown automaton. The language $L_{\mathrm{match}}$ is deterministic since it is accepted by the deterministic pushdown automaton $M_{\mathrm{match}}$.

Not all context-free languages are deterministic. The language

$$L_{\mathrm{pal}} = \{w \in \{0, 1\}^* \mid w^R = w\} \ ,$$

the set of *palindromes* over $\{0, 1\}$, is an example of a context-free language which is not deterministic.

$L_{\mathrm{pal}}$ is generated by the context-free grammar

$$G_{\mathrm{pal}} = (\{0, 1, S\}, \{0, 1\}, \{S \to \varepsilon \mid 0 \mid 1 \mid 0S0 \mid 1S1\}, S) \ .$$

The predictive machine for $G_{\mathrm{pal}}$ accepts a palindrome by pushing input symbols into the stack until it decides to guess the centre of the palindrome. This guessing is done by applying the action $SI \to I$ (an even-length palindrome) or one of the actions $SI \to 0I, SI \to 1I$ (an odd-length palindrome).

It should be fairly obvious that no pushdown automaton can decide the centre of the palindrome deterministically. It should also be obvious that, for a pushdown automaton to accept a palindrome, it must determine its centre. We state without formal proof

**Proposition 5.10** *The language $L_{\mathrm{pal}}$ is not deterministic.*   $\square$

The existence of context-free languages that are not deterministic means that there cannot exist any algorithm for making pushdown automata deterministic. This is in contrast to the fact that for finite automata such an algorithm does exist.

Finally we note that if the centres of the palindromes are distinguished by marking them by a special symbol, the language becomes deterministic. We leave it as an exercise to show that the language

$$L_{\mathrm{cpal}} = \{wcw^R \,|\, w \in \{0, 1\}^*\}$$

is a deterministic context-free language over $\{0, 1, c\}$, where $c \notin \{0, 1\}$. We call this language the set of *palindromes with centre marker c*.

We summarize in the following theorem the results of this section and Section 4.5.

**Theorem 5.11** (*Characterizations of Context-Free Languages*) *The following state-ments are logically equivalent for all languages $L$ over an alphabet $T$:*

(1) *$L$ is the language generated by some context-free grammar with terminal alphabet $T$.*

(2) *$L$ is the language generated by some canonical two-form grammar with terminal alphabet $T$.*

(3) *$L$ is the language generated by some Chomsky normal-form grammar with terminal alphabet $T$.*

(4) *$L$ is the language accepted by some pushdown automaton with input alphabet $T$.*

(5) *$L$ is the language accepted by some normal-form pushdown automaton with input alphabet $T$.*

*Moreover, if $D$ is a description of $L$ belonging to any of the above classes of context-free language descriptions, then $D$ can be transformed into equivalent descriptions belonging to the other classes.*   $\square$

We conclude this section by defining for pushdown automata the time and space complexity of accepting a given sentence. In the sequel, we shall often relate the time complexity of accepting a given sentence to the time complexity of generating the same sentence in a context-free grammar.

Let $M$ be a pushdown automaton with input alphabet $T$, initial stack contents $\gamma_s$, and set of final stack contents $F$. We define for all $w \in L(M)$

$$\text{TIME}_M(w) = \min\{\text{TIME}_M(\$\gamma_s\mathsf{l}w\$, \$\gamma\mathsf{l}\$)\mid\gamma\in F\} \ ,$$
$$\text{SPACE}_M(w) = \min\{\text{SPACE}_M(\$\gamma_s\mathsf{l}w\$, \$\gamma\mathsf{l}\$)\mid\gamma\in F\} \ ,$$

where $\text{TIME}_M(\phi_1, \phi_2)$ denotes the time complexity and $\text{SPACE}_M(\phi_1, \phi_2)$ the space complexity, of deriving $\phi_2$ from $\phi_1$ in $M$ (see Section 1.6).

$\text{TIME}_M(w)$ is called the *time complexity*, and $\text{SPACE}_M(w)$ the *space complexity*, *of accepting w in M. M accepts w in time t if* $\text{TIME}_M(w) \leqslant t$ *and accepts w in space s if* $\text{SPACE}_M(w) \leqslant s$. *M runs in time* $T(n)$ *(respectively, in space* $S(n)$*) if M accepts every sentence of length n in time* $T(n)$ *(respectively, in space* $S(n)$*).*

For example, in the pushdown automaton $M_{\text{match}}$ we have

$$\text{TIME}_{M_{\text{match}}}(0^n1^n) = 2n+1 \ ,$$
$$\text{SPACE}_{M_{\text{match}}}(0^n1^n) = 2n+4 \ .$$

## 5.2 Left Parsers and Right Parsers

Let $G = (V, T, P, S)$ be a grammar and $w$ a sentence in $L(G)$. A rule string $\pi$ in $P^*$ is a *left parse of w in G* if the start symbol $S$ leftmost derives $w$ in $G$ using $\pi$, or $S \underset{\text{lm}}{\overset{\pi}{\Longrightarrow}} w$ in $G$. Similarly, a rule string $\pi$ is a *right parse of w in G* if $S$ rightmost derives $w$ using the reversal $\pi^R$ of $\pi$, or $S \underset{\text{rm}}{\overset{\pi^R}{\Longrightarrow}} w$ in $G$.

A (possibly nondeterministic) RAM program is a *left parser* for a grammar $G$ if it recognizes the language $L(G)$ and produces for each sentence in $L(G)$ at least one left parse in $G$. A *right parser* for $G$ is defined similarly.

The results of Chapter 4 imply that a left parse and a right parse of a sentence $w$ each uniquely define a derivation tree for $w$. Moreover, this derivation tree can easily be constructed from either of the parses. This means that any left or right parser of a grammar $G$, besides being a recognizer for $L(G)$, can be regarded as a program that produces a derivation tree for each sentence in $L(G)$.

The difference between a left parser and a right parser lies in the manner in which the derivation tree is produced. A left parser builds the derivation tree in a top-down manner, in the order implied by the leftmost derivation, while a right parser builds the tree in a bottom-up manner, in the order implied by the reversal of the rightmost derivation.

Parsers that build the derivation tree in a top-down manner are often referred to in the literature as *top-down parsers*, and those that build the tree in a bottom-up manner as *bottom-up parsers*. Left parsers constitute the most important subclass of top-down parsers and right parsers the most important subclass of bottom-up parsers.

The formal model we shall use for parsers is obtained from pushdown automata by adding an "output effect". A pushdown automaton with an output effect will be called a "pushdown transducer".

Formally, $M$ is a *pushdown transducer with output alphabet $\Delta$ and output effect $\tau$*, written $(M, \tau)$, if $M$ is a pushdown automaton and $\tau$ is a homomorphism from $P^*$ to $\Delta^*$, where $P$ is the set of rules of $M$.

Let $w$ be a sentence in $L(M)$. An action string $\pi'$ is a *parse of $w$ in $M$* if the initial configuration for $w$ derives an accepting configuration in $M$ using $\pi'$. A pushdown transducer $(M, \tau)$ *produces output $\pi$ for $w$* if $\tau(\pi') = \pi$ for some parse $\pi'$ of $w$ in $M$.

A pushdown transducer $M$ is a *left parser* (resp. *right parser*) for a grammar $G$ if it satisfies the following:

(1) The input alphabet of $M$ is the terminal alphabet of $G$.
(2) $L(M) = L(G)$.
(3) The output alphabet of $M$ is the set of rules of $G$.
(4) Any output produced by $M$ for a sentence $w \in L(G)$ is a left parse (resp. right parse) of $w$ in $G$.

Note that the definition guarantees that a left parser (right parser) always produces at least one left parse (right parse) for any sentence in the language. However, it need not produce all the parses.

We can readily obtain a left parser for a grammar $G$ from its predictive machine by adding an output effect defined as follows:

(1) $\tau(A\mathsf{l} \to \omega^R\mathsf{l}) = A \to \omega$.
(2) $\tau(a\mathsf{l}a \to \mathsf{l}) = \varepsilon$.

This parser is called the *produce-shift parser* for $G$. It is a special case of a "strong LL($k$) parser", which will be defined in the next section.

In the produce-shift parser for $G_{\text{match}}$, the output effect $\tau$ is defined as follows:

$$r_1 = S\mathsf{l} \to \mathsf{l} \,, \qquad \tau(r_1) = S \to \varepsilon \,.$$
$$r_2 = S\mathsf{l} \to \mathsf{l}S0\mathsf{l} \,, \qquad \tau(r_2) = S \to 0S1 \,.$$
$$r_3 = 0\mathsf{l}0 \to \mathsf{l} \,, \qquad \tau(r_3) = \varepsilon.$$
$$r_4 = 1\mathsf{l}1 \to \mathsf{l} \,, \qquad \tau(r_4) = \varepsilon \,.$$

The parses produced for the sentences $\varepsilon$, $0011$, $0^n1^n$ are:

$$\tau(r_1) = S \to \varepsilon \,,$$
$$\tau(r_2 r_3 r_2 r_3 r_1 r_4 r_4) = (S \to 0S1)(S \to 0S1)(S \to \varepsilon) \,,$$
$$\tau((r_2 r_3)^n r_1 r_4^n) = (S \to 0S1)^n(S \to \varepsilon), \ n \geq 0 \,.$$

(The computations on these sentences were given in the previous section.)

In the following series of lemmas we prove that the produce-shift parser for any grammar $G$ is indeed a left parser for $G$.

**Lemma 5.12** *Let $G=(V, T, P, S)$ be a grammar and $(M, \tau)$ its produce-shift parser. Further, let $\gamma$ be a string in $V^*$, $w$ a string in $T^*$, $\Phi$ a string over the alphabet of $M$, and $\pi'$ an action string such that*

$$(a) \qquad \$\gamma \mathsf{I} w\$ \xRightarrow{\pi'} \Phi \quad \text{in } M .$$

*Then for some strings $x$, $y$ and $\psi$,*

$$w = xy, \quad \Phi = \$\psi \mathsf{I} y\$, \quad |\pi'| = |\tau(\pi')| + |x| ,$$

$$(b) \qquad \text{and} \quad \gamma^R \xRightarrow[\text{lm}]{\tau(\pi')} x\psi^R \quad \text{in } G .$$

*Proof.* The proof is by induction on the length of the action string $\pi'$. If $\pi' = \varepsilon$, then $\Phi = \$\gamma \mathsf{I} w\$$, and statements (b) hold when we choose $x = \varepsilon$, $y = w$, and $\psi = \gamma$. Note that, since $\tau$ is a homomorphism, $\tau(\varepsilon) = \varepsilon$. This proves the base case.

To prove the induction step, we assume that $\pi'$ is of the form $r'\pi''$, where $r'$ is a single action, and, as an induction hypothesis, that the lemma holds for the action string $\pi''$. If $r'$ is a produce action for some rule $A \to \omega$ in $P$, then (a) implies that, for some strings $\delta$ and $\gamma_1$,

$$\$\gamma \mathsf{I} w\$ = \$\delta A \mathsf{I} w\$ \xRightarrow{r'} \$\delta \omega^R \mathsf{I} w\$$$

$$= \$\gamma_1 \mathsf{I} w\$ \xRightarrow{\pi''} \Phi \text{ in } M . \tag{5.1}$$

Then we have

$$\gamma^R = (\delta A)^R = A\delta^R \xRightarrow[\text{lm}]{\tau(r')} \omega\delta^R = (\delta\omega^R)^R = \gamma_1^R \text{ in } G . \tag{5.2}$$

On the other hand, if we apply the induction hypothesis to the second derivation segment in (5.1), we can conclude that, for some strings $x$, $y$ and $\psi$,

$$w = xy, \quad \Phi = \$\psi \mathsf{I} y\$, \quad |\pi''| = |\tau(\pi'')| + |x| ,$$

$$\text{and } \gamma_1^R \xRightarrow[\text{lm}]{\tau(\pi'')} x\psi^R \text{ in } G . \tag{5.3}$$

By combining (5.2) and (5.3) it is then easy to see that statements (b) hold. Note that $\tau(r')\tau(\pi'') = \tau(r'\pi'') = \tau(\pi')$.

We have yet to consider the case in which $r'$ is a shift action on some terminal $a$. Then statement (a) implies that, for some strings $\gamma_1$ and $z$,

$$\$\gamma \mathsf{I} w\$ = \$\gamma_1 a \mathsf{I} az\$ \xRightarrow{r'} \$\gamma_1 \mathsf{I} z\$ \xRightarrow{\pi''} \Phi \text{ in } M . \tag{5.4}$$

Applying the induction hypothesis to the second derivation segment in (5.4) we can conclude that, for some strings $x'$, $y$ and $\psi$,

$$z = x'y, \quad \Phi = \$\psi \mathbin| y\$, \quad |\pi''| = |\tau(\pi'')| + |x'|, \quad \text{and} \quad \gamma_1^R \xRightarrow[\text{lm}]{\tau(\pi'')} x'\psi^R \text{ in } G \ . \tag{5.5}$$

Statements (b) then hold if we choose $x = ax'$. Note that $w = az$, $\gamma^R = a\gamma_1^R$, and $\tau(\pi'') = \tau(r')\tau(\pi'') = \tau(r'\pi'') = \tau(\pi')$.   $\square$

**Lemma 5.13** *If $(M, \tau)$ is the produce-shift parser for a grammar $G$, then $L(M) \subseteq L(G)$, and $\tau(\pi')$ is a left parse of a sentence $w$ in $G$ whenever $\pi'$ is a parse of $w$ in $M$. Moreover, $TIME_G(w) \leqslant TIME_M(w) - |w|$.*

*Proof.* Set $\gamma = S$ and $\Phi = \$\mathbin|\$$ in Lemma 5.12.   $\square$

**Lemma 5.14** *Let $G = (V, T, P, S)$ be a grammar and $(M, \tau)$ its produce-shift parser. Further, let $\gamma$ and $\psi$ be strings in $V^*$, $x$ a string in $T^*$, and $\pi$ a rule string in $P^*$ such that*

(a)
$$\gamma^R \xRightarrow[\text{lm}]{\pi} x\psi^R \quad \text{in } G \ , \quad \text{and}$$

*either $\psi^R = \varepsilon$ or $1: \psi^R$ is a nonterminal.*

*Then for some action string $\pi'$,*

(b)
$$\tau(\pi') = \pi, \quad |\pi'| = |\pi| + |x|, \quad \text{and}$$

$$\$\gamma \mathbin| xy\$ \xRightarrow{\pi'} \$\psi \mathbin| y\$ \quad \text{in } M$$

*for all strings $y \in T^*$.*

*Proof.* The proof is by induction on the length of the rule string $\pi$. In the base case we have $\pi = \varepsilon$, and so $\gamma^R = x\psi^R$. Since $M$ has a shift action on all terminals in $T$, we then have

$$\$\gamma \mathbin| xy\$ = \$\psi x^R \mathbin| xy\$ \xRightarrow{\pi'} \$\psi \mathbin| y\$ \quad \text{in } M \ , \tag{5.6}$$

where $\pi'$ is the $|x|$-length string of shift actions on terminals occurring in $x$. Since $\tau(\pi') = \varepsilon$, statements (b) hold.

To prove the induction step, we assume that $\pi$ is of the form $\pi_1 r$, where $r$ is a rule $A \to \omega$, and, as an induction hypothesis, that the lemma holds for the rule string $\pi_1$. We have

$$\gamma^R \xRightarrow[\text{lm}]{\pi_1} x_1 \psi_1^R = x_1 A\delta \xRightarrow[\text{lm}]{r} x_1 \omega\delta = x\psi^R \quad \text{in } G \tag{5.7}$$

for some strings $\psi_1$, $\delta \in V^*$ and $x_1 \in T^*$. Here $x = x_1 z$ and $\omega\delta = z\psi^R$ for some $z$, because $\psi^R$ is empty or begins with a nonterminal. Since $\psi_1^R = A\delta$ and hence begins with a nonterminal, we can apply the induction hypothesis to the first derivation segment in (5.7) and conclude that, for some action string $\pi_1'$,

$$\tau(\pi_1') = \pi_1, \quad |\pi_1'| = |\pi_1| + |x_1| , \quad \text{and}$$

$$\$\gamma | x_1 y_1 \$ \overset{\pi_1'}{\Longrightarrow} \$\psi_1 | y_1 \$ \quad \text{in } M , \tag{5.8}$$

where $y_1$ denotes the string $zy$. Thus we have

$$\$\gamma | xy\$ = \$\gamma | x_1 zy\$ \overset{\pi_1'}{\Longrightarrow} \$\psi_1 | zy\$ = \$\delta^R A | zy\$ . \tag{5.9}$$

On the other hand, $M$ has the produce action $r' = A| \to \omega^R |$, which implies that

$$\$\delta^R A | zy\$ \overset{r'}{\Longrightarrow} \$\delta^R \omega^R | zy\$ = \$(\omega\delta)^R | zy\$ = \$\psi z^R | zy\$ . \tag{5.10}$$

Since $M$ has a shift action on all terminals in $T$, we can conclude that

$$\$\psi z^R | zy\$ \overset{\pi_2'}{\Longrightarrow} \$\psi | y\$ , \tag{5.11}$$

where $\pi_2'$ is the $|z|$-length string of shift actions on the terminals ocurring in $z$. Choosing $\pi' = \pi_1' r' \pi_2'$ and combining statements (5.8)–(5.11), we see finally that statements (b) hold. Note that $\tau(\pi') = \tau(\pi_1')\tau(r')\tau(\pi_2') = \pi_1 r = \pi$, and that $|\pi'| = |\pi_1'| + 1 + |\pi_2'| = |\pi_1| + |x_1| + 1 + |\pi_2'| = |\pi_1 r| + |x_1 z| = |\pi| + |x|.$ $\quad\square$

**Lemma 5.15** *If $(M, \tau)$ is the produce-shift parser for a grammar $G$, then $L(G) \subseteq L(M)$, and for any left parse $\pi$ of a sentence $w$ in $G$, $\tau(\pi') = \pi$ for some parse $\pi'$ of $w$ in $M$. Moreover, $TIME_M(w) \leqslant TIME_G(w) + |w|$.*

*Proof.* Set $\gamma = S$, $x = w$, and $\psi = y = \varepsilon$ in Lemma 5.14. Recall that if $S \Rightarrow^n w$, then $S \underset{\text{lm}}{\Rightarrow}{}^n w$ (see Theorem 4.2).    $\square$

Lemmas 5.13 and 5.15 together imply

**Theorem 5.16** *The produce-shift parser $M$ for a grammar $G$ is a left parser for $G$. Moreover, for each sentence $w \in L(G)$, $M$ produces all left parses of $w$ in $G$, and $TIME_M(w) = TIME_G(w) + |w|.$*    $\square$

The last part of Theorem 5.16 implies (via Corollary 4.26) that the produce-shift parser for any grammar $G$ runs in time linear in the length of the sentence.

Next we consider a pushdown transducer which is a right parser for grammar $G = (V, T, P, S)$. This parser is called the *shift-reduce parser* for $G$. The stack alphabet of the parser is $V$, the input alphabet is $T$, the initial stack contents is $\varepsilon$, the set of final stack contents is $\{S\}$, and the set of actions consists of all rules of the forms

(ra)   $\omega | \to A |$    "reduce by $A \to \omega$",   for rule $A \to \omega$ in $P$ ,
(sa)   $| a \to a |$      "shift $a$",   for terminal $a$ in $T$ .

Here (ra) is a *reduce action* and (sa) a *shift action*. The output effect $\tau$ is defined by

(1)   $\tau(\omega | \to A |) = A \to \omega$.
(2)   $\tau(| a \to a |) = \varepsilon$.

The shift-reduce parser for $G_{\text{match}}$ has the following actions:

$$r_1 = | \to S|, \qquad \tau(r_1) = S \to \varepsilon .$$
$$r_2 = 0S1| \to S|, \qquad \tau(r_2) = S \to 0S1 .$$
$$r_3 = |0 \to 0|, \qquad \tau(r_3) = \varepsilon .$$
$$r_4 = |1 \to 1|, \qquad \tau(r_4) = \varepsilon .$$

The following statements are true for this machine:

$$\$|\$ \xRightarrow{r_1} \$S|\$ ,$$

$$\$|0011\$ \xRightarrow{r_3} \$0|011\$ \xRightarrow{r_3} \$00|11\$ \xRightarrow{r_1} \$00S|11\$$$

$$\xRightarrow{r_4} \$00S1|1\$ \xRightarrow{r_2} \$0S|1\$ \xRightarrow{r_4} \$0S1|\$ \xRightarrow{r_2} \$S|\$ ,$$

$$\$|0^n1^n\$ \xRightarrow{r_3^n} \$0^n|1^n\$ \xRightarrow{r_1} \$0^n S|1^n\$ \xRightarrow{(r_4 r_2)^n} \$S|\$, \qquad n \geqslant 0 .$$

The parses produced for the accepted strings $\varepsilon$, 0011, $0^n 1^n$ are:

$$\tau(r_1) = S \to \varepsilon ,$$

$$\tau(r_3 r_3 r_1 r_4 r_2 r_4 r_2) = (S \to \varepsilon)(S \to 0S1)(S \to 0S1) ,$$

$$\tau(r_3^n r_1 (r_4 r_2)^n) = (S \to \varepsilon)(S \to 0S1)^n, \qquad n \geqslant 0 .$$

In the following we show that the shift-reduce parser for $G$ is indeed a right parser for $G$.

**Lemma 5.17** *Let $G = (V, T, P, S)$ be a grammar and $(M, \tau)$ its shift-reduce parser. Further, let $\gamma$ be a string in $V^*$, $w$ a string in $T^*$, $\Phi$ a string over the alphabet of $M$, and $\pi'$ an action string such that*

(a)      $\$\gamma | w\$ \xRightarrow{\pi'} \Phi$   *in $M$ .*

*Then for some strings $x$, $y$ and $\psi$,*

(b)      $w = xy, \qquad \Phi = \$\psi | y\$, \qquad |\pi'| = |\tau(\pi')| + |x| ,$
        *and*   $\psi \xRightarrow[\text{rm}]{\tau(\pi')^R} \gamma x$   *in $G$ .*

*Proof.* The proof is by induction on the length of the action string $\pi'$. If $\pi' = \varepsilon$, then $\Phi = \$\gamma\,|\,w\$$, and statements (b) hold when we choose $x = \varepsilon$, $y = w$, and $\psi = \gamma$. This proves the base case.

To prove the induction step, we assume that $\pi'$ is of the form $r'\pi''$, where $r'$ is a single action. As an induction hypothesis, we assume that the lemma holds for the action string $\pi''$. If $r'$ is a reduce action for some rule $A \to \omega$ in $P$, then for some strings $\delta$ and $\gamma_1$,

$$\$\gamma\,|\,w\$ = \$\delta\omega\,|\,w\$ \overset{r'}{\Longrightarrow} \$\delta A\,|\,w\$ = \$\gamma_1\,|\,w\$ \overset{\pi''}{\Longrightarrow} \Phi \quad \text{in } M \ . \tag{5.12}$$

Then we have

$$\gamma_1 = \delta A \overset{\tau(r')}{\underset{rm}{\Longrightarrow}} \delta\omega = \gamma \quad \text{in } G \ . \tag{5.13}$$

On the other hand, we can apply the induction hypothesis to the second derivation segment in (5.12) and conclude that, for some strings $x$, $y$ and $\psi$,

$$w = xy \ , \qquad \Phi = \$\psi\,|\,y\$ \ , \qquad |\pi''| = |\tau(\pi'')| + |x| \ ,$$

$$\text{and} \quad \psi \overset{\tau(\pi'')^R}{\underset{rm}{\Longrightarrow}} \gamma_1 x \quad \text{in } G \ . \tag{5.14}$$

By combining (5.13) and (5.14) it is then easy to see that statements (b) hold. Note that $\tau(\pi'')^R \tau(r') = (\tau(r')\tau(\pi''))^R = \tau(r'\pi'')^R = \tau(\pi')^R$.

We have yet to consider the case in which $r'$ is a shift action on some terminal $a$. Then for some strings $\gamma_1$ and $z$,

$$\$\gamma\,|\,w\$ = \$\gamma\,|\,az\$ \overset{r'}{\Longrightarrow} \$\gamma a\,|\,z\$ = \$\gamma_1\,|\,z\$ \overset{\pi''}{\Longrightarrow} \Phi \quad \text{in } M \ . \tag{5.15}$$

Applying the induction hypothesis to the second derivation segment in (5.15) we can conclude that, for some strings $x'$, $y$ and $\psi$,

$$z = x'y, \qquad \Phi = \$\psi\,|\,y\$ \ , \qquad |\pi''| = |\tau(\pi'')| + |x'| \ ,$$

$$\text{and} \quad \psi \overset{\tau(\pi'')^R}{\underset{rm}{\Longrightarrow}} \gamma_1 x' \quad \text{in } G \ . \tag{5.16}$$

Statements (b) then hold if we choose $x = ax'$. Note that $\tau(r') = \varepsilon$ and that $\gamma_1 = \gamma a$ and $w = az$.   $\square$


**Lemma 5.18** *If $(M, \tau)$ is the shift-reduce parser for a grammar $G$, then $L(M) \subseteq L(G)$, and $\tau(\pi')$ is a right parse of a sentence $w$ in $G$ whenever $\pi'$ is a parse of $w$ in $M$. Moreover, $TIME_G(w) \leqslant TIME_M(w) - |w|$.*


*Proof.* Set $\gamma = \varepsilon$ and $\Phi = \$S\,|\,\$$ in Lemma 5.17.   $\square$

**Lemma 5.19** *Let $G = (V, T, P, S)$ be a grammar and $(M, \tau)$ its shift-reduce parser. Further, let $\gamma$ and $\psi$ be strings in $V^*$, $x$ a string in $T^*$, and $\pi$ a rule string in $P^*$ such that*

(a)
$$\psi \overset{\pi^R}{\underset{rm}{\Longrightarrow}} \gamma x \quad in\ G,\ and$$

$$either\ \gamma = \varepsilon\ or\ \gamma{:}1\ is\ a\ nonterminal.$$

*Then for some action string $\pi'$,*

(b)
$$\tau(\pi') = \pi, \quad |\pi'| = |\pi| + |x|, \quad and$$

$$\$\gamma\mathbf{I}xy\$ \overset{\pi'}{\Longrightarrow} \$\psi\mathbf{I}y\$ \quad in\ M$$

*for all strings $y \in T^*$.*

*Proof.* The proof is by induction on the length of the rule string $\pi$. In the base case we have $\pi = \varepsilon$, and so $\psi = \gamma x$. Since $M$ has a shift action on all terminals in $T$, we then have

$$\$\gamma\mathbf{I}xy\$ \overset{\pi'}{\Longrightarrow} \$\gamma x\mathbf{I}y\$ = \$\psi\mathbf{I}y\$ \quad in\ M\ , \tag{5.17}$$

where $\pi'$ is the $|x|$-length string of shift actions on the terminals occurring in $x$. Since $\tau(\pi') = \varepsilon$, statements (b) hold.

To prove the induction step, we assume that $\pi$ is of the form $r\pi_1$, where $r$ is a rule $A \to \omega$. As an induction hypothesis, we assume that the lemma holds for the rule string $\pi_1$. We have

$$\psi \overset{\pi_1^R}{\underset{rm}{\Longrightarrow}} \gamma_1 x_1 = \delta A x_1 \overset{r}{\underset{rm}{\Longrightarrow}} \delta\omega x_1 = \gamma x \quad in\ G \tag{5.18}$$

for some strings $\gamma_1, \delta \in V^*$ and $x_1 \in T^*$. Here $x = zx_1$ and $\delta\omega = \gamma z$ for some $z$, because $\gamma$ is empty or ends with a nonterminal. Since $\gamma_1 = \delta A$, and hence ends with a nonterminal, we can apply the induction hypothesis to the first derivation segment in (5.18) and conclude that, for some action string $\pi'_1$,

$$\tau(\pi'_1) = \pi_1, \quad |\pi'_1| = |\pi_1| + |x_1|\ , \quad and$$

$$\$\gamma_1\mathbf{I}x_1y\$ \overset{\pi'_1}{\Longrightarrow} \$\psi\mathbf{I}y\$ \quad in\ M\ . \tag{5.19}$$

Thus we have

$$\$\delta A\mathbf{I}x_1y\$ = \$\gamma_1\mathbf{I}x_1y\$ \overset{\pi'_1}{\Longrightarrow} \$\psi\mathbf{I}y\$\ . \tag{5.20}$$

On the other hand, $M$ has the reduce action $r' = \omega\mathbf{I} \to A\mathbf{I}$, which implies that

$$\$\delta\omega\mathbf{I}x_1y\$ \overset{r'}{\Longrightarrow} \$\delta A\mathbf{I}x_1y\$\ . \tag{5.21}$$

Since $M$ has a shift action on all terminals in $T$, we can conclude that

$$\$\gamma\mathbf{I}xy\$ = \$\gamma\mathbf{I}zx_1y\$ \overset{\pi_2'}{\Longrightarrow} \$\gamma z\mathbf{I}x_1y\$ = \$\delta\omega\mathbf{I}x_1y\$ \; , \tag{5.22}$$

where $\pi_2'$ is the $|z|$-length string of shift actions on the terminals occurring in $z$. Choosing $\pi' = \pi_2'r'\pi_1'$ and combining statements (5.19)–(5.22) we see finally that statements (b) hold. Note that $\tau(\pi') = \tau(\pi_2')\tau(r')\tau(\pi_1') = r\pi_1 = \pi$, and that $|\pi'| = |\pi_2'| + 1 + |\pi_1'| = |z| + 1 + |\pi_1| + |x_1| = |r\pi_1| + |zx_1| = |\pi| + |x|$.  $\square$

**Lemma 5.20** *If $(M, \tau)$ is the shift-reduce parser for a grammar $G$, then $L(G) \subseteq L(M)$, and for any right parse $\pi$ of a sentence $w$ in $G$, $\tau(\pi') = \pi$ for some parse $\pi'$ of $w$ in $M$. Moreover, $TIME_M(w) \leqslant TIME_G(w) + |w|$.*

*Proof.* Set $\psi = S$, $x = w$, and $\gamma = y = \varepsilon$ in Lemma 5.19. Recall that if $S \Rightarrow^n w$, then $S \underset{rm}{\Longrightarrow}^n w$ (see Theorem 4.2).  $\square$

By Lemmas 5.18 and 5.20 we have

**Theorem 5.21** *The shift-reduce parser $M$ for a grammar $G$ is a right parser for $G$. Moreover, for each sentence $w \in L(G)$, $M$ produces all right parses of $w$ in $G$, and $TIME_M(w) = TIME_G(w) + |w|$.*  $\square$

A practical parser should be deterministic and halt on all inputs. This is not the case for the produce-shift and shift-reduce parsers presented above, which are almost always nondeterministic. Recall that the produce-shift parser is nondeterministic whenever there is a "produce-produce conflict", i.e., a pair of distinct produce actions

$$A\mathbf{I} \to \omega_1^R\mathbf{I}\,, \quad A\mathbf{I} \to \omega_2^R\mathbf{I}\;.$$

The shift-reduce parser can be nondeterministic under even weaker conditions. Any pair of actions of the form

$$\omega\mathbf{I} \to A\mathbf{I}, \quad \mathbf{I}a \to a\mathbf{I}$$

causes nondeterminism, since both these rules can be applied to any configuration of the form $\$\gamma\omega\mathbf{I}ay\$$. (This type of nondeterminism might be called a "shift-reduce conflict".) Also, a pair of distinct reduce actions

$$\omega_1\mathbf{I} \to A_1\mathbf{I}, \quad \omega_2\mathbf{I} \to A_2\mathbf{I}$$

causes nondeterminism whenever $\omega_1$ is a suffix of $\omega_2$ or vice versa (a "reduce-reduce conflict").

Since there exist context-free languages that are not accepted by any deterministic pushdown automaton, we cannot hope to construct a deterministic parser for every context-free grammar if the parser is supposed to function like a pushdown transducer. Of course, this does not mean that we are unable to parse deterministically every context-free grammar. It is not hard to augment the Cocke-Kasami-Younger recognition algorithm (see Section 4.7) so as to emit a parse for the sentence in the transformed canonical two-form grammar. From this parse it is possible to reconstruct a parse for the sentence in the original grammar (the transformation into canonical two-form can be done so that a "cover" is obtained; see Section 6.6). Earley's recognition algorithm, which works directly on the original grammar, is even easier to augment with a parsing effect. However, both of these algorithms require time nonlinear in $n$ to process an input of length $n$, whereas parsers obtained via pushdown automata run in linear time.

We conclude this section by presenting a simple method for constructing deterministic left parsers. The method works for a proper subclass of context-free grammars called "simple grammars". More general methods for parser construction will be considered in Sections 5.3 and 5.7 (and in later chapters).

A grammar $G = (V, T, P, S)$ is in *Greibach normal-form* if its rules are of the forms

(1)  $A \rightarrow a\beta$, where $a \in T$ and $\beta \in (V \setminus \{S\})^*$.
(2)  $S \rightarrow \varepsilon$.

In a Greibach normal-form grammar, then, the right-hand side of a rule cannot begin with a nonterminal. Moreover, the right-hand side can be empty only in the case of the rule $S \rightarrow \varepsilon$. Also note that the start symbol $S$ does not appear in the right-hand side of any rule.

**Proposition 5.22** *Any grammar $G$ with terminal alphabet $T$ can be transformed in time $O(|G|^3)$ into an equivalent Greibach normal-form grammar with terminal alphabet $T$.*   $\square$

In the produce-shift parser for a Greibach normal-form grammar the actions are of the following forms:

| action $r$: | $\tau(r)$: |
|---|---|
| $A\mathsf{I} \rightarrow \beta^R a\mathsf{I}$ | $A \rightarrow a\beta$ |
| $S\mathsf{I} \rightarrow \mathsf{I}$ | $S \rightarrow \varepsilon$ |
| $a\mathsf{I}a \rightarrow \mathsf{I}$ | $\varepsilon$ |

An application of the produce action $A\mathsf{I} \rightarrow \beta^R a\mathsf{I}$ can lead to the acceptance of the input string only if the current input symbol is $a$, because after the application of this produce action the only applicable action is the shift action $a\mathsf{I}a \rightarrow \mathsf{I}$. This means that, without changing the accepted language, we can add to the action $A\mathsf{I} \rightarrow \beta^R a\mathsf{I}$ a *one-symbol lookahead a*, as follows:

$$A\mathsf{I}a \rightarrow \beta^R a\mathsf{I}a \ .$$

Similarly, we can add to the action $S\mathsf{I} \rightarrow \mathsf{I}$ the lookahead symbol $\$$:

$$S\mathsf{I}\$ \rightarrow \mathsf{I}\$ \ .$$

Observe that this action only comes into effect in the configuration $S I S$, because, by definition, $S$ does not appear in the right-hand side of any rule.

A parser obtained in this way is deterministic if and only if the grammar has no pair of distinct rules of the form

$$A \to a\beta_1, \qquad A \to a\beta_2 .$$

A Greibach normal-form grammar that has this property is called a *simple grammar*, or *s-grammar*.

Grammars for programming languages are usually not *s*-grammars. However, many subsets of programming languages can be generated by *s*-grammars. As an example, consider the grammar with rules

$$S \to \textbf{begin } C ,$$
$$C \to \textbf{end} \,|\, a \,;\, C \,|\, \textbf{begin } C \,;\, C .$$

The actions of the deterministic produce-shift parser for this grammar are:

| action $r$: | $\tau(r)$: |
|---|---|
| $S$ I **begin** $\to C$ **begin** I **begin** | $S \to \textbf{begin } C$ |
| $C$ I **end** $\to$ **end** I **end** | $C \to \textbf{end}$ |
| $C$ I $a \to C$ ; $a$ I $a$ | $C \to a$ ; $C$ |
| $C$ I **begin** $\to C$ ; $C$ **begin** I **begin** | $C \to \textbf{begin } C$ ; $C$ |
| **begin** I **begin** $\to$ I | $\varepsilon$ |
| **end** I **end** $\to$ I | $\varepsilon$ |
| $a$ I $a \to$ I | $\varepsilon$ |
| ; I ; $\to$ I | $\varepsilon$ |

We say that a language over an alphabet $T$ is a *simple language*, or *s-language*, if it is the language generated by some *s*-grammar with terminal alphabet $T$.

The family of *s*-languages is a proper subfamily of the LL(1) languages (see the following sections).

## 5.3  Strong LL($k$) Parsing

In this section we consider the general problem of adding lookahead into nondeterministic produce-shift parsers in order to make them deterministic. We shall show that, for any context-free grammar, one can obtain a left parser from the produce-shift parser by adding to the produce actions a lookahead string of length $k \geq 0$. Grammars for which this left parser is deterministic will be called strong LL($k$) grammars. Properties of these grammars will be considered in Section 5.4.

First we note that adding lookahead to the actions of a pushdown transducer only restricts the applicability of the actions and hence certainly cannot extend the language accepted, nor the set of outputs produced for a given sentence. More generally, we have

**Fact 5.23** Let $M$ and $M'$ be pushdown transducers with the same stack alphabet, terminal alphabet, output alphabet, initial stack contents and set of final stack contents such that each action of $M'$ is of the form

$$\delta\alpha|xyz\to\delta\beta|yz \ ,$$

where $\alpha|xy\to\beta|y$ is an action of $M$ mapped to the same output string. Then $L(M')\subseteq L(M)$, any computation of $M'$ is a computation of $M$, and any output produced by $M'$ for a sentence $w\in L(M')$ is also produced by $M$ for $w$.    $\square$

Thus, the problem in adding lookahead to the produce actions of a produce-shift parser is how to do so without decreasing the language accepted or the set of left parses produced.

We start by considering the grammar $G_{\text{block}}$, which has the following rules:

$$S\to E\,|\,B \ ,$$
$$E\to\varepsilon \ ,$$
$$B\to a\,|\,\textbf{begin } S\ C\ \textbf{end} \ ,$$
$$C\to\varepsilon\,|\,; S\ C \ .$$

If the right-hand side of a rule begins with a terminal, we can proceed as for a Greibach normal-form grammar and use the terminal as the sole lookahead string for that rule. We then get the following produce actions:

$$r_1 = B\ |\ a\to a\ |\ a \ ,$$
$$r_2 = B\ |\ \textbf{begin}\to\textbf{end}\ C\ S\ \textbf{begin}\ |\ \textbf{begin} \ ,$$
$$r_3 = C\ |\ ;\to C\ S\ ;\ |\ ; \ .$$

If the right-hand side of a rule begins with a nonterminal, the first symbol of any terminal string derived by that nonterminal is a legal current input symbol when the left-hand side of the rule is on top of the stack. As the terminal strings derived by the nonterminal $B$ begin either with $a$ or $\textbf{begin}$, we get

$$r_4 = S\ |\ a\to B\ |\ a \ ,$$
$$r_5 = S\ |\ \textbf{begin}\to B\ |\ \textbf{begin} \ .$$

If the first symbol in the right-hand side derives the empty string $\varepsilon$, we must also consider the terminal strings derived by the second symbol in the right-hand side, and if this derives $\varepsilon$, we must consider the third, and so on. The whole right-hand side may in fact derive $\varepsilon$. In this case we must also consider the terminals that can legally *follow* the left-hand side, i.e., terminals that appear immediately after the left-hand side in some sentential form of the grammar. For example, $\textbf{end}$ is a legal follower of the nonterminal $C$ because

$$S\Rightarrow B\Rightarrow\textbf{begin } S\ C\ \textbf{end}$$

holds in $G_{block}$. Thus we get the action

$$r_6 = C \text{ I end} \to \text{ I end} \ .$$

On the other hand, it is obvious that no other terminal can legally follow $C$.

The legal followers of the nonterminal $S$ include **end** and the semicolon, by virtue of the following:

$$S \Rightarrow B \Rightarrow \textbf{begin } S \ C \textbf{ end} \Rightarrow \textbf{begin } S \textbf{ end} \ ,$$
$$S \Rightarrow B \Rightarrow \textbf{begin } S \ C \textbf{ end} \Rightarrow \textbf{begin } S \ ; \ S \ C \textbf{ end} \ .$$

On the other hand, it easy to see that no other terminal can follow $S$ in any sentential form. Thus we get, for the rule $S \to E$,

$$r_7 = S \text{ I end} \to E \text{ I end} \ ,$$
$$r_8 = S \text{ I } ; \to E \text{ I } ; \ .$$

The legal followers of the nonterminal $E$ are clearly the same as for $S$. So we get, for the rule $E \to \varepsilon$,

$$r_9 = E \text{ I end} \to \text{ I end} \ ,$$
$$r_{10} = E \text{ I } ; \to \text{ I } ; \ .$$

Of course, in this case it is not actually necessary to add any lookahead because there is only one produce action for $E$ in the produce-shift parser.

If a nonterminal can appear as the last symbol of a sentential form, as is the case here with $S$, $E$ and $B$, we must also regard the end marker $ as a legal follower of that nonterminal. Thus the rules $S \to E$ and $E \to \varepsilon$ lead to the additional produce actions

$$r_{11} = S \text{ I } \$ \to E \text{ I } \$ \ ,$$
$$r_{12} = E \text{ I } \$ \to \text{ I } \$ \ .$$

Without these actions the parser would not accept the empty string $\varepsilon$.

The resulting parser is in this case deterministic. The adding of one-symbol lookahead has removed the nondeterminism from the produce actions for the nonterminals $S$, $B$ and $C$. That the parser still accepts the whole language generated by the grammar should be clear from the following derivations. First, the parser accepts $\varepsilon$:

$$\$ \ S \text{ I } \$ \overset{r_{11}}{\Longrightarrow} \$ \ E \text{ I } \$ \overset{r_{12}}{\Longrightarrow} \$ \text{ I } \$ \ .$$

The parse produced is $(S \to E)(E \to \varepsilon)$. Second, the parser accepts the sentence

$$\textbf{begin } a \ ; \ \textbf{begin } a \ ; \ ; \ \textbf{end end} \ ,$$

by virtue of the following derivation:

$$\$ \ S \text{ I } \textbf{begin } a \ ; \ \textbf{begin } a \ ; \ ; \ \textbf{end end} \ \$$$
$$\overset{r_5}{\Longrightarrow} \$ \ B \text{ I } \textbf{begin } a \ ; \ \textbf{begin } a \ ; \ ; \ \textbf{end end} \ \$$$

$\overset{r_2}{\Longrightarrow}$ \$ end $C$ $S$ **begin** I **begin** $a$ ; **begin** $a$ ; ; **end end** \$

$\Longrightarrow$ \$ **end** $C$ $S$ I $a$ ; **begin** $a$ ; ; **end end** \$

$\overset{r_4}{\Longrightarrow}$ \$ **end** $C$ $B$ I $a$ ; **begin** $a$ ; ; **end end** \$

$\overset{r_1}{\Longrightarrow}$ \$ **end** $C$ $a$ I $a$ ; **begin** $a$ ; ; **end end** \$

$\Longrightarrow$ \$ **end** $C$ I ; **begin** $a$ ; ; **end end** \$

$\overset{r_3}{\Longrightarrow}$ \$ **end** $C$ $S$ ; I ; **begin** $a$ ; ; **end end** \$

$\Longrightarrow$ \$ **end** $C$ $S$ I **begin** $a$ ; ; **end end** \$

$\overset{r_5}{\Longrightarrow}$ \$ **end** $C$ $B$ I **begin** $a$ ; ; **end end** \$

$\overset{r_2}{\Longrightarrow}$ \$ **end** $C$ **end** $C$ $S$ **begin** I **begin** $a$ ; ; **end end** \$

$\Longrightarrow$ \$ **end** $C$ **end** $C$ $S$ I $a$ ; ; **end end** \$

$\overset{r_4}{\Longrightarrow}$ \$ **end** $C$ **end** $C$ $B$ I $a$ ; ; **end end** \$

$\overset{r_1}{\Longrightarrow}$ \$ **end** $C$ **end** $C$ $a$ I $a$ ; ; **end end** \$

$\Longrightarrow$ \$ **end** $C$ **end** $C$ I ; ; **end end** \$

$\overset{r_3}{\Longrightarrow}$ \$ **end** $C$ **end** $C$ $S$ ; I ; ; **end end** \$

$\Longrightarrow$ \$ **end** $C$ **end** $C$ $S$ I ; **end end** \$

$\overset{r_8}{\Longrightarrow}$ \$ **end** $C$ **end** $C$ $E$ I ; **end end** \$

$\overset{r_{10}}{\Longrightarrow}$ \$ **end** $C$ **end** $C$ I ; **end end** \$

$\overset{r_3}{\Longrightarrow}$ \$ **end** $C$ **end** $C$ $S$ ; I ; **end end** \$

$\Longrightarrow$ \$ **end** $C$ **end** $C$ $S$ I **end end** \$

$\overset{r_7}{\Longrightarrow}$ \$ **end** $C$ **end** $C$ $E$ I **end end** \$

$\overset{r_9}{\Longrightarrow}$ \$ **end** $C$ **end** $C$ I **end end** \$

$\overset{r_6}{\Longrightarrow}$ \$ **end** $C$ **end** I **end end** \$

$\Longrightarrow$ \$ **end** $C$ I **end** \$

$\overset{r_6}{\Longrightarrow}$ \$ **end** I **end** \$

$\Longrightarrow$ \$ I \$ .

The parse produced is $(S{\rightarrow}B)$ $(B{\rightarrow}\textbf{begin}\ S\ C\ \textbf{end})$ $(S{\rightarrow}B)$ $(B{\rightarrow}a)$ $(C{\rightarrow}; S\ C)$ $(S{\rightarrow}B)$ $(B{\rightarrow}\textbf{begin}\ S\ C\ \textbf{end})$ $(S{\rightarrow}B)$ $(B{\rightarrow}a)$ $(C{\rightarrow}; S\ C)$ $(S{\rightarrow}E)$ $(E{\rightarrow}\varepsilon)$ $(C{\rightarrow}; S\ C)$ $(S{\rightarrow}E)$ $(E{\rightarrow}\varepsilon)$ $(C{\rightarrow}\varepsilon)$ $(C{\rightarrow}\varepsilon)$.

   The parser presented above is an example of a "strong LL(1) parser". Here "LL" means that the input string is parsed from Left to right and that a Left parse is produced, while "1" means that lookahead strings of length at most one are used. The prefix "strong" refers to the parser construction method used, which is simpler than the general "canonical" method, and hence usually requires stronger properties of the grammar if a deterministic parser is to be produced. (The canonical $LL(k)$ parsing method will be discussed in Chapter 8).

In the general case the lookahead strings are of length at most $k$, where $k$ is some natural number. It is obvious that the longer the lookahead strings are, the larger is the class of grammars for which the method yields a deterministic parser.

Let $G=(V, T, P, S)$ be a grammar, $k$ a natural number and $\gamma$ a string in $V^*$. We define

$$FIRST_{G,k}(\gamma)=k:L_G(\gamma) ,$$
$$FOLLOW_{G,k}(\gamma)= \{y\in T^* \mid S\Rightarrow^* \alpha\gamma\beta \text{ in } G \quad \text{and} \quad y\in FIRST_{G,k}(\beta)$$
$$\text{for some } \alpha, \beta\in V^*\} .$$

In other words, $FIRST_{G,k}(\gamma)$ denotes the set of all prefixes $k:x$, where $x$ is a terminal string derived by $\gamma$, and $FOLLOW_{G,k}(\gamma)$ denotes the set of all $k:x$, where $x$ is a terminal string following $\gamma$ in some sentential form of $G$. (Recall from Section 1.2 that $k:x$ is the $k$-length prefix of $x$ if $k<|x|$, and $x$ otherwise.)

If no ambiguity arises, we may abbreviate $FIRST_{G,k}$ to $FIRST_k$ and $FOLLOW_{G,k}$ to $FOLLOW_k$. We may also generalize $FIRST_k$ to sets $W\subseteq V^*$ in the natural way, i.e.,

$$FIRST_k(W)= \bigcup_{\gamma\in W} FIRST_k(\gamma) .$$

The following fact is often used (without being stated explicitly) in proving properties of $LL(k)$ and other parsers.

**Fact 5.24** In any grammar, for all strings $\alpha$, $\beta$, $\gamma$ and natural numbers $k$, $n$,

(a) $FIRST_k(\alpha\beta\gamma)=k:FIRST_{k+n}(\alpha\beta\gamma)=FIRST_k(\alpha FIRST_{k+n}(\beta) \gamma).$

(b) $FOLLOW_k(\gamma)=k:FOLLOW_{k+n}(\gamma)=FIRST_k(FOLLOW_{k+n}(\gamma)).$   $\square$

If a lookahead string remains shorter than $k$ (which may happen when a nonterminal is followed in some sentential form by a terminal string shorter than $k$), then we must "pad" it with the end marker $\$$. Note that, if we wish to obtain a deterministic parser, we cannot allow some lookahead string to be a proper prefix of another. For example, in the strong $LL(1)$ parser for $G_{block}$ we cannot use the empty string $\varepsilon$ in place of $\$$ in the actions $r_{11}$ and $r_{12}$, because then these actions would be applicable whenever the actions $r_4, r_5, r_7, r_8$ and $r_9, r_{10}$ are. The padding with $\$$ is most conveniently done by augmenting the grammar with this new terminal and with a new starting rule $S'\to\$S\$$.

Formally, the $\$$-*augmented grammar* for $G=(V, T, P, S)$ is the grammar $G'=(V\cup\{S',\$\}, T\cup\{\$\}, P\cup\{S'\to\$S\$\}, S')$, where we assume that the new symbols $\$$ and $S'$ do not appear in $V$.

We often use the short-hand notations $\text{FIRST}'_k$ and $\text{FOLLOW}'_k$ for the operators $\text{FIRST}_{G',k}$ and $\text{FOLLOW}_{G',k}$ of the \$-augmented grammar $G'$ for $G$, especially when in the same context the short-hand notations $\text{FIRST}_k$ and $\text{FOLLOW}_k$ (for $G$) are used.

**Fact 5.25** In any grammar,

$$\text{FOLLOW}'_k(\gamma) = k : \text{FOLLOW}_k(\gamma)\,\$$$

for all strings $\gamma$.   $\square$

Now let $G = (V, T, P, S)$ be a grammar and $k$ a natural number. The *strong LL(k) parser* (or *SLL(k) parser*) for $G$ is the pushdown transducer with stack alphabet $V$, input alphabet $T$, initial stack contents $S$, set of final stack contents $\{\varepsilon\}$, and set of actions consisting of all rules of the forms

$(pa)$ $A|y \rightarrow \omega^R|y$        "produce by rule $A \rightarrow \omega$ on lookahead $y$",
$(sa)$ $a|a \rightarrow |$            "shift $a$".

Here $A \rightarrow \omega$ is a rule in $P$, $a$ is a terminal in $T$, and $y \in \text{FIRST}'_k(\omega\text{FOLLOW}'_k(A))$. The output effect $\tau$ is defined by

(1) $\tau(A|y \rightarrow \omega^R|y) = A \rightarrow \omega$.
(2) $\tau(a|a \rightarrow |) = \varepsilon$.

We have immediately

**Fact 5.26** For any reduced grammar $G$, the SLL(0) parser for $G$ is just the produce-shift parser for $G$.   $\square$

Returning to $G_{\text{block}}$, we have

$$\text{FIRST}'_1(a\ \text{FOLLOW}'_1(B)) = \{a\}\ ,$$
$$\text{FIRST}'_1(\textbf{begin}\ S\ C\ \textbf{end}\ \text{FOLLOW}'_1(B)) = \{\textbf{begin}\}\ .$$

Hence the SLL(1) parser for $G_{\text{block}}$ has the produce actions $r_1$ and $r_2$. Furthermore,

$$\text{FIRST}'_1(;\ S\ C\ \text{FOLLOW}'_1(C)) = \{;\}\ ,$$
$$\text{FIRST}'_1(B\ \text{FOLLOW}'_1(S)) = \text{FIRST}'_1(B) = \{a, \textbf{begin}\}\ ,$$

so the produce actions $r_3$, $r_4$ and $r_5$ are also present. Finally,

$$\text{FIRST}'_1(\varepsilon\ \text{FOLLOW}'_1(C)) = \text{FOLLOW}'_1(C) = \{\textbf{end}\}\ ,$$
$$\text{FIRST}'_1(E\ \text{FOLLOW}'_1(S)) = \text{FOLLOW}'_1(S) = \{\textbf{end}, ; , \$\}\ ,$$
$$\text{FIRST}'_1(\varepsilon\ \text{FOLLOW}'_1(E)) = \text{FOLLOW}'_1(E) = \{\textbf{end}, ; , \$\}\ ,$$

so we also get the produce actions $r_6$ to $r_{12}$.

For $k=2$ we have in $G_{\text{block}}$

$$\text{FIRST}'_2(a \ \text{FOLLOW}'_2(B)) = \text{FIRST}'_2(a \ \text{FOLLOW}'_1(B))$$
$$= \text{FIRST}'_2(a\{\text{end}, ;, \$\}) = \{a \ \text{end}, a \ ;, a\$\} \ ,$$
$$\text{FIRST}_2(\text{begin } S \ C \ \text{end } \text{FOLLOW}_2(B))$$
$$= \text{FIRST}_2(\text{begin } S \ C \ \text{end})$$
$$= \text{begin } \text{FIRST}_1(S \ C \ \text{end})$$
$$= \text{begin}\{a, \text{begin}, ;, \text{end}\}$$
$$= \{\text{begin } a, \text{begin begin}, \text{begin } ;, \text{begin end}\} \ .$$

Hence the SLL(2) parser for $G_{\text{block}}$ has the following produce actions for $B$:

$$B \mid a \ \text{end} \to a \mid a \ \text{end} \ ,$$
$$B \mid a \ ; \ \to a \mid a \ ; \ ,$$
$$B \mid a \ \$ \to a \mid a \ \$ \ ,$$
$$B \mid \text{begin } a \to \text{end } C \ S \ \text{begin} \mid \text{begin } a \ ,$$
$$B \mid \text{begin begin} \to \text{end } C \ S \ \text{begin} \mid \text{begin begin} \ ,$$
$$B \mid \text{begin } ; \ \to \text{end } C \ S \ \text{begin} \mid \text{begin } ; \ ,$$
$$B \mid \text{begin end} \to \text{end } C \ S \ \text{begin} \mid \text{begin end} \ .$$

We now establish the correctness of the SLL($k$) parser, i.e., show that it is always a left parser for the grammar. First we note that Lemmas 5.12 and 5.13 hold as such for the SLL($k$) parser, because they hold for the produce-shift parser (SLL(0) parser): recall from Fact 5.23 that the addition of lookahead cannot extend the language accepted nor the set of parses produced.

In the following are restated Lemmas 5.12 and 5.13 for SLL($k$) parsers.

**Lemma 5.27** *Let $G=(V, T, P, S)$ be a grammar, $k$ a natural number, and $(M, \tau)$ the SLL($k$) parser for $G$. Further, let $\gamma$ be a string in $V^*$, $w$ a string in $T^*$, $\Phi$ a string over the alphabet of $M$, and $\pi'$ an action string such that*

(a)   $\$\gamma \mid w\$ \ \overset{\pi'}{\Longrightarrow} \ \Phi$   *in M.*

*Then for some strings $x$, $y$ and $\psi$,*

(b)
$$w = xy, \quad \Phi = \$\psi \mid y\$, \quad |\pi'| = |\tau(\pi')| + |x| \ ,$$

$$\text{and} \quad \gamma^R \ \overset{\tau(\pi')}{\underset{\text{lm}}{\Longrightarrow}} \ x\psi^R \quad \text{in } G \ .$$

$\square$

**Lemma 5.28** *If $(M, \tau)$ is the SLL($k$) parser for a grammar $G$, then $L(M) \subseteq L(G)$, and $\tau(\pi')$ is a left parse of a sentence $w$ in $G$ whenever $\pi'$ is a parse of $w$ in $M$. Moreover, $TIME_G(w) \leqslant TIME_M(w) - |w|$.*   $\square$

The counterpart of Lemma 5.14 runs as follows.

**Lemma 5.29** *Let $G = (V, T, P, S)$ be a grammar, $k$ a natural number, and $(M, \tau)$ the SLL($k$) parser for $G$. Further, let $\gamma$ and $\psi$ be strings in $V^*$, $x$ and $y$ strings in $T^*$, and $\pi$ a rule string in $P^*$ such that*

(a)
$$\gamma^R \xrightarrow[\mathrm{lm}]{\pi} x\psi^R \text{ in } G, \quad k : y \in \mathrm{FIRST}_k(\psi^R \mathrm{FOLLOW}_k(\gamma^R)) ,$$

*and either $\psi^R = \varepsilon$ or $1 : \psi^R$ is a nonterminal .*

*Then for some action string $\pi'$*

(b)
$$\tau(\pi') = \pi, \quad |\pi'| = |\pi| + |x|, \quad and$$

$$\$\gamma \mathbf{l} xy\$ \xrightarrow{\pi'} \$\psi \mathbf{l} y\$ \text{ in } M .$$

*Proof.* As in Lemma 5.14, the proof is by induction on the length of the rule string $\pi$. The proof of the base case is as in Lemma 5.14. (The additional condition on $k : y$ is not needed.)

The proof of the induction step requires some additions. As in the proof of Lemma 5.14, we conclude from (a) that

$$\gamma^R \xrightarrow[\mathrm{lm}]{\pi_1} x_1 \psi_1^R = x_1 A\delta \xrightarrow[\mathrm{lm}]{r} x_1 \omega\delta = x_1 z\psi^R = x\psi^R ,$$

where $\pi_1 r = \pi$. Let $y_1 = zy$. Since $k : y \in \mathrm{FIRST}_k(\psi^R \mathrm{FOLLOW}_k(\gamma^R))$, we must have $k : y_1 \in \mathrm{FIRST}_k(z\psi^R \mathrm{FOLLOW}_k(\gamma^R))$. Since $\psi_1^R$ derives $z\psi^R$, we then have

$$k : y_1 \in \mathrm{FIRST}_k(\psi_1^R \mathrm{FOLLOW}_k(\gamma^R)) .$$

The induction hypothesis now implies that, for some action string $\pi'_1$,

$$\tau(\pi'_1) = \pi_1, \quad |\pi'_1| = |\pi_1| + |x_1|, \text{ and}$$

$$\$\gamma \mathbf{l} xy\$ = \$\gamma \mathbf{l} x_1 zy\$ = \$\gamma \mathbf{l} x_1 y_1\$ \xrightarrow{\pi'_1} \$\psi_1 \mathbf{l} y_1\$ = \$\delta^R A \mathbf{l} y_1\$ .$$

Now $\mathrm{FIRST}_k(\delta \mathrm{FOLLOW}_k(\gamma^R))$ is contained in $\mathrm{FOLLOW}_k(A)$, since $\gamma^R$ derives $x_1 A\delta$. Thus $\mathrm{FIRST}_k(\omega\delta \mathrm{FOLLOW}_k(\gamma^R))$ is contained in $\mathrm{FIRST}_k(\omega \mathrm{FOLLOW}_k(A))$. But $k : y_1 \in \mathrm{FIRST}_k(\omega\delta \mathrm{FOLLOW}_k(\gamma^R))$ (recall that $\omega\delta = z\psi^R$). Thus we have

$$k : y_1 \in \mathrm{FIRST}_k(\omega \mathrm{FOLLOW}_k(A)) ,$$

which in turn implies

$$k : y_1\$ \in \mathrm{FIRST}'_k(\omega \mathrm{FOLLOW}'_k(A)) .$$

So $M$ has a produce action, $r'$, for $A \to \omega$ on lookahead $k : y_1 \$$, and this is applicable to the configuration $\$ \delta^R A | y_1 \$$, i.e.,

$$\$ \delta^R A | y_1 \$ \xrightarrow{r'} \$ \delta^R \omega^R | y_1 \$ = \$(\omega \delta)^R | zy\$ = \$\psi z^R | zy\$ \ .$$

The rest of the proof then proceeds as in Lemma 5.14.  $\square$

**Lemma 5.30** *If $(M, \tau)$ is the SLL(k) parser for a grammar $G$, then $L(G) \subseteq L(M)$, and for any left parse $\pi$ of a sentence $w$ in $G$, $\tau(\pi') = \pi$ for some parse $\pi'$ of $w$ in $M$. Moreover, $TIME_M(w) \leqslant TIME_G(w) + |w|$.*

*Proof.* Set $\gamma = S$, $x = w$, and $\psi = y = \varepsilon$ in Lemma 5.29. Note that $k : \varepsilon$ is always in $\text{FOLLOW}_k(S) = \text{FIRST}_k(\varepsilon^R \text{FOLLOW}_k(S^R))$.  $\square$

By Lemmas 5.28 and 5.30 we have

**Theorem 5.31** *The SLL(k) parser $M$ for a grammar $G$ is a left parser for $G$, for all $k \geqslant 0$. Moreover, for each sentence $w \in L(G)$, $M$ produces all left parses of $w$ in $G$, and $TIME_M(w) = TIME_G(w) + |w|$.*  $\square$

## 5.4 Strong LL(k) Grammars

We say that grammar $G$ is *strong LL(k)* (or *SLL(k)*) if its SLL(k) parser is deterministic. A language over an alphabet $T$ is *strong LL(k)* (or *SLL(k)*) if it is the language generated by some SLL(k) grammar with terminal alphabet $T$.

Later, in Chapter 8, we shall show that the family of SLL(k) languages in fact coincides with the family of LL(k) languages, the family of languages generated by general LL(k) grammars. In this section we shall derive grammatical characterizations for the SLL(k) property of grammars. These will be of use in proving other results on SLL(k) grammars and in comparing the class of SLL(k) grammars with other related grammar classes. First, we require two lemmas.

**Lemma 5.32** *Let $G = (V, T, P, S)$ be a grammar, $\alpha$ and $\beta$ strings in $V^*$, $X$ and $Y$ symbols in $V$, $x$ and $y$ strings in $T^*$, and $n$ a natural number such that*

$$Y \Rightarrow^n \alpha X \beta, \quad \alpha \Rightarrow^* x, \quad and \quad \beta \Rightarrow^* y \quad in \ G \ .$$

*Then for some string $\gamma \in V^*$,*

$$Y \underset{lm}{\Longrightarrow}^* xX\gamma \quad and \quad \gamma \Rightarrow^* y \quad in \ G \ .$$

*Proof.* The proof is by induction on $n$. The base case $n = 0$ is trivial, because then $\alpha = \beta = \varepsilon$, $X = Y$, $x = y = \varepsilon$, and we can choose $\gamma = \varepsilon$. To prove the induction step, we assume that $n>0$ and, as an induction hypothesis, that the lemma holds for $n-1$. We have to consider three cases:

(a) $Y\Rightarrow^{n-1}\alpha'A\beta'\Rightarrow\alpha'\omega\beta'=\alpha'\omega\delta X\beta=\alpha X\beta.$

(b) $Y\Rightarrow^{n-1}\alpha'A\beta'\Rightarrow\alpha'\omega\beta'=\alpha'\psi X\delta\beta'=\alpha X\delta\beta'=\alpha X\beta.$

(c) $Y\Rightarrow^{n-1}\alpha'A\beta'\Rightarrow\alpha'\omega\beta'=\alpha X\psi\omega\beta'=\alpha X\beta.$

Here $\alpha'$, $\beta'$, $\delta$, $\psi$ are strings in $V^*$ and $A\rightarrow\omega$ is some rule in $P$. In case (a) we have $\beta'=\delta X\beta$. Thus

$$Y\Rightarrow^{n-1}\alpha''X\beta, \qquad \alpha''\Rightarrow^* x, \qquad \text{and} \qquad \beta\Rightarrow^* y \quad \text{in } G\ .$$

where we have written $\alpha''$ in place of $\alpha'A\delta$. The claim then follows from the induction hypothesis. In case (b) we have $\alpha=\alpha'\psi$ and $\beta=\delta\beta'$, which means that $x$ can be written as $x'z$, and $y$ as $vy'$, where $x'$ is derived by $\alpha'$, $z$ is derived by $\psi$, $v$ derived by $\delta$, and $y'$ is derived by $\beta'$. Thus we have

$$Y\Rightarrow^{n-1}\alpha'A\beta', \qquad \alpha'\Rightarrow^* x', \qquad \text{and} \qquad \beta'\Rightarrow^* y' \quad \text{in } G\ .$$

Applying the induction hypothesis, we conclude that, for some $\gamma'\in V^*$,

$$Y \underset{\text{lm}}{\Rightarrow}{}^* x'A\gamma' \qquad \text{and} \qquad \gamma'\Rightarrow^* y' \quad \text{in } G\ .$$

But then we have

$$Y \underset{\text{lm}}{\Rightarrow}{}^* x'A\gamma' \underset{\text{lm}}{\Rightarrow} x'\omega\gamma'=x'\psi X\delta\gamma'\ .$$

By Theorem 4.2, $\psi$ leftmost derives $z$. We therefore have

$$Y \underset{\text{lm}}{\Rightarrow}{}^* x'\psi X\delta\gamma' \underset{\text{lm}}{\Rightarrow}{}^* x'zX\delta\gamma'=xX\delta\gamma', \qquad \text{and}$$

$$\delta\gamma'\Rightarrow^* vy'=y \quad \text{in } G\ .$$

The claim then follows by choosing $\gamma=\delta\gamma'$. In case (c) we have $\alpha'=\alpha X\psi$ and $\psi\omega\beta'=\beta$. Thus

$$Y\Rightarrow^{n-1}\alpha X\beta'', \qquad \alpha\Rightarrow^* x, \qquad \text{and} \qquad \beta''\Rightarrow^* y \quad \text{in } G\ ,$$

where we have written $\beta''$ in place of $\psi A\beta'$. The claim then follows from the induction hypothesis. $\square$

Lemma 5.32 yields

**Lemma 5.33** *Let $G=(V, T, P, S)$ be a reduced grammar. Then*

$$\text{FOLLOW}_k(X)=\{y\in T^*\mid S \underset{\text{lm}}{\Rightarrow}{}^* xX\beta \text{ and } y\in \text{FIRST}_k(\beta) \text{ for some } x\in T^*$$

$$\text{and } \beta\in V^*\}$$

*for all symbols $X\in V$.* $\square$

We say that a pair of produce actions

$$A_1 \mathbin{|} y_1 \to \omega_1^R \mathbin{|} y_1, \quad A_2 \mathbin{|} y_2 \to \omega_2^R \mathbin{|} y_2$$

*exhibits a produce-produce conflict if* $A_1 = A_2$, $y_1 = y_2$, *and* $\omega_1 \neq \omega_2$.
A nonterminal $A$ *has the* SLL($k$) *property if*

$$\mathrm{FIRST}_k(\omega_1 \mathrm{FOLLOW}_k(A)) \cap \mathrm{FIRST}_k(\omega_2 \mathrm{FOLLOW}_k(A)) = \varnothing$$

for all pairs of distinct rules $A \to \omega_1 \mathbin{|} \omega_2$ in the grammar.

**Theorem 5.34** (*Characterizations of SLL($k$) Grammars*) *The following statements are logically equivalent for all reduced grammars $G$ and natural numbers $k$.*

(a) *The SLL($k$) parser for $G$ is deterministic.*
(b) *No pair of produce actions in the SLL($k$) parser for $G$ exhibits a produce-produce conflict.*
(c) *All nonterminals of $G$ have the SLL($k$) property.*
(d) *The conditions*

$$S \underset{\mathrm{lm}}{\Longrightarrow}{}^* x_1 A \delta_1 \underset{\mathrm{lm}}{\Longrightarrow} x_1 \omega_1 \delta_1 \underset{\mathrm{lm}}{\Longrightarrow}{}^* x_1 y_1,$$

$$S \underset{\mathrm{lm}}{\Longrightarrow}{}^* x_2 A \delta_2 \underset{\mathrm{lm}}{\Longrightarrow} x_2 \omega_2 \delta_2 \underset{\mathrm{lm}}{\Longrightarrow}{}^* x_2 y_2, \quad and$$

$$k : y_1 = k : y_2$$

*always imply that* $\omega_1 = \omega_2$.

*Proof.* Let $M$ be the SLL($k$) parser for $G$. We consider the converse of statement (a), namely the statement

$$M \text{ is nondeterministic} . \tag{5.23}$$

This is equivalent to the statement

$$\begin{cases} M \text{ has distinct produce actions} \\ A \mathbin{|} y' \to \omega_1^R \mathbin{|} y' \quad \text{and} \quad A \mathbin{|} y'z \to \omega_2^R \mathbin{|} y'z \ . \end{cases} \tag{5.24}$$

By definition, this in turn is equivalent to the statement

$$\begin{cases} A \to \omega_1 \mathbin{|} \omega_2 \text{ are rules of } G \ , \\ y' \in \mathrm{FIRST}_k'(\omega_1 \mathrm{FOLLOW}_k'(A)) \ , \\ y'z \in \mathrm{FIRST}_k'(\omega_2 \mathrm{FOLLOW}_k'(A)) \ , \\ \text{and either } \omega_1 \neq \omega_2 \text{ or } z \neq \varepsilon \ , \end{cases} \tag{5.25}$$

which by Fact 5.25 is equivalent to

$$\begin{cases} A \to \omega_1 | \omega_2 \text{ are rules of } G \ , \\ y' = k\!:\!y\$ \text{ for some } y \in \text{FIRST}_k(\omega_1 \text{FOLLOW}_k(A)) \ , \\ y'z = k\!:\!v\$ \text{ for some } v \in \text{FIRST}_k(\omega_2 \text{FOLLOW}_k(A)) \ , \\ \text{and either } \omega_1 \neq \omega_2 \text{ or } z \neq \varepsilon \ . \end{cases} \qquad (5.26)$$

Since $v$ does not contain \$, $y' = k\!:\!y\$$ cannot be a proper prefix of $k\!:\!v\$ = y'z$. Thus $z = \varepsilon$ and $y = v$ in (5.26), and hence $z = \varepsilon$ in (5.24). But then (5.24) is equivalent to the converse of statement (b), and (5.26) is equivalent to the statement

$$\begin{cases} A \to \omega_1 | \omega_2 \text{ are distinct rules of } G, \text{ and} \\ y \in \text{FIRST}_k(\omega_1 \text{FOLLOW}_k(A)) \cap \\ \text{FIRST}_k(\omega_2 \text{FOLLOW}_k(A)) \ . \end{cases} \qquad (5.27)$$

This is just the converse of statement (c). By Lemma 5.33, statement (5.27) is also equivalent to

$$\begin{cases} S \underset{\text{lm}}{\Longrightarrow}^* x_1 A \delta_1 \ , \quad y \in \text{FIRST}_k(\omega_1 \delta_1) \ , \\ \\ S \underset{\text{lm}}{\Longrightarrow}^* x_2 A \delta_2 \ , \quad y \in \text{FIRST}_k(\omega_2 \delta_2) \ , \\ \\ \text{and } A \to \omega_1 | \omega_2 \text{ are distinct rules of } G \ , \end{cases} \qquad (5.28)$$

which by Theorem 4.2 is equivalent to the converse of statement (d).   □

**Theorem 5.35** *For all natural numbers* $k$, *the class of SLL(*k*) grammars is properly contained in the class of SLL(*k* + 1) grammars.*

*Proof.* That any SLL(*k*) grammar is also an SLL(*k* + 1) grammar is seen easily from any of the characterizations given·in Theorem 5.34. Note that, by Fact 5.24,

$$\text{FIRST}_k(\omega\text{FOLLOW}_k(A))$$
$$= \text{FIRST}_k(\omega\text{FIRST}_k(\text{FOLLOW}_{k+1}(A)))$$
$$= \text{FIRST}_k(\omega\text{FOLLOW}_{k+1}(A))$$
$$= k\!:\text{FIRST}_{k+1}(\omega\text{FOLLOW}_{k+1}(A)) \ .$$

Thus the intersection

$$\text{FIRST}_{k+1}(\omega_1\text{FOLLOW}_{k+1}(A)) \cap \text{FIRST}_{k+1}(\omega_2\text{FOLLOW}_{k+1}(A))$$

must be empty whenever the intersection

$$\text{FIRST}_k(\omega_1\text{FOLLOW}_k(A)) \cap \text{FIRST}_k(\omega_2\text{FOLLOW}_k(A))$$

is empty. Hence, by characterization (b) in Theorem 5.34, the grammar is SLL(*k* + 1) whenever it is SLL(*k*). Using characterization (a) (i.e., the definition) we come to the same conclusion by noting that, if $k$-length lookahead strings in the produce actions are sufficient to make the parser deterministic, then $(k + 1)$-length lookahead strings are certainly sufficient.

The fact that, for all $k$, there are $SLL(k + 1)$ grammars which are not $SLL(k)$ can be seen by considering the grammars $G_k = (\{S, a\}, \{a\}, \{S \to a^k | a^{k+1}\}, S)$.  $\square$

The following proposition states that the families of $SLL(k)$ languages, for $k = 0, 1, \ldots$, form a properly increasing hierarchy.

**Proposition 5.36**  *For all $k \geqslant 1$, the language*

$$L_k = \{a^n w \mid n \geqslant 1 \ \text{and} \ w \in \{b, c, b^k d\}^n\}$$

*is $SLL(k)$ but not $SLL(k - 1)$.*  $\square$

The observation stated in the next theorem is important. As we shall see, the same result can be proved for all the other classes of deterministically parsable grammars ($LR(k)$, $LL(k)$ etc) considered in this book.

**Theorem 5.37**  *Any $SLL(k)$ grammar is unambiguous.*

*Proof.* Let $M$ be the $SLL(k)$ parser for an $SLL(k)$ grammar $G$. By definition, $M$ is deterministic. Thus, since no action of $M$ is applicable to the accepting configuration $\$I\$$, $M$ has exactly one accepting computation on each sentence $w \in L(G)$, or equivalently each $w \in L(G)$ has exactly one parse in $M$. This means that $M$ can produce exactly one left parse for $w$ in $G$. On the other hand, by Theorem 5.31, $M$ produces all the left parses. So each $w \in L(G)$ has exactly one left parse in $G$, which means that $G$ is unambiguous.  $\square$

We say that a configuration $\Phi$ of a pushdown automaton $M$ is *looping* if for all natural numbers $n$ there is a configuration $\Phi_n$ such that

$$\Phi \Rightarrow^n \Phi_n \quad \text{in } M .$$

**Fact 5.38**  If $\Phi$ is a looping configuration of a pushdown automaton $M$, then there is an input string $y$ and an infinite sequence of stack strings $\gamma_0, \gamma_1, \ldots$ such that

$$\Phi \Rightarrow^* \$\gamma_0 I y\$ \quad \text{and} \quad \$\gamma_i I y\$ \Rightarrow \$\gamma_{i+1} I y\$ \quad \text{in } M$$
$$\forall i \geqslant 0.  \square$$

**Fact 5.39**  A pushdown automaton $M$ loops forever on an input string $w$ if and only if the initial configuration for $w$ is looping in $M$.  $\square$

We say that a nonterminal $A$ of a grammar $G$ is *left-recursive* if $A \Rightarrow^+ A\beta$ in $G$ for some string $\beta$. A grammar $G$ is *left-recursive* if it has a left-recursive nonterminal.

The following two theorems indicate the relationship between left-recursive nonterminals in a grammar $G$ and looping configurations in the $SLL(k)$ parser for $G$.

**Theorem 5.40** *Let $G = (V, T, P, S)$ be a reduced left-recursive grammar. Then the SLL(k) parser M for G loops forever on some sentence $w \in L(G)$.*

*Proof.* Since $G$ is left-recursive and reduced, Lemma 5.32 implies that

$$S \underset{\mathrm{lm}}{\Longrightarrow}{}^* xA\delta, \quad A \underset{\mathrm{lm}}{\overset{\pi}{\Longrightarrow}} A\beta, \quad A \Rightarrow^* u,$$

$$\beta \Rightarrow^* v, \quad \text{and} \quad \delta \Rightarrow^* z$$

for some nonterminal $A$, nonempty rule string $\pi \in P^*$, strings $\beta, \delta \in V^*$, and strings $x$, $u, v, z \in T^*$. Let $y = uv^k z$ and, for all $n \geq 0$, $\psi_n = (A\beta^n \delta)^R$. Then we have, for all $n \geq k$,

$$S \underset{\mathrm{lm}}{\Longrightarrow}{}^* xA\delta \underset{\mathrm{lm}}{\overset{\pi^n}{\Longrightarrow}} xA\beta^n \delta = x\psi_n^R ,$$

$$k : y = k : uv^k z \in \mathrm{FIRST}_k(\psi_n^R) \subseteq \mathrm{FIRST}_k(\psi_n^R \mathrm{FOLLOW}_k(S)) .$$

Note that if $v = \varepsilon$, then $uv^n z = uv^k z$ for all $n$, and if $v \neq \varepsilon$, then $k : uv^n z = k : uv^k z$ for all $n \geq k$. By Lemma 5.29, we can then conclude that, for all $n \geq k$, there exists an action string $\pi_n'$ such that

$$|\pi_n'| \geq |\pi^n|, \quad \text{and} \quad \$S\mathsf{I}xy\$ \overset{\pi_n'}{\Longrightarrow} \$\psi_n \mathsf{I}y\$ \quad \text{in } M .$$

Since $\pi \neq \varepsilon$, the initial configuration $\$S\mathsf{I}xy\$$ is looping. Moreover, $xy$ belongs to $L(G)$, since

$$S \Rightarrow^* xA\delta \overset{\pi^k}{\Longrightarrow} xA\beta^k \delta \Rightarrow^* xuv^k z = xy .$$

$\square$


**Corollary 5.41** *A reduced left-recursive grammar is not SLL(k) for any $k \geq 0$.*

*Proof.* By Theorem 5.40, the SLL($k$) parser for the grammar loops forever on some sentence $w$. Since the parser must also accept $w$, it must have an accepting computation on $w$. Therefore, it cannot be deterministic. (Note that the accepting configuration $\$\mathsf{I}\$$ is never looping, since no action is applicable to it.) By definition, the grammar is therefore not SLL($k$). $\square$


Next we shall prove the converse of Theorem 5.40, namely that looping forever implies left-recursiveness. We need the following lemma.


**Lemma 5.42** *Let $G = (V, T, P, S)$ be a grammar and, for all natural numbers $i$, $A_i$ a nonterminal, $\delta_i$ a string in $V^*$, and $r_i$ a rule in $P$ such that*

$$A_i \delta_i \underset{\mathrm{lm}}{\overset{r_i}{\Longrightarrow}} A_{i+1} \delta_{i+1} \quad \text{in } G \quad \text{for all} \quad i \in \mathbb{N} .$$

*Then $A_i$ is left-recursive for some $i \in \mathbb{N}$.*

*Proof.* Let $i_0$ be an index corresponding to a shortest string $\delta_i$, so that

$$|\delta_{i_0}| \leqslant |\delta_i| \quad \text{for all } i \geqslant 0 \ .$$

Inductively, for all $k > 0$ let $i_k$ be an index corresponding to a shortest string $\delta_i$ with $i > i_{k-1}$, so that

$$i_k > i_{k-1}, \quad \text{and} \quad |\delta_{i_k}| \leqslant |\delta_i| \quad \text{for all } i \geqslant i_k \ .$$

Then we have

$$A_{i_k} \delta_{i_k} \xRightarrow[\text{lm}]{\pi_k} A_{i_{k+1}} \delta_{i_{k+1}} \quad \text{in } G \quad \text{for all } k \geqslant 0 \ ,$$

where $\pi_k$ denotes the rule string $r_{i_k} \ldots r_{i_{k+1}-1}$. Since $|\pi_k| = |i_{k+1} - i_k| > 0$, there exist strings $\alpha_k, \beta_k \in V^*$ and rule strings $\pi_k'$ and $\pi_k''$ for all $k \geqslant 0$, such that

$$\pi_k = \pi_k' \pi_k'', \quad A_{i_k} \xRightarrow[\text{lm}]{\pi_k'} \alpha_k, \quad \delta_{i_k} \xRightarrow[\text{lm}]{\pi_k''} \beta_k, \quad \alpha_k \beta_k = A_{i_{k+1}} \delta_{i_{k+1}} \ ,$$

$$|\pi_k'| > 0, \quad \text{and whenever } |\pi_k''| > 0, \text{ then } \alpha_k \in T^* \ .$$

So we have

$$A_{i_k} \delta_{i_k} \xRightarrow[\text{lm}]{\pi_k'} \alpha_k \delta_{i_k} \xRightarrow[\text{lm}]{\pi_k''} \alpha_k \beta_k = A_{i_{k+1}} \delta_{i_{k+1}} \ ,$$

where $\pi_k' \pi_k'' = \pi_k$. Here $\alpha_k \delta_{i_k} = A_j \delta_j$, where $j = i_k + |\pi_k'|$. Since $|\delta_{i_k}| \leqslant |\delta_j|$, $\alpha_k$ must be of the form $A_j \alpha_k'$, for some $\alpha_k'$. Since $\alpha_k$ therefore does not belong to $T^*$, $\pi_k''$ must be empty and hence $j = i_{k+1}$, which means that

$$A_{i_k} \xRightarrow{\pi_k'} \alpha_k = A_{i_{k+1}} \alpha_k' \quad \text{for all } k \geqslant 0 \ .$$

But then

$$A_{i_k} \Rightarrow^+ A_{i_{k+n}} \alpha_{k+n-1}' \ldots \alpha_{k+1}' \alpha_k' \quad \text{for all } k \geqslant 0 \quad \text{and} \quad n > 0 \ ,$$

so it follows that some $A_{i_k}$ is left-recursive.  $\square$

We are now in a position to prove

**Theorem 5.43** *Let $M$ be the SLL(k) parser for a grammar $G$. If some configuration is looping in $M$, then $G$ is left-recursive.*

*Proof.* If $\Phi$ is a looping configuration of $M$ then, by Fact 5.38, there is an input string $y$, an infinite sequence of strings $\gamma_0, \gamma_1, \ldots$, and an infinite sequence of actions $r_0', r_1', \ldots$ such that $\Phi \Rightarrow^* \$\gamma_0 \mathbf{I} y\$$ and $\$\gamma_i \mathbf{I} y\$ \xRightarrow{r_i'} \$\gamma_{i+1} \mathbf{I} y\$$ in $M$

for all $i \geqslant 0$. Here the actions $r_i'$ must all be produce actions, so each $\gamma_i$ is of the form $\delta_i^R A_i$, where $A_i$ is a nonterminal and $\delta_i$ is some string. Moreover, Lemma 5.27 implies that, for all $i \geqslant 0$,

$$A_i \delta_i = (\delta_i^R A_i)^R = \gamma_i^R \overset{\tau(r_i)}{\underset{\text{lm}}{\Longrightarrow}} \gamma_{i+1}^R = (\delta_{i+1}^R A_{i+1})^R = A_{i+1}\delta_{i+1} \ .$$

Since $|\tau(r_i')| = 1$, we conclude by Lemma 5.42 that $G$ must be left-recursive. $\quad\square$

Theorems 5.40 and 5.43 together yield

**Theorem 5.44** *Let $G$ be a reduced grammar and $k$ a natural number. Then $G$ is left-recursive if and only if the $SLL(k)$ parser for $G$ loops forever on some sentence in $L(G)$.* $\quad\square$

Let $M$ be a pushdown automaton with input alphabet $T$ and let $w$ be a nonsentence, i.e., a string in $T^* \backslash L(M)$. We say that $M$ *detects an error in $w$* if $M$ has a computation on $w$ that ends in an error configuration. (Recall that an error configuration is one to which no action is applicable.)

Any pushdown automaton $M$ either detects an error in a nonsentence $w$ or loops forever on $w$. (As $M$ can be nondeterministic, it may even do both.) Clearly, a practical parser should always detect an error in every nonsentence. Theorem 5.43 states that, for any non-left-recursive grammar, the $SLL(k)$ parser has this property. Thus, by Corollary 5.41, error detection is guaranteed at least when the grammar is reduced and $SLL(k)$. In fact, it turns out that a stronger result can be proved: the $SLL(k)$ parser of any grammar always detects an error in any nonsentence, regardless of whether the grammar is or is not $SLL(k)$. This result is most conveniently proved using some properties of the "viable suffixes" of the grammar (see Chapter 8).

## 5.5 Construction of Strong LL(1) Parsers

In this section we shall demonstrate how the results of Chapter 2, and in particular those of Section 2.4, can be used to derive an efficient algorithm for constructing the $SLL(k)$ parser for a given grammar. For simplicity, and because parsers with lookahead length $k > 1$ are seldom used in practice, we restrict ourselves to the case $k = 1$.

First we note

**Fact 5.45** The size of the $SLL(k)$ parser for a grammar $G = (V, T, P, S)$ is $O(k \cdot |T|^k \cdot |G|)$.

*Proof.* The length of the produce action $A\,|\,y \to \omega^R\,|\,y$ is at most $|A\omega| + 2k + 2$, and there are at most $|T|^k \cdot |P|$ distinct produce actions. $\quad\square$

Let $G=(V, T, P, S)$ be a grammar and let **begins, ends, adjoins** and **terminal** be relations on $V^*$ defined by

$X$ **begins** $A$ if $G$ has a rule $A \to \alpha X \beta$, where $\alpha \Rightarrow^* \varepsilon$ ,

$X$ **ends** $A$ if $G$ has a rule $A \to \alpha X \beta$, where $\beta \Rightarrow^* \varepsilon$ ,

$X$ **adjoins** $Y$ if $G$ has a rule $A \to \alpha X \gamma Y \beta$, where $\gamma \Rightarrow^* \varepsilon$ ,

$X$ **terminal** $Y$ if $Y$ is a terminal in $T$ and $X = Y$ .

In Chapter 4 we showed that the nullable nonterminals in any grammar $G$ can be found in time $O(|G|)$ (see Theorem 4.14). We therefore have

**Lemma 5.46** *The following statements hold for all grammars* $G$:

(1) *The relations* **begins, ends** *and* **terminal** *for* $G$ *are of size* $O(|G|)$ *and can be computed from* $G$ *in time* $O(|G|)$.

(2) *The relation* **adjoins** *for* $G$ *is of size* $O(|G|^2)$ *and can be computed from* $G$ *in time* $O(|G|^2)$.

(3) *If* $G$ *is* $\varepsilon$-free, *the relation* **adjoins** *is of size* $O(|G|)$ *and can be computed from* $G$ *in time* $O(|G|)$.

$\square$

First we shall show how the sets $\mathrm{FIRST}_1(X)$ and $\mathrm{FOLLOW}_1(A)$ are obtained via the relations **begins, ends, adjoins** and **terminal**.

**Lemma 5.47** *Let* $G=(V, T, P, S)$ *be a grammar. Then the following implications hold for all symbols* $X, Y \in V$ *and natural numbers* $n$:

(1)  $Y$ **begins**$^n$ $X$ *implies* $X \underset{\mathrm{lm}}{\Rightarrow}^m Y\beta$ *for some* $\beta \in V^*$ *and* $m \geqslant n$.

(2)  $X \Rightarrow^n Y\beta$ *implies* $Y$ **begins**$^m X$ *for some* $m \leqslant n$.

(3)  $Y$ **ends**$^n X$ *implies* $X \underset{\mathrm{rm}}{\Rightarrow}^m \alpha Y$ *for some* $\alpha \in V^*$ *and* $m \geqslant n$.

(4)  $X \Rightarrow^n \alpha Y$ *implies* $Y$ **ends**$^m X$ *for some* $m \leqslant n$.

*Proof.* Four simple inductions on $n$. We leave the details for the exercises.    $\square$

In order to compute the $\mathrm{FIRST}_1$ sets we define a relational expression **first-of** = **terminal begins***.

**Lemma 5.48** *Let* $G=(V, T, P, S)$ *be a grammar. Then for all symbols* $a, X \in V$, $a \in \mathrm{FIRST}_1(X)$ *implies* $a$ **first-of** $X$. *Moreover, if* $G$ *is reduced then the converse also holds.*

*Proof.* By definition, $a \in \mathrm{FIRST}_1(X)$ if and only if $a$ is a terminal in $T$ and $X \Rightarrow^* ay$ for some string $y \in T^*$. Thus, by Lemma 5.47, $a \in \mathrm{FIRST}_1(X)$ implies $a$ **first-of** $X$.

Conversely, if $a$ **first-of** $X$, then $a$ is a terminal and, by Lemma 5.47, $X \Rightarrow^* a\beta$ for some $\beta \in V^*$. If $G$ is reduced, then $\beta$ derives some $y \in T^*$, so $a \in \mathrm{FIRST}_1(X)$ as claimed. $\square$

**Theorem 5.49** *Given any reduced grammar* $G = (V, T, P, S)$ *and symbol* $X \in V$, *the set* $FIRST_1(X)$ *can be computed in time* $O(|G|)$. *Moreover, the collection of all sets* $FIRST_1(X)$, *for* $X \in V$, *can be computed in time* $O(|T| \cdot |G|)$.

*Proof.* By Lemma 5.48, the set $\mathrm{FIRST}_1(X) \setminus \{\varepsilon\}$ is obtained as the image of $\{X\}$ under the relation denoted by the relational expression **first-of**$^{-1}$. By Lemma 5.46 and Theorem 2.28, this image can be computed in time $O(|G|)$. On the other hand, by Theorem 4.14, the set of nullable symbols in $V$ can be computed in time $O(|G|)$. Thus the set $\mathrm{FIRST}_1(X)$ can be computed in time $O(|G|)$. Theorem 2.29 in turn implies that the whole relation denoted by **first-of**$^{-1}$ can be computed in time $O(|T| \cdot |G|)$. Note that $T$ is the range of the expression. This means that the collection of all sets $\mathrm{FIRST}_1(X) \setminus \{\varepsilon\}$, and hence all sets $\mathrm{FIRST}_1(X)$, can be computed in time $O(|T| \cdot |G|)$. $\square$

In order to compute $\mathrm{FOLLOW}_1(X)$, we define a relational expression **follows** $=$ **first-of adjoins**$^{-1}$ (**ends**$^{-1}$)*. Note that here **first-of** denotes a subexpression rather than its value, so that **follows** is actually the expression

$$\textbf{terminal begins* adjoins}^{-1}\ (\textbf{ends}^{-1})*\ .$$

We shall show that, in a reduced grammar, a terminal $a$ belongs to $\mathrm{FOLLOW}_1(X)$ if and only if $a$ **follows** $X$. For this we need the following lemma, which is illustrated in Figure 5.1.

**Lemma 5.50** *Let* $G = (V, T, P, S)$ *be a grammar. Further, let* $A$ *be a nonterminal,* $X$ *and* $Y$ *symbols in* $V$, $\gamma$, $\psi$ *and* $\delta$ *strings in* $.V^*$, *and* $\pi$ *a rule string in* $P^*$ *such that*

$$(a)\quad A \overset{\pi}{\Longrightarrow} \gamma X \psi Y \delta \quad and \quad \psi \Rightarrow^* \varepsilon \quad in\ G\ .$$

*Then there are symbols* $X', Y' \in V$, *a rule* $r' = B \to \alpha X' \psi' Y' \beta$ *in* $P$, *and strings* $\gamma', \delta', \alpha', \beta' \in V^*$ *such that*

$$A \overset{\pi'}{\Longrightarrow} \gamma' B \delta' \overset{r'}{\Longrightarrow} \gamma' \alpha X' \psi' Y' \beta \delta'\ ,$$
$$(b)$$
$$X' \underset{rm}{\Longrightarrow}^* \alpha' X, \quad \psi' \Rightarrow^* \varepsilon, \quad and \quad Y' \underset{lm}{\Longrightarrow}^* Y \beta' \quad in\ G\ ,$$

*where* $\pi' r'$ *is a prefix of* $\pi$. *In other words, in the derivation of* $\gamma X \psi Y \delta$ *from* $A$ *there is a step showing that* $X$ *and* $Y$ *"originate" from a pair of adjoining symbols in the right-hand side of the same rule.*

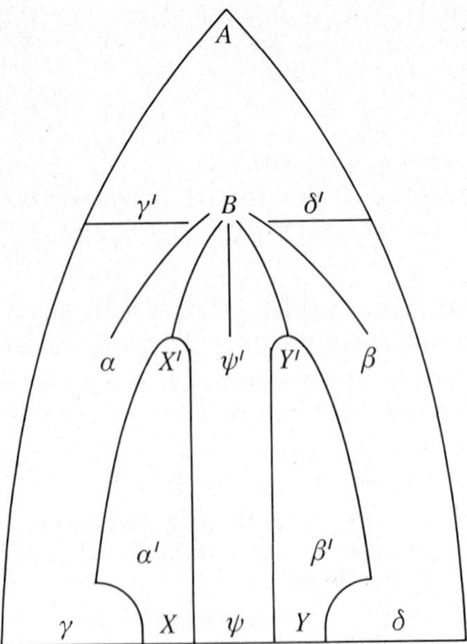

**Figure 5.1** A derivation tree ilustrating Lemma 5.50. Here $X'$ **adjoins** $Y'$, $X$ **ends*** $X'$, and $Y$ **begins*** $Y'$

*Proof.* The proof is by induction on the length of the rule string $\pi$. The base case $|\pi|=1$ is trivial, because then we can choose $X'=X$, $Y'=Y$, $r'=\pi=A\rightarrow\gamma X\psi Y\delta$, $\pi'=\varepsilon$, $\gamma'=\delta'=\alpha'=\beta'=\varepsilon$ and $\psi'=\psi$.

To prove the induction step, we assume that $\pi$ is of the form $\pi_1 r$, where $r$ is a rule $A_1\rightarrow\omega_1$ and $\pi_1$ is a rule string of length at least one. As an induction hypothesis, we assume that the lemma holds for $\pi_1$. We have

$$A \overset{\pi_1}{\Longrightarrow} \gamma_1 A_1 \delta_1 \overset{r}{\Longrightarrow} \gamma_1 \omega_1 \delta_1 = \gamma X\psi Y\delta$$

for some $\gamma_1$ and $\delta_1$. We have to consider six cases:

*Case 1:* $\omega_1$ is contained in $\gamma$, i.e., for some $\delta_1, \delta_1''$,

$$\gamma_1\omega_1\delta_1=\gamma_1\omega_1\delta_1'\delta_1''=\gamma\delta_1''=\gamma X\psi Y\delta .$$

Then $\gamma_1 A_1\delta_1=\gamma_1 A_1\delta_1' X\psi Y\delta$, and the claim follows directly from the induction hypothesis.

*Case 2:* $\omega_1$ contains $X$ but not $Y$, i.e., for some $\alpha', \psi', \psi''$,

$$\gamma_1\omega_1\delta_1=\gamma_1\alpha' X\psi'\delta_1=\gamma X\psi'\delta_1=\gamma X\psi'\psi'' Y\delta=\gamma X\psi Y\delta .$$

Then $\gamma_1 A_1\delta_1=\gamma_1 A_1\psi'' Y\delta$, where $\psi''\Rightarrow^* \varepsilon$ and $A_1 \underset{rm}{\Longrightarrow} \omega_1 = \alpha' X\psi' \underset{rm}{\Longrightarrow}^* \alpha' X$. (Note that $\psi' \Rightarrow^* \varepsilon$ implies, by Theorem 4.2, that $\psi' \underset{\mathrm{rm}}{\Rightarrow}{}^* \varepsilon$.) The claim follows by applying the induction hypothesis to the symbols $A_1$ and $Y$.

*Case 3:* $\omega_1$ is contained in $\psi$, i.e., for some $\psi', \psi''$,

$$\gamma_1 \omega_1 \delta_1 = \gamma X \psi' \omega_1 \delta_1 = \gamma X \psi' \omega_1 \psi'' Y\delta = \gamma X \psi Y\delta \ .$$

Then $\gamma_1 A_1 \delta_1 = \gamma X \psi' A_1 \psi'' Y\delta$, where $\psi' A_1 \psi'' \Rightarrow^* \varepsilon$. The claim follows from the induction hypothesis.

*Case 4:* $\omega_1$ contains $Y$ but not $X$, i.e., for some $\beta', \psi', \psi''$,

$$\gamma_1 \omega_1 \delta_1 = \gamma_1 \psi'' Y\beta' \delta_1 = \gamma_1 \psi'' Y\delta = \gamma X \psi' \psi'' Y\delta = \gamma X \psi Y\delta \ .$$

Then $\gamma_1 A_1 \delta_1 = \gamma X \psi' A_1 \delta_1$, where $\psi' \Rightarrow^* \varepsilon$ and $A_1 \underset{\mathrm{lm}}{\Rightarrow} \omega_1 = \psi'' Y\beta' \underset{\mathrm{lm}}{\Rightarrow}{}^* Y\beta'$. (Note that $\psi'' \Rightarrow^* \varepsilon$ implies $\psi'' \underset{\mathrm{lm}}{\Rightarrow}{}^* \varepsilon$.) The claim follows by applying the induction hypothesis to the symbols $X$ and $A_1$.

*Case 5:* $\omega_1$ is contained in $\delta$, i.e., for some $\gamma_1', \gamma_1''$,

$$\gamma_1 \omega_1 \delta_1 = \gamma_1' \gamma_1'' \omega_1 \delta_1 = \gamma_1' \delta = \gamma X \psi Y\delta \ .$$

Then $\gamma_1 A_1 \delta_1 = \gamma X \psi Y\gamma_1'' A_1 \delta_1$, and the claim follows directly from the induction hypothesis.

*Case 6:* $\omega_1$ contains both $X$ and $Y$, i.e., for some $\alpha, \beta$,

$$\gamma_1 \omega_1 \delta_1 = \gamma_1 \alpha X \psi Y\beta \delta_1 = \gamma X \psi Y\beta \delta_1 = \gamma X \psi Y\delta \ .$$

Statements (b) then hold if we choose $X' = X$, $Y' = Y$, $r' = r$, $\gamma' = \gamma_1$, $\delta' = \delta_1$, $\alpha' = \beta' = \varepsilon$, and $\pi' = \pi_1$.   $\square$

We are now able to prove

**Lemma 5.51** *Let $G = (V, T, P, S)$ be a grammar. Then for all symbols $a$, $X \in V$, $a \in FOLLOW_1(X)$ implies $a$ **follows** $X$. Moreover, if $G$ is reduced then the converse also holds.*

*Proof.* First we note that, by Lemma 5.47, the statement

$$X \textbf{ ends* } X' \textbf{ adjoins } Y' \ (\textbf{terminal begins*})^{-1} \, a \tag{5.29}$$

is always logically equivalent to

$$\begin{cases} a \in T, \text{ and for some } B, \alpha, \psi', \beta, \alpha', \beta' \ , \\ B \to \alpha X' \psi' Y' \beta \in P, \ X' \Rightarrow^* \alpha' X, \ \psi' \Rightarrow^* \varepsilon \ , \\ \text{and } Y' \Rightarrow^* a\beta' \ . \end{cases} \tag{5.30}$$

On the other hand, the terminal $a$ belongs to $\text{FOLLOW}_1(X)$ if and only if

$$S \Rightarrow^* \gamma X a y \text{ for some } \gamma \in V^* \text{ and } y \in T^* . \tag{5.31}$$

Now if (5.31) is true for the terminal $a$, Lemma 5.50 implies that (5.30) is true for some symbols $X'$ and $Y'$. As (5.30) is equivalent to (5.29), we conclude that $a \in \text{FOLLOW}_1(X)$ implies $a$ **follows** $X$. Conversely, if (5.29) holds for some symbols $X'$ and $Y'$, then (5.30) holds for $X'$ and $Y'$. If $G$ is reduced, (5.30) implies that $S$ derives $\gamma' B\delta$ for some $\gamma'$, $\delta \in V^*$, and $\beta' \beta\delta$ derives some $y \in T^*$. Then

$$S \Rightarrow^* \gamma' B\delta \Rightarrow \gamma' \alpha X' \psi' Y' \beta\delta \Rightarrow^* \gamma' \alpha\alpha' X a\beta' \beta\delta \Rightarrow^* \gamma' \alpha\alpha' X a y , \tag{5.32}$$

which means that (5.31) holds, and hence $a \in \text{FOLLOW}_1(X)$.   $\square$

Using the result of Lemma 5.51, we obtain an algorithm for computing the set $\text{FOLLOW}_1(X)$ for a given symbol $X$ in a grammar $G$. Unfortunately, the time complexity of this algorithm is not linear in $|G|$ if we make explicit use of the relation **adjoins**, because then the size of the relational expression given in Lemma 5.51 is $O(|G|^2)$ and not $O(|G|)$. However, it turns out that there exists a relational expression of size $O(|G|)$ which denotes **adjoins**, so that a linear time-bounded algorithm is obtained.

Let $G = (V, T, P, S)$ be a grammar and let the dot ($\bullet$) be a new symbol not found in $V$. We call any rule of the form $A \rightarrow \alpha \bullet \beta$, where $A \rightarrow \alpha\beta$ is a rule in $P$, a *position* (or an *item core*) of $G$.

The following observation is important.

**Fact 5.52** The number of distinct positions of a grammar $G = (V, T, P, S)$ cannot exceed $|G|$. Moreover, if each symbol in $V$ appears in some rule in $P$, then the number of distinct positions of $G$ is equal to $|G|$.   $\square$

For a grammar $G = (V, T, P, S)$, let **points**, **passes-any**, and **passes-null** be relations on $V \cup \{r \mid r \text{ is a position of } G\}$ defined by

(a) $A \rightarrow \alpha \bullet X\beta$ **points** $X$.
(b) $A \rightarrow \alpha \bullet X\beta$ **passes-any** $A \rightarrow \alpha X \bullet \beta$.
(c) $A \rightarrow \alpha \bullet X\beta$ **passes-null** $A \rightarrow \alpha X \bullet \beta$, if $X \Rightarrow^* \varepsilon$.

In each case, $A \rightarrow \alpha X\beta$ is a rule in $P$ and $X$ is a symbol in $V$. Each relation is of size $O(|G|)$ and can be computed from $G$ in time $O(|G|)$.

Now $X$ **adjoins** $Y$ if and only if there is a rule $A \rightarrow \alpha X\gamma Y\beta$ in $P$ such that

$$X \textbf{ points}^{-1} A \rightarrow \alpha \bullet X\gamma Y\beta \textbf{ passes-any } A \rightarrow \alpha X \bullet \gamma Y\beta \textbf{ passes-null*}$$
$$A \rightarrow \alpha X\gamma \bullet Y\beta \textbf{ points } Y .$$

We therefore have

**Lemma 5.53** *In any grammar G,*

$$\textbf{points}^{-1}\ \textbf{passes-any passes-null*}\ \textbf{points} = \textbf{adjoins.}\quad \square$$

In other words, the relation **adjoins** for $G$ is the value of the relational expression **points**$^{-1}$ **passes-any passes-null* points**, which is of size $O(|G|)$.

From now on, we assume that wherever **adjoins** appears it stands for the expression and not its value. Accordingly, we take **follows** to be the expression

$$\textbf{terminal begins*}\ (\textbf{points}^{-1}\ \textbf{passes-any passes-null*}\ \textbf{points})^{-1}\ (\textbf{ends}^{-1})^*\ .$$

**Theorem 5.54** *Given any reduced grammar $G = (V, T, P, S)$ and symbol $X \in V$, the set $FOLLOW_1(X)$ can be computed in time $O(|G|)$. Moreover, the collection of all sets $FOLLOW_1(X)$, for $X \in V$, can be computed in time $O(|T| \cdot |G|)$.*

*Proof.* By Lemmas 5.51 and 5.53, the set $FOLLOW_1(X) \setminus \{\varepsilon\}$ is obtained as the image **follows**$^{-1}(X)$. The relational expression **follows**$^{-1}$ is of size $O(|G|)$ and has range $T$. From Theorem 2.28 we conclude that the set $FOLLOW_1(X) \setminus \{\varepsilon\}$ can be computed in time $O(|G|)$. By Theorem 2.29, we see that the collection of all sets $FOLLOW_1(X) \setminus \{\varepsilon\}$, $X \in V$, can be computed in time $O(|T| \cdot |G|)$. To compute the sets $FOLLOW_1(X)$, we use the fact that the empty string $\varepsilon$ belongs to $FOLLOW_1(X)$ if and only if $X$ **ends*** $S$ (see Lemma 5.47). By Theorem 2.28, the image **ends***$(S)$ can be computed in time $O(|G|)$.   $\square$

We now consider the construction of the actions of the SLL(1) parser for a reduced grammar $G = (V, T, P, S)$. First we note that the shift actions are trivial to construct; the time needed is $O(|T|)$. In order to construct the produce actions we need, for each rule $A \to \omega$ in $P$, the set

$$FIRST'_1(\omega FOLLOW'_1(A))$$

of all lookahead symbols for produce actions for $A \to \omega$. Here $FIRST'_1$ and $FOLLOW'_1$ denote the $FIRST_1$ and $FOLLOW_1$ functions of the \$-augmented grammar $G'$ for $G$.

One way to determine the lookahead sets involves precomputing the sets $FIRST'_1(X)$ and $FOLLOW'_1(X)$ for all symbols $X$ in the \$-augmented grammar $G'$. Assume $\omega = X_1 \ldots X_n$, where $X_1, \ldots, X_n$ $(n \geqslant 0)$ are single symbols. If, for some $i < n$, $X_1, \ldots, X_i$ are nullable but $X_{i+1}$ is not, then $FIRST'_1(\omega FOLLOW'_1(A))$ is obtained as the union of the sets $FIRST'_1(X_1) \setminus \{\varepsilon\}, \ldots, FIRST'_1(X_i) \setminus \{\varepsilon\}$, and $FIRST'_1(X_{i+1})$. If all the symbols $X_1, \ldots, X_n$ are nullable, then $FIRST'_1(\omega FOLLOW'_1(A))$ is obtained as the union of the sets $FIRST'_1(X) \setminus \{\varepsilon\}, \ldots,$ $FIRST'_1(X_n) \setminus \{\varepsilon\}$, and $FOLLOW'_1(A) \setminus \{\varepsilon\}$. Once the sets $FIRST'_1(X)$ and $FOLLOW'_1(X)$ have been computed for all $X \in V$ (and the set of nullable symbols has been determined), the time needed to compute a single set $FIRST'_1(\omega FOLLOW'_1(A))$ is $O(|\omega| \cdot |T|)$, and hence the time needed to determine all lookahead sets $FIRST'_1(\omega FOLLOW'_1(A))$, for $A \to \omega$ in $P$, is $O(|G| \cdot |T|)$. From Theorems 5.49 and 5.54, it follows that the total time needed to construct the actions of the SLL(1) parser for $G$ is $O(|T| \cdot |G|)$.

Following the approach usually taken in practice, we assume that the scanner is organized as a subroutine of the parser and that it operates incrementally, producing one token at a time. The parser calls the scanner whenever the current input symbol has been shifted and a new one must be determined. A call *scan* in the parser causes the next token to be extracted from the input string and stored in a global variable *token*. This has two fields, corresponding to the components of the pairs $(x, m)$. The field denoted by *token.kind* contains $m$, the token class name of the token, while the other field (not considered here) contains $x$, the actual character string of the token.

Now we are ready to describe the schemes for generating the parsing program for a grammar. First we consider the *stack implemention*: the schemes for program generation are shown in Figures 5.2 to 5.4, and an example is given in Figure 5.5.

```
empty;
push(eof-token);
push(S);
scan;
repeat
      pop(symbol);
      case symbol of
            X₁: parse(X₁);
            X₂: parse(X₂);
                  ⋮
            Xₙ: parse(Xₙ)
      end
until isempty;
```

**Figure 5.2** Program scheme for the stack implementation of the SLL(1) parser. The set $\{X_1, \ldots, X_n\}$ consists of all symbols of the grammar, including *eof-token* (i.e., \$). The contents of the program segments "*parse(X_i)*" are shown in Figure 5.3 (for nonterminal $X_i$) and Figure 5.4 (for terminal or end marker $X_i$)

```
parse(A)=
      if token.kind in FIRST'₁(X₁₁ ... X₁ₙ₁ FOLLOW'₁(A)) then
      begin
            write "A→X₁₁ ... X₁ₙ₁";
            push(X₁ₙ₁); ... ; push(X₁₁)
      end else
      if token.kind in FIRST'₁(X₂₁ ... X₂ₙ, FOLLOW'₁(A)) then
      begin
            write "A→X₂₁ ... X₂ₙ₂";
            push(X₂ₙ₂); ... ; push(X₂₁)
      end else
            ⋮
      if token.kind in FIRST'₁(Xₘ₁ ... Xₘₙₘ FOLLOW'₁(A)) then
      begin
            write "A→Xₘ₁ ... Xₘₙₘ";
            push(Xₘₙₘ); ... ; push(Xₘ₁)
      end else
            error ("No A can start with this.")
```

**Figure 5.3** Parsing program for a nonterminal $A$ in the stack implementation of the SLL(1) parser. The rules of $A$ are

$$A \to X_{11} \ldots X_{1n_1} \,|\, X_{21} \ldots X_{2n_2} \,|\, \ldots \,|\, X_{m1} \ldots X_{mn_m}$$

```
parse(a) =
    if token.kind = a then
        scan
    else
        error ("a expected.")

parse(eof-token) =
    if token.kind ≠ eof-token then
        error ("End-of-input expected.")
```

**Figure 5.4** Parsing programs for a terminal $a$ and the end marker $ (*eof-token*) in the stack implementation of the SLL(1) parser

```
parse(S) =
        if token.kind in {a-token, begin-keyword} then
        begin
            write "S→B";
            push(B)
        end else
        if token.kind in {end-keyword, semicolon,
        eof-token} then begin
            write "S→E";
            push(E)
        end else
            error ("No S can start with this.")

parse(E) =
        if token.kind in {end-keyword, semicolon,
        eof-token} then begin
            write "E→ε";
        end else
            error ("No E can start with this.")

parse(B) =
        if token.kind in {a-token} then begin
            write "B→a";
            push (a-token)
        end else
        if token.kind in {begin-keyword} then begin
            write "B→begin S C end";
            push(end-keyword); push(C); push(S);
            push(begin-keyword)
        end else
            error ("No B can start with this.")

parse(C) =
        if token.kind in {end-keyword} then begin
            write "C→ε";
        end else
        if token.kind in {semicolon} then begin
            write "C→; S C";
            push(C); push(S); push(semicolon)
        end else
            error ("No C can start with this.")
```

**Figure 5.5** Parsing programs for nonterminals in the stack implementation of the SLL(1) parser for the grammar $G_{block}$, which has the rules $S→E\,|\,B$, $E→ε$, $B→a\,|\,$**begin** $S\,C\,$**end**, and $C→ε\,|\,;\,S\,C$

The stack implementation involves a stack that can contain any symbol of the grammar, including the end marker $ (*eof-token*). The stack is operated using the operations *empty, push, pop,* and *isempty*. The operation *empty* initializes the stack to empty. The operation *push(X)* pushes symbol $X$ onto the stack, while *pop(symbol)* pops the topmost symbol off the stack and stores it in the variable *symbol*. The operation *isempty* returns true if the stack is empty, and false otherwise. Initially the symbols $ and $S$ (in this order) are pushed onto the stack.

The effects of the actions of the SLL(1) parser are simulated in the obvious way. To determine which action to apply next, the topmost symbol is popped off the stack. If the popped symbol is a terminal $a$, the effect of the shift action

$$a \mid a \rightarrow \mid$$

is obtained by comparing the popped terminal with the current input symbol and, if they are equal, scanning the next token. If on the contrary the popped symbol is a nonterminal $A$, then the appropriate produce action

$$A \mid a \rightarrow \omega^R \mid a$$

is selected by examining the current input symbol. The symbols in the right-hand side $\omega$ are then pushed onto the stack in reverse order.

The simulation continues until one of the following happens: (1) the stack is empty and the current input symbol is $; (2) the stack is empty but the current input symbol is not $; (3) the stack is nonempty but no action is applicable. In case (1) the parser accepts its input. In cases (2) and (3) an *error handling procedure, error,* is called with an appropriate error message as a parameter. The call *error(m)* writes the message $m$ and terminates the processing (or, preferably, performs some recovery action so as to allow parsing to continue; see the exercises).

In the *recursive descent implementation* of the SLL(1) parser no explicit use is made of a stack. Instead, the parsing program is divided up into a set of *parsing procedures,* which can call each other recursively. An implicit stack of activation records needed to implement the parsing procedures then corresponds to the explicit stack of grammar symbols.

For each nonterminal $A$ of the grammar, there is a parsing procedure also called $A$. Schemes for generating this procedure are given in Figures 5.6 and 5.7. The task of procedure $A$ is to parse the sentences derived by the grammar $(V, T, P, A)$ obtained from $G$ by regarding $A$ as the start symbol. Procedure $A$ is called whenever the current input symbol should start a sentence in the language $L(A)$. Procedure $A$ parses this sentence and then returns control to the calling procedure. Upon return from $A$, scanning of the input has advanced so that the current input symbol should now be a legal follower of $A$.

The main program for the parser consists of a call to $S$, the parsing procedure for the start symbol of the grammar (see Figure 5.8). This call is preceded by a scan of the first symbol in the input string. Upon return from this call to $S$, the current input symbol must be checked to see if it is the end marker (cf. the corresponding check in the stack implementation of the SLL(1) parser).

The parsing procedures for the nonterminals of $G_{block}$ are shown in Figure 5.9.

**procedure** $A$;
**begin**
      **if** *token.kind* **in** $\text{FIRST}'_1(\omega_1\text{FOLLOW}'_1(A))$ **then begin**
          write "$A\rightarrow\omega_1$";
          *parse*$(\omega_1)$
      **end else**
      **if** *token.kind* **in** $\text{FIRST}'_1(\omega_2\text{FOLLOW}'_1(A))$ **then begin**
          write "$A\rightarrow\omega_2$";
          *parse*$(\omega_2)$
      **end else**
          $\vdots$
      **if** *token.kind* **in** $\text{FIRST}'_1(\omega_n\text{FOLLOW}'_1(A))$ **then begin**
          write "$A\rightarrow\omega_n$";
          *parse*$(\omega_n)$
      **end else**
          *error*("No $A$ can start with this.")
**end**;

**Figure 5.6** Parsing procedure for a nonterminal $A$ in the recursive descent implementation of the SLL(1) parser. The rules of $A$ are $A\rightarrow\omega_1|\omega_2|\ldots|\omega_n$. The contents of the program segments "*parse*$(\omega_i)$" are shown in Figure 5.7

*parse*$(a\beta)=$
    *scan*;
    *check*$(\beta)$

*parse*$(A\beta)=$
    $A$;
    *check*$(\beta)$

*check*$(a\beta)=$
    **if** *token.kind*$=a$ **then**
        *scan*
    **else**
        *error*("$a$ expected.");
    *check*$(\beta)$

*check*$(A\beta)=$
    *parse*$(A\beta)$

*parse*$(\varepsilon)=check(\varepsilon)=\varepsilon$

**Figure 5.7** Parsing programs for suffixes of right-hand sides in the recursive descent implementation of the SLL(1) parser. Here $a$ is a terminal, $A$ is a nonterminal, and $\beta$ is a string in $V^*$. The equations define the meaning of "*parse*$(\gamma)$" and "*check*$(\gamma)$" inductively on the length of string $\gamma\in V^*$

*scan*;
$S$;
**if** *token.kind* $\neq$ *eof-token* **then**
    *error*("End-of-input expected.");

**Figure 5.8** Main program for the recursive descent implementation of the SLL(1) parser. Here $S$ is the parsing procedure for the start symbol of the grammar

```
procedure S;
begin
        if token.kind in {a-token, begin-keyword} then
        begin
            write "S→B";
            B;
        end else
        if token.kind in {end-keyword, semicolon,
        eof-token} then begin
            write "S→E";
            E;
        end else
            error("No S can start with this.")
end;

procedure E;
begin
        if token.kind in {end-keyword, semicolon,
        eof-token} then begin
            write "E→ε";
        end else
            error("No E can start with this.")
end;

procedure B;
begin
        if token.kind in {a-token} then begin
            write "B→a";
            scan;
        end else
        if token.kind in {begin-keyword} then begin
            write "B→begin S C end";
            scan;
            S;
            C;
            if token.kind = end-keyword then
                scan
            else
                error("end-keyword expected.");
        end else
            error("No B can start with this.")
end;

procedure C;
begin
        if token.kind in {end-keyword} then begin
            write "C→ε";
        end else
        if token.kind in {semicolon} then begin
            write "C→; S C";
            scan;
            S;
            C;
        end else
            error("No C can start with this.")
end;
```

**Figure 5.9** Parsing procedures for nonterminals in the recursive descent implementation of the SLL(1) parser for $G_{block}$

## 5.7 Simple Precedence Parsing

In this section we shall discuss briefly the problem of making shift-reduce parsers deterministic. As for SLL(1) parsers, we add a one-symbol lookahead to the actions. Besides this, we add a one-symbol "lookback" into the stack. The lookahead and lookback symbols are determined via certain "precedence relations" on the alphabet of the grammar. The resulting parser is called a "simple precedence parser". The parser can only be constructed for $\varepsilon$-free grammars, and a deterministic parser is obtained for a subclass of $\varepsilon$-free grammars called "simple precedence grammars".

Let $G=(V, T, P, S)$ be an $\varepsilon$-free grammar and let **begins, ends, adjoins** and **terminal** be relations as defined in Section 5.5. The (*Wirth-Weber*) *precedence relations* for $G$, denoted by $\doteq$, $<$, $>$, are relations on $V$ defined by

$$\doteq \;=\; \textbf{adjoins} \;,$$
$$< \;=\; \textbf{adjoins } (\textbf{begins}^+)^{-1} \;,$$
$$> \;=\; \textbf{ends}^+ \textbf{ adjoins } (\textbf{begins}^*)^{-1} \textbf{ terminal} \;.$$

The union $\doteq \cup <$ is often denoted by $\lessdot$.

By Lemma 5.46 and Theorem 2.29 we have

**Theorem 5.57** *Given any $\varepsilon$-free grammar $G=(V, T, P, S)$, the precedence relations for $G$ can be computed in time $O(|V| \cdot |G|)$.*  $\square$

From the definitions of **begins, ends, adjoins** and **terminal**, and Lemma 5.47, we have

**Lemma 5.58** *Let $\doteq$, $<$, and $>$ be the precedence relations for an $\varepsilon$-free grammar $G$. Then for all symbols $X$ and $Y$ of $G$,*

(1) $X \doteq Y$ *if and only if $G$ has a rule $A \to \alpha X Y \beta$.*

(2) $X < Y$ *if and only if $G$ has a rule $A \to \alpha X Y' \beta$, where $Y' \underset{\text{lm}}{\Longrightarrow}^+ Y\delta$ for some string $\delta$.*

(3) $X \lessdot Y$ *if and only if $G$ has a rule $A \to \alpha X Y' \beta$, where $Y' \underset{\text{lm}}{\Longrightarrow}^* Y\delta$ for some string $\delta$.*

(4) $X > Y$ *if and only if $Y$ is a terminal of $G$ and $G$ has a rule $A \to \alpha X' Y' \beta$, where $X' \underset{\text{rm}}{\Longrightarrow}^+ \gamma X$ and $Y' \underset{\text{lm}}{\Longrightarrow}^* Y\delta$ for some strings $\gamma$ and $\delta$.*

$\square$

As an example, consider the grammar $G_{\text{dblock}}$, which has the following rules:

$$S \to a \mid \textbf{begin } D \; L \; \textbf{end} \;,$$
$$D \to d \;,$$
$$L \to ; S \mid L ; S \;.$$

In the $-augmented grammar for $G_{dblock}$ we have

$$\$ \doteq S \doteq \$ \ ,$$
$$\textbf{begin} \doteq D \doteq L \doteq \textbf{end} \ ,$$
$$L \doteq ; \ \doteq S \ ,$$
$$\$ \lessdot a \ , \ \$ \lessdot \textbf{begin} \ ,$$
$$\textbf{begin} \lessdot d \ ,$$
$$D \lessdot ; \, , \ D \lessdot L \ ,$$
$$; \ \lessdot a, \ ; \ \lessdot \textbf{begin} \ ,$$
$$d \gtrdot ; \, ,$$
$$S \gtrdot \textbf{end}, \ a \gtrdot \textbf{end}, \ \textbf{end} \gtrdot \textbf{end} \ ,$$
$$S \gtrdot ; \, , \ a \gtrdot ; \, , \ \textbf{end} \gtrdot ; \, ,$$
$$a \gtrdot \$, \ \textbf{end} \gtrdot \$ \ .$$

Let $G = (V, T, P, S)$ be an $\varepsilon$-free grammar and $\doteq, \ \lessdot, \ \gtrdot$ the precedence relations for the $-augmented grammar $G'$ for $G$. The *simple precedence parser* for $G$ is the pushdown transducer with stack alphabet $V$, input alphabet $T$, initial stack contents $\varepsilon$, set of final stack contents $\{S\}$, and set of actions consisting of all rules of the forms

(ra) $X\omega|a \rightarrow XA|a$        "reduce by $A \rightarrow \omega$ on
                                    lookback $X$ and lookahead $a$" ,

(sa) $Y|b \rightarrow Yb|$            "shift $b$ on lookback $Y$" .

Here $A \rightarrow \omega$ is a rule in $P$, $X$ and $Y$ are symbols in $V \cup \{\$\}$, $a$ is a terminal in $T \cup \{\$\}$, and $b$ is a terminal in $T$ such that

$$X \lessdot 1:\omega, \quad \omega:1 \gtrdot a, \quad \text{and} \quad Y \lesseqgtr b \ .$$

The output effect $\tau$ is defined by

(1) $\tau(X\omega|a \rightarrow XA|a) = A \rightarrow \omega$ .
(2) $\tau(Y|b \rightarrow Yb|) = \varepsilon$ .

Theorem 5.57 implies


**Theorem 5.59** *Given any $\varepsilon$-free grammar $G = (V, T, P, S)$, the simple precedence parser for $G$ is of size $O(|V| \cdot |T| \cdot |G|)$ and can be constructed from $G$ in time $O(|V| \cdot |T| \cdot |G|)$.* $\square$

The simple precedence parser for $G_{dblock}$ has the following reduce actions

$$\$ \, a|\textbf{end} \rightarrow \$ \, S|\textbf{end} \ ,$$
$$\$ \, a|; \rightarrow \$ \, S|; \ ,$$
$$\$ \, a|\$ \rightarrow \$ \, S|\$ \ ,$$
$$; \, a|\textbf{end} \rightarrow ; \, S|\textbf{end} \ ,$$

$$; a \textbf{I} ; \rightarrow ; S \textbf{I} ; \ ,$$
$$; a \textbf{I} \$ \rightarrow ; S \textbf{I} \$ \ ,$$
$$\$\,\textbf{begin}\ D\ L\ \textbf{end}\ \textbf{I}\ \textbf{end} \rightarrow \$\,S\,\textbf{I}\,\textbf{end}\ ,$$
$$\$\,\textbf{begin}\ D\ L\ \textbf{end}\ \textbf{I}\,; \rightarrow \$\,S\,\textbf{I};\ ,$$
$$\$\,\textbf{begin}\ D\ L\ \textbf{end}\ \textbf{I}\,\$ \rightarrow \$\,S\,\textbf{I}\,\$\ ,$$
$$; \textbf{begin}\ D\ L\ \textbf{end}\ \textbf{I}\ \textbf{end} \rightarrow ; S\,\textbf{I}\,\textbf{end}\ ,$$
$$; \textbf{begin}\ D\ L\ \textbf{end}\ \textbf{I}\,; \rightarrow ; S\,\textbf{I};\ ,$$
$$; \textbf{begin}\ D\ L\ \textbf{end}\ \textbf{I}\,\$ \rightarrow ; S\,\textbf{I}\,\$\ ,$$
$$\textbf{begin}\ d\ \textbf{I}\,; \rightarrow \textbf{begin}\ D\ \textbf{I};\ ,$$
$$D\ ;\ S\ \textbf{I}\ \textbf{end} \rightarrow D\ L\ \textbf{I}\ \textbf{end}\ ,$$
$$D\ ;\ S\ \textbf{I}\,; \rightarrow D\ L\ \textbf{I};\ ,$$
$$D\ L\ ;\ S\ \textbf{I}\ \textbf{end} \rightarrow D\ L\ \textbf{I}\ \textbf{end}\ ,$$
$$D\ L\ ;\ S\ \textbf{I}\,; \rightarrow D\ L\ \textbf{I};\ .$$

The shift actions are

$$\$\,\textbf{I}\,a \rightarrow \$\,a\,\textbf{I}\ ,$$
$$;\,\textbf{I}\,a \rightarrow ;\,a\,\textbf{I}\ ,$$
$$\textbf{begin}\,\textbf{I}\,d \rightarrow \textbf{begin}\ d\,\textbf{I}\ ,$$
$$\$\,\textbf{I}\,\textbf{begin} \rightarrow \$\,\textbf{begin}\,\textbf{I}\ ,$$
$$;\,\textbf{I}\,\textbf{begin} \rightarrow ;\,\textbf{begin}\,\textbf{I}\ ,$$
$$L\,\textbf{I}\,; \rightarrow L\,;\,\textbf{I}\ ,$$
$$D\,\textbf{I}\,; \rightarrow D\,;\,\textbf{I}\ ,$$
$$L\,\textbf{I}\,\textbf{end} \rightarrow L\,\textbf{end}\,\textbf{I}\ .$$

The parser is clearly deterministic in this case.

For any $\varepsilon$-free grammar $G$, the actions of the simple precedence parser are restrictions of the actions of the nondeterministic shift-reduce parser defined in Section 5.2. This means (by Fact 5.23) that we may restate Lemmas 5.17 and 5.18 for simple precedence parsers.

**Lemma 5.60** *Let $G=(V,\ T,\ P,\ S)$ be an $\varepsilon$-free grammar and $(M,\ \tau)$ its simple precedence parser. Further, let $\gamma$ be a string in $V^*$, $w$ a string in $T^*$, $\Phi$ a string over the alphabet of $M$, and $\pi'$ an action string such that*

(a) $$\$\gamma\,\textbf{I}\,w\$ \overset{\pi'}{\Longrightarrow} \Phi \quad \text{in } M \ .$$

*Then for some strings $x$, $y$ and $\psi$,*

(b)
$$w = xy, \quad \Phi = \$\psi\,\textbf{I}\,y\,\$, \quad |\pi'| = |\tau(\pi')| + |x| \ ,$$
$$\text{and} \quad \psi \xRightarrow[\text{rm}]{\tau(\pi')^R} \gamma x \quad \text{in } G \ .$$

$\square$

**Lemma 5.61** *If $(M,\ \tau)$ is the simple precedence parser for an $\varepsilon$-free grammar $G$, then $L(M) \subseteq L(G)$, and $\tau(\pi')$ is a right parse of a sentence $w$ in $G$ whenever $\pi'$ is a parse of $w$ in $M$. Moreover, $TIME_G(w) \leqslant TIME_M(w) - |w|$.* $\square$

To prove the counterpart of Lemma 5.19 we need the following result.

**Lemma 5.62** *Let $G=(V, T, P, S)$ be an $\varepsilon$-free grammar. Then for all symbols $X$ and $Y$ in $V$, nonterminals $A$, and terminals $a$,*

*(1) If $X \leqslant A$ and $G$ has a rule $A \to Y\beta$, then $X \lessdot Y$.*
*(2) If $A(\leqslant \cup \gtrdot) a$ and $G$ has a rule $A \to \alpha X$, then $X \gtrdot a$.*

*Proof.* If $X \leqslant A$ then, by Lemma 5.58, $G$ has a rule $B \to \alpha' X Y' \beta'$, where $Y' \underset{\text{lm}}{\Longrightarrow}{}^* A\delta$ for some string $\delta$. But then for any rule $A \to Y\beta$ of $G$, $Y' \underset{\text{lm}}{\Longrightarrow}{}^+ Y\beta\delta$, which implies, again by Lemma 5.58, that $X \lessdot Y$. Thus statement (1) is true. To prove statement (2), let $A(\leqslant \cup \gtrdot)a$. By Lemma 5.58, $G$ has a rule $B \to \alpha' X' Y' \beta'$, where $X' \underset{\text{rm}}{\Longrightarrow}{}^* \gamma A$ and $Y' \underset{\text{lm}}{\Longrightarrow}{}^* a\delta$ for some strings $\gamma$ and $\delta$. But then for any rule $A \to \alpha X$, $X' \underset{\text{rm}}{\Longrightarrow}{}^+ \gamma\alpha X$, which implies, again by Lemma 5.58, that $X \gtrdot a$.    $\square$

A string $\gamma \in V^*$ is a *valid stack string* of the simple precedence parser for a grammar $G=(V, T, P, S)$ if it is empty or is of the form $X_1 \ldots X_n$, where $X_1, \ldots, X_n$ are symbols in $V$ such that

$$\$ \leqslant X_1 \leqslant X_2 \leqslant \ldots \leqslant X_n$$

holds in the $\$$-augmented grammar for $G$. In other words, any two successive symbols in the string $\$\gamma$ must be $\leqslant$-related.

We can now prove

**Lemma 5.63** *Let $G=(V, T, P, S)$ be an $\varepsilon$-free grammar and $(M, \tau)$ its simple precedence parser. Further, let $\gamma$ and $\psi$ be strings in $V^*$, $x$ and $y$ strings in $T^*$, and $\pi$ a rule string in $P^*$ such that*

$$(a) \begin{cases} \psi \underset{\text{rm}}{\overset{\pi^R}{\Longrightarrow}} \gamma x \text{ in } G, \ \psi \text{ is a valid stack string }, \\[2mm] \$\psi : 1(\leqslant \cup \gtrdot) 1 : y\,\$, \text{ and} \\[2mm] \text{either } \gamma = \varepsilon \text{ or } \gamma : 1 \text{ is a nonterminal }. \end{cases}$$

*Then for some action string $\pi'$,*

$$(b) \begin{cases} \tau(\pi') = \pi, \ |\pi'| = |\pi| + |x| , \\[2mm] \gamma \text{ is a valid stack string, } \$\gamma : 1(\leqslant \cup \gtrdot) 1 : xy\$, \text{ and} \\[2mm] \$\gamma \mid xy\$ \overset{\pi'}{\Longrightarrow} \$\psi \mid y\$ \text{ in } M . \end{cases}$$

*Proof.* The proof is by induction on the length of the rule string $\pi$. In the base case we have $\pi = \varepsilon$, and so $\psi = \gamma x$. Since any two successive symbols in $\$\psi$ are $\leqslant$-related, $M$ can shift the terminals in $x$, i.e.,

$$\$\gamma\mathbin{\mathsf{l}} xy\$ \xRightarrow{\pi'} \$\gamma x\mathbin{\mathsf{l}} y\$ = \$\psi\mathbin{\mathsf{l}} y\$ \text{ in } M\,, \tag{5.33}$$

where $\pi'$ is an $|x|$-length string of shift actions. Statements (b) then hold because $\tau(\pi')=\varepsilon$, $\psi=\gamma x$ is a valid stack string, and $\$\psi:1\,(\leqslant\cup\gtrdot)\,1:y\$$.

To prove the induction step, we assume that $\pi$ is of the form $r\pi_1$, where $r$ is a rule $A\to\omega$. As an induction hypothesis, we assume that the lemma holds for the rule string $\pi_1$. We have

$$\psi \xRightarrow[\mathrm{rm}]{\pi_1^R} \gamma_1 x_1 = \delta A x_1 \xRightarrow[\mathrm{rm}]{r} \delta\omega x_1 = \gamma x \quad \text{in } G \tag{5.34}$$

for some strings $\gamma_1, \delta \in V^*$ and $x_1 \in T^*$. Here $x = zx_1$ and $\delta\omega = yz$ for some $z$, because $\gamma$ is empty or ends with a nonterminal. Since $\gamma_1 = \delta A$, and hence ends with a nonterminal, we can apply the induction hypothesis to the first derivation segment in (5.34) and conclude that, for some action string $\pi'_1$,

$$\left\{ \begin{array}{l} \tau(\pi'_1)=\pi_1,\ |\pi'_1|=|\pi_1|+|x_1|\,, \\[2mm] \gamma_1 \text{ is a valid stack string, } \$\gamma_1:1\,(\leqslant\cup\gtrdot)1:x_1\,y\$\,, \\[2mm] \$\gamma_1\mathbin{\mathsf{l}} x_1 y\$ \xRightarrow{\pi'_1} \$\psi\mathbin{\mathsf{l}} y\$ \text{ in } \ M\,. \end{array} \right. \tag{5.35}$$

Thus we have

$$\$\delta A\mathbin{\mathsf{l}} x_1\,y\$ = \$\gamma_1\mathbin{\mathsf{l}} x_1 y\$ \xRightarrow{\pi'_1} \$\psi\mathbin{\mathsf{l}} y\$\,. \tag{5.36}$$

Moreover, we can conclude from Lemma 5.62 that $\$\delta:1 \lessdot 1:\omega$ and $\omega:1 \gtrdot 1:x_1 y\$$. Hence $M$ has a reduce action $r'$ for $A\to\omega$ on lookahead $1:x_1 y\$$ and lookback $\$\delta:1$, and we have

$$\$\delta\omega\mathbin{\mathsf{l}} x_1 y\$ \xRightarrow{r'} \$\delta A\mathbin{\mathsf{l}} x_1 y\$\,. \tag{5.37}$$

Here $\delta\omega$ is a valid stack string because $\delta$ is a prefix of the valid stack string $\gamma_1$, $\$\delta:1 \lessdot 1:\omega$, and any two successive symbols in $\omega$ are $\doteq$-related. Since $\delta\omega = yz$, $M$ can then shift the terminals in $z$, i.e.,

$$\$\gamma\mathbin{\mathsf{l}} xy\$ = \$\gamma\mathbin{\mathsf{l}} zx_1 y\$ \xRightarrow{\pi'_2} \$\gamma z\mathbin{\mathsf{l}} x_1 y\$ = \$\delta\omega\mathbin{\mathsf{l}} x_1 y\$\,, \tag{5.38}$$

where $\pi'_2$ is a $|z|$-length string of shift actions. Choosing $\pi' = \pi'_2 r'\pi'_1$ and combining statements (5.35)–(5.38) we finally conclude that statements (b) hold. Recall that $yz = \delta\omega$ is a valid stack string, and that $yz:1 = \omega:1 \gtrdot 1:x_1 y\$$, where $zx_1 y\$ = xy\$$.  $\square$

**Lemma 5.64** *If $(M, \tau)$ is the simple precedence parser for an $\varepsilon$-free grammar $G$, then $L(G) \subseteq L(M)$, and for any right parse $\pi$ of a sentence $w$ in $G$, $\tau(\pi')=\pi$ for some parse $\pi'$ of $w$ in $M$. Moreover, $TIME_M(w)\leqslant TIME_G(w)+|w|$.*

*Proof.* Set $\psi = S$, $x = w$, and $\gamma = y = \varepsilon$ in Lemma 5.63. Note that $\$ \doteq S \doteq \$$.   □

By Lemmas 5.61 and 5.64 we have

**Theorem 5.65** *The simple precedence parser M for any $\varepsilon$-free grammar G is a right parser for G. Moreover, for each sentence $w \in L(G)$, M produces all right parses of w in G, and $TIME_M(w) = TIME_G(w) + |w|$.*   □

We say that an $\varepsilon$-free grammar $G = (V, T, P, S)$ is a *simple precedence grammar* if its simple precedence parser is deterministic and, in addition, $S \Rightarrow^+ S$ is impossible in G.

The additional requirement that the start symbol must not nontrivially derive itself is necessary if we want all simple precedence grammars to be unambiguous. Note that the simple precedence parser for the ambiguous grammar $(\{S, a\}, \{a\}, \{S \to S|a\}, S)$ is deterministic. It has the actions

$$\$S|\$ \to \$S|\$, \qquad \$a|\$ \to \$S|\$, \qquad \$|a \to \$a| \ .$$

**Theorem 5.66** *Any simple precedence grammar is unambiguous.*

*Proof.* Let $M$ be the simple precedence parser for a simple precedence grammar $G$. By definition, $M$ is deterministic. Moreover, $S \Rightarrow^+ S$ is not possible in $G$. Thus, by Lemma 5.60, $\$S|\$ \Rightarrow^+ \$S|\$$ is not possible in $M$. Together with the determinism, this means that $M$ has exactly one accepting computation on each $w \in L(G)$, and hence produces for each such $w$ exactly one right parse in $G$. On the other hand, by Theorem 5.65, $M$ produces all the right parses. So each $w \in L(G)$ has exactly one right parse in $G$, which means, by Theorem 4.12, that $G$ is unambiguous.   □

Next we shall derive a grammatical characterization of the simple precedence grammars.

**Lemma 5.67** *Let $G = (V, T, P, S)$ be a reduced $\varepsilon$-free grammar. Then for all symbols $Z \in V$,*

$$X' \leqslant Z \, (\leqslant \cup \gtrdot) \, a$$

*holds in the $\$$-augmented grammar $G'$ for $G$, for some symbol $X' \in V \cup \{\$\}$ and terminal $a \in T \cup \{\$\}$.*

*Proof.* Since $G'$ is reduced, we have

$$S' \Rightarrow^* \gamma Z a \delta \quad \text{in } G'$$

for some $\gamma \in \$V^*$ and $a\delta \in (T \cup \{\$\})(V \cup \{\$\})^*$. Let $X = \gamma:1$. Then, by Lemma 5.50, $G'$ has a rule $B \to \alpha X'Z'\beta$, where $Z' \underset{\text{lm}}{\Rightarrow}^* Z\beta'$ for some string $\beta'$. By Lemma 5.58, $X' \leqslant Z$. Now let $Y = a$. By Lemma 5.50, $G'$ has a rule $B \to \alpha Z'Y'\beta$, where $Z' \underset{\text{rm}}{\Rightarrow}^* \alpha'Z$ and $Y' \underset{\text{lm}}{\Rightarrow}^* Y\beta' = a\beta'$ for some strings $\alpha'$ and $\beta'$. But then, by Lemma 5.58, either $Z \leqslant a$ or $Z \gtrdot a$.   □

**Theorem 5.68** *Let $G=(V, T, P, S)$ be an $\varepsilon$-free grammar. The simple precedence parser M for G is deterministic whenever the following conditions are satisfied:*

*(a) $(\lessdot \cap \gtrdot) = \varnothing$.*

*(b) G is invertible, i.e., no two rules in G have identical right-hand sides.*

*(c) For all symbols X, Y and rules $A \to \alpha X Y \beta$ and $B \to Y\beta$, $X \lessdot Y$ is impossible.*

*Conversely, if M is deterministic then all of the above conditions hold provided that G is reduced.*

*Proof.* M is nondeterministic if and only if it has one of the following pairs of distinct actions

(1) $X\,|\,a \to Xa\,|$,     $Y\alpha X\,|\,a \to YA\,|\,a$.

(2) $X\omega\,|\,a \to XA\,|\,a$,     $X\omega\,|\,a \to XB\,|\,a$.

(3) $Z\alpha X Y\beta\,|\,a \to ZA\,|\,a$,     $X Y\beta\,|\,a \to XB\,|\,a$.

Here (1) represents a "shift-reduce conflict" and (2) and (3) "reduce-reduce conflicts". By definition, $X(\lessdot \cap \gtrdot)\,a$ in (1) and $X \lessdot Y$ in (3). Thus we see that, if $M$ is nondeterministic, then one of the statements (a), (b) or (c) is false.

We now assume that $G$ is reduced and prove the converse. First, if $X(\lessdot \cap \gtrdot)$ $a$ for some $X$ and $a$, then $M$ has the shift action $X\,|\,a \to Xa\,|$. Moreover, by Lemma 5.58, the \$-augmented grammar $G'$ for $G$ has a rule $A' \to \alpha' X' Y'\beta'$, where $X' \underset{\mathrm{rm}}{\Longrightarrow}^{+} \gamma X$ and $Y' \underset{\mathrm{lm}}{\Longrightarrow}^{*} a\delta$ for some $\gamma$ and $\delta$. Thus $G$ has a rule $A \to \alpha X$. Since $G'$ is reduced, we conclude from Lemma 5.67 that $Y \lessdot A$ for some symbol $Y$. By Lemma 5.62, $Y \lessdot 1: \alpha X$. But then $M$ has the reduce action $Y\alpha X\,|\,a \to YA\,|\,a$. So we have shown that the converse of statement (a) implies the existence of a pair of actions of the form (1). Next, if $G$ is not invertible, it has a pair of distinct rules $A \to \omega$, $B \to \omega$. By Lemma 5.67, $X \lessdot A$ and $A\,(\lessdot \cup \gtrdot)\,a$ for some symbol $X$ and terminal $a \in T \cup \{\$\}$. By Lemma 5.62, $X \lessdot 1:\omega$ and $\omega:1 \gtrdot a$. But then $M$ has the pair of actions (2). So we have shown that the converse of statement (b) implies the existence of a pair of distinct actions of the form (2). Finally, let $G$ have rules $A \to \alpha X Y\beta$ and $B \to Y\beta$. By Lemma 5.67, $Z \lessdot A$ and $A\,(\lessdot \cup \gtrdot)\,a$ for some symbol $Z$ and terminal $a \in T \cup \{\$\}$. By Lemma 5.62, $Z \lessdot 1:\alpha X Y\beta$ and $\alpha X Y\beta:1 \gtrdot a$, which means that $M$ has the action $Z\alpha X Y\beta\,|\,a \to ZA\,|\,a$. Moreover, as $Y\beta:1 = \alpha X Y\beta:1$, $M$ has the action $X Y\beta\,|\,a \to XB\,|\,a$ whenever $X \lessdot Y$. Thus, the converse of statement (c) implies the existence of a pair of actions of the form (3).  □

**Corollary 5.69** *A reduced $\varepsilon$-free grammar $G=(V, T, P, S)$ is simple precedence if and only if the following conditions are satisfied:*

*(a) $(\lessdot \cap \gtrdot) = \varnothing$.*

*(b) G is invertible.*

*(c) For all symbols X, Y and rules $A \to \alpha X Y\beta$ and $B \to Y\beta$, $X \lessdot Y$ is impossible.*

*(d) $S \Rightarrow^{+} S$ is impossible.*

□

**Corollary 5.70** *An ε-free grammar $G=(V, T, P, S)$ is simple precedence whenever the following conditions are satisfied:*

*(a)* $(\lessdot \cap \gtrdot) = (\lessdot \cap \doteq) = \emptyset$.
*(b) G is invertible.*
*(c) $S \Rightarrow^+ S$ is impossible.*

□

**Theorem 5.71** *Given any reduced ε-free grammar $G=(V, T, P, S)$, it is decidable in deterministic time $O(|V| \cdot |G|)$ whether or not G is simple precedence.*

*Proof.* By Theorem 5.57, the relations $\lessdot$ and $\gtrdot$ can be computed in time $O(|V| \cdot |G|)$. Thus it is possible to test in time $O(|V| \cdot |G|)$ whether or not conditions (a) and (c) of Corollary 5.69 hold. The invertibility condition (b) is trivial to test in time $O(|G|)$. To test condition (d), we note that $S \Rightarrow^+ S$ if and only if $S$ belongs to the closure **unit-rule**$^+(S)$, where **unit-rule** is the relation defined by

$$A \text{ \textbf{unit-rule} } B \quad \text{if } A \rightarrow B \text{ is a rule of } G \ .$$

By Theorem 2.28, the closure **unit-rule**$^+(S)$ can be computed in time $O(|G|)$. Thus, by Corollary 5.69, $G$ can be tested for the simple precedence property in deterministic time $O(|V| \cdot |G|)$.   □

## Exercises

5.1   Prove that $L(M_{\text{match}}) = L_{\text{match}}$ for the pushdown automaton $M_{\text{match}}$ given in Section 5.1.

5.2   Prove Facts 5.1 and 5.2.

5.3   Give deterministic pushdown automata that accept the following languages

a) $\{0^m 1^n \mid m \leqslant n\}$.
b) $L_{\text{cpal}} = \{wcw^R \mid w \in \{0, 1\}^*\}, c \neq 0, 1$.
c) $\{w \in \{0, 1\}^* \mid w \text{ consists of an equal number of ones and zeros}\}$.

5.4   Give pushdown automata that accept the following languages:

a) $\{0, 1\}^* \setminus \{0^n 1^n 0^n \mid n \geqslant 1\}$.
b) $\{0, 1\}^* \setminus \{ww \mid w \in \{0, 1\}^*\}$.

(*Hint:* Use nondeterministic automata that guess why their input is not in the language and check that the guess is correct.)

5.5  Prove Proposition 5.5. What is the complexity of your transformation? Can you obtain a polynomial time bound?

5.6  Let $M$ be a pushdown automaton with a *bounded stack*, i.e., there is a constant $k \geqslant 0$, depending only on $M$, such that in all accepting computations of $M$ the stack is no higher than $k$ in any configuration. Show that $M$ can be transformed in time $O(|M|^k)$ into an equivalent finite automaton. Thus pushdown automata with a bounded stack can only accept regular languages.

5.7  Define the notion of "workspace complexity" for pushdown automata.

5.8  Give an $s$-grammar that is equivalent to the grammar $G_{\text{match}}$. Also give the deterministic produce-shift parser for your grammar.

5.9  Show that any context-free language can be accepted by a pushdown automaton that runs *in real time*, i.e., in time $n$.
(*Hint*: You may use the result of Proposition 5.22.)

5.10  Show that the family of regular languages is a proper subfamily of the family of $s$-languages.

5.11  Let $M$ be a pushdown automaton with initial stack contents $\gamma_s$. We say that $M$ has the *correct prefix property* if the statement

$$\$\gamma_s \mathbf{l} xy\$ \Rightarrow^* \$\gamma \mathbf{l} y\$ \quad \text{in } M$$

can be true only if $x$ is a prefix of some sentence in $L(M)$.

a) Show that the shift-reduce parser of a grammar does not in general have the correct prefix property.
b) Show that the produce-shift parser of any reduced grammar has the correct prefix property.
c) Show that the produce-shift parser of a non-reduced grammar need not have the correct prefix property.

5.12  What is the workspace complexity of accepting a sentence in a) a produce-shift parser, b) a shift-reduce parser? (Cf. Exercise 5.7.)

5.13  Prove Facts 5.24 and 5.25.

5.14  Give the SLL(1) parser for the grammar $G_{\text{exp}}$ with rules

$$\begin{aligned}
E &\to TE' , \\
E' &\to \varepsilon \mid + TE' , \\
T &\to FT' , \\
T' &\to \varepsilon \mid * FT' , \\
F &\to a \mid (E) .
\end{aligned}$$

The terminal alphabet of $G_{\text{exp}}$ is $\{a, +, *, ), (\}$, and its nonterminal alphabet is $\{E, E', T, T', F\}$, where $E$ is the start symbol. Simulate the behavior of the parser on the following input strings:

a) $a$     b) $a+a*a+a$         c) $((a*(a+a))$
d) $\varepsilon$     e) $(a$               f) $aa$

**5.15** Give all the produce actions of the SLL(2) parser for $G_{\text{block}}$.

**5.16** Give the SLL(2) parser for the grammar $G_{\text{exp}}$ of Exercise 5.14. Simulate the behavior of the parser on the following input strings:

a) $\varepsilon$         b) $(a$           c) $aa$

**5.17** Prove the analogue of Lemma 5.32 for rightmost derivations: if in a grammar $G$

$$Y \Rightarrow^n \alpha X \beta, \quad \alpha \Rightarrow^* x, \quad \text{and} \quad \beta \Rightarrow^* y ,$$

then for some $\gamma$

$$Y \underset{\text{rm}}{\Longrightarrow}^* \gamma X y \quad \text{and} \quad \gamma \Rightarrow^* x \quad \text{in } G .$$

(*Hint*: There is a quicker way to obtain the result than following the proof of Lemma 5.32.)

**5.18** Does Lemma 5.33 hold if $X$ is allowed to be any string in $V^*$?

**5.19** Show that no SLL(0) language can contain more than one sentence.

**5.20** Consider the grammar

$$S \rightarrow A = A | (S) ,$$
$$A \rightarrow a | (A) .$$

a) Give the SLL(2) parser for the grammar.
b) Show that the grammar is not SLL($k$) for any $k$.
c) Show that the grammar generates a deterministic language.
d) Is the language generated by the grammar SLL($k$) for some $k$?

**5.21** Show that the languages $L_k$ given in Proposition 5.36 are SLL($k$). Can you find an $\varepsilon$-free SLL($k$) grammar for $L_k$?

**5.22** Show that a non-reduced SLL($k$) grammar can contain left-recursive non-terminals.

5.23  Show that a language is an $s$-language if and only if it is the language generated by some $\varepsilon$-free SLL(1) grammar.

5.24  Show that the set of all regular expressions over any alphabet $T$ is an $s$-language over the alphabet $T \cup \{\underline{\varepsilon}, \underline{\varnothing}, *, \cdot, \cup, ), (\}$.

5.25  Give a deterministic pushdown automaton that does not detect an error in some nonsentence.

5.26  What exactly is the difference between the behavior of the SLL($k+1$) parser for an SLL($k$) grammar and the behavior of the SLL($k$) parser for the same grammar? Might it sometimes be beneficial to use, say, the SLL(2) or SLL(3) parser even when a grammar is SLL(1)?

5.27  Prove Lemma 5.47.

5.28  Give relational expressions for computing the sets $\mathrm{FIRST}_2(X)$ and $\mathrm{FOLLOW}_2(X)$ for a symbol $X$. What is the complexity of the resulting algorithm? Can you generalize your construction to $\mathrm{FIRST}_k(X)$ and $\mathrm{FOLLOW}_k(X)$?

5.29  Consider the behavior of the SLL(1) parser for $G_{\mathrm{block}}$ in the case of the erroneous string

**begin** $a$; **begin**; $a\ a$ **end end** .

a) Give the contents of the stack of the parser at the time of error detection, assuming that the stack implementation is used.
b) Give the stack of activation records of the recursive descent parsing procedures at the time of error detection.
c) What is the error message issued?

5.30  A configuration of a recursive descent parsing program can be represented as a string of positions in the grammar. Recall from Section 5.5 that a *position* is a dotted rule $A \rightarrow \alpha \cdot \beta$, where $A \rightarrow \alpha\beta$ is a rule of the grammar. For each possible stack of activation records of the parsing procedures $A_1, \ldots, A_n$ there is a unique string of positions

$$A_1 \rightarrow \alpha_1 \cdot \beta_1, \ldots, A_n \rightarrow \alpha_n \cdot \beta_n .$$

Here $A_i \rightarrow \alpha_i \cdot \beta_i$ means that the flow of control in the parsing procedure $A_i$ is in the segment corresponding to the right-hand side $\alpha_i\beta_i$, and that the parsing has advanced over $\alpha_i$.

a) Using positions, represent the configuration of the recursive descent parser fot $G_{\mathrm{block}}$ at the time it detects the error in the string given in the previous exercise.

   b) Using positions, relate the configurations of the recursive descent parser to the leftmost derivations in the grammar.

   c) Use this relationship to obtain a correctness proof for the recursive descent parsing method.

**5.31** Give a) the stack implementation, b) the recursive descent implementation for the SLL(1) parser for the grammar $G_{exp}$ of Exercise 5.14.

**5.32** Augment the recursive descent parser for $G_{exp}$ with the construction of the derivation tree.

**5.33** Augment the recursive descent parser for $G_{exp}$ so as to transform the parsed expression into the corresponding postfix form. The *postfix-form* expressions are generated by the grammar

$$S \to SS + \,|\, SS * \,|\, a \ .$$

**5.34** Write a program that transforms any regular expression over $\{0,1\}$ into an equivalent finite automaton. You may assume that a scanner for these regular expressions is available.

**5.35** Write a program that transforms any regular expression $E$ over $\{0,1\}$ into a regular expression denoting $L(E)^R$.

**5.36** In this exercise we consider a means of optimizing the implementations of SLL(1) parsers. The parsing programs given in Section 5.6 can be shortened and speeded up a little by making use of default actions. A produce action for some rule $A \to \omega$ is a *default action* if it is applied without checking that the current input symbol is a legal lookahead. A default action thus behaves like the produce action $A| \to \omega^R|$ in the predictive machine, or SLL(0) parser, of the grammar. However, a default action for the rule $A \to \omega$ is applied only when no produce actions for other rules of $A$ are applicable. Figure 5.10 shows the parsing procedure for a nonterminal $A$ when default actions are used in conjunction with the recursive descent implementation of the SLL(1) parser.

   a) Carry out this optimization in the case of the SLL(1) parser for $G_{block}$. Choose as the default action a produce action for a rule with a nullable right-hand side if possible.

   b) Why does the optimization work? That is, why is the parsing program still a valid left parser for the grammar after the introduction of default actions?

   c) What is the overall effect of the use of default actions on the behaviour of the parser?

**5.37** Consider the recursive descent implementation of the SLL(1) parser for $G_{exp}$. Optimize this implementation by means of default actions.

```
procedure A;
begin
      if token.kind in FIRST'₁(ω₁ FOLLOW'₁(A)) then begin
          write "A→ω₁";
          parse(ω₁)
      end else
              ⋮
      if token.kind in FIRST'₁(ω_{n-1} FOLLOW'₁(A)) then begin
          write "A→ω_{n-1}";
          parse(ω_{n-1})
      end else begin
          write "A→ω_n";
          check(ω_n)
      end
end;
```

**Figure 5.10** Parsing procedure for a nonterminal $A$ in the recursive descent implementation of the SLL(1) parser when default actions are used. The rules of $A$ are: $A \rightarrow \omega_1 | \ldots | \omega_n$. The produce action for $A \rightarrow \omega_n$ has been chosen as the default action

5.38  In this exercise we consider another way of optimizing the SLL(1) parser. The number of recursive calls of parsing procedures in recursive descent parsers can be reduced by handling immediate right recursion in a special way. A grammar has *immediate right recursion* if it contains a rule of the form $A \rightarrow \alpha A$. The produce actions for these rules can be implemented by iteration, as shown in Figure 5.11.

a) Carry out this optimization in the case of the SLL(1) parser for $G_{\text{block}}$.
b) Why does the optimization work?

5.39  Consider the implementation of the SLL(1) parser for $G_{\text{exp}}$ suggested in Exercise 5.37. Elaborate this implementation further by handling immediate right recursion as suggested in the previous exercise.

```
procedure A;
begin
      while token.kind in FIRST₁(α) do begin
          write "A→αA";
          parse(α)
      end;
      if token.kind in FIRST'₁(β₁ FOLLOW'₁(A)) then begin
          write "A → β₁";
          parse(β₁)
      end else
              ⋮
      if token.kind in FIRST'₁(β_n FOLLOW'₁(A)) then begin
          write "A → β_n";
          parse(β_n)
      end
end;
```

**Figure 5.11** Parsing procedure for a nonterminal $A$ in the recursive descent implementation of the SLL(1) parser. The rules of $A$ are: $A \rightarrow \alpha A | \beta_1 | \ldots | \beta_n$

5.40 In this exercise we consider the handling of *syntax errors* in parsing. A practical parser should never quit the parsing process upon the detection of the first syntax error. Instead, it should proceed with the processing of the input string so that as many errors as possible can be detected and reported in the same run. To do this, the parser must be augmented with some *error recovery mechanism*, the task of which is to get the parser back into normal parsing mode after an error has been detected. As an example, we consider the recursive descent parser for $G_{block}$ and augment it with a simple error recovery mechanism, often referred to as "panic mode recovery". The error recovery mechanism is in this case embedded into the error handling procedure *error* (see Figure 5.12). The idea is to scan the input string until some "safe" symbol is encountered. In the case of $G_{block}$ we regard as safe symbols the keywords **begin** and **end** and the delimiter *semicolon*. Note that these are either starters or followers of major syntactic entities of the language. To guarantee that the scanning will not continue over the end of the input string, we always include the end marker $ in the set of safe symbols. After a safe symbol has been scanned, the rest of the recovery action depends on whether the safe symbol is a starter or a follower. If it is a follower, the control is simply passed back to the calling parsing procedure. Otherwise, a further parsing procedure is called, for a nonterminal whose starter the safe symbol is, after which control is finally passed back to the original calling procedure. To analyze this error recovery mechanism, consider the erroneous string

**begin** *a* **begin** *a a* **end** ; **end** ; **begin** *x* **end** **begin** .

    a) At which point does the error recovering parser issue error messages, and what are these messages?

    b) Evaluate the quality of the messages. Which of the messages are misleading? Which are totally *extraneous*, i.e., reports on nonexistent errors?

    c) Is some error left undetected?

    d) How large a portion of the input string is processed in normal parsing mode?

    e) Does the use of default actions affect the quality of the error recovery?

    f) Find ways to improve the quality of the error recovery.

```
procedure error (message m);
begin
      write m;
      while not (token.kind in {begin-keyword,
      end-keyword, semicolon, eof-token}) do
            scan;
      if token.kind = begin-keyword then
            B
      else if token.kind = semicolon then
            C
end;
```

**Figure 5.12** Error handling procedure for the recursive descent parser for $G_{block}$. A simple error recovery method called "panic mode" is used

g) How well do you think the panic mode recovery mechanism of $G_{block}$ generalizes to real programming languages? Can you formalize the panic mode recovery mechanism so that it applies to any SLL(1) grammar?

**5.41**  Augment the recursive descent parser for $G_{exp}$ with panic mode error recovery.

**5.42**  Design an error recovery mechanism that can be incorporated into the stack implementation of the SLL(1) parser. Analyze the behaviour of the parser for $G_{block}$ in the case of the erroneous string given in Exercise 5.40 when the parser has been augmented with your error recovery mechanism.

**5.43**  Give examples of grammars for which

a) $\doteq$ is neither reflexive, symmetric nor transitive.
b) $<$ is neither irreflexive nor transitive.
c) $\leqslant$ is neither reflexive, antisymmetric nor transitive.
d) $>$ is neither irreflexive nor transitive.

**5.44**  Show that, in a reduced $\varepsilon$-free grammar,

$$\text{FOLLOW}'_1(X) = \{a \in T \cup \{\$\} \mid X (\leqslant \cup >) a\}$$

for any symbol $X$.

**5.45**  Give the simple precedence parsers for the following grammars:

a) The grammar of Exercise 5.20.
b) $E \rightarrow E + T \mid + T \mid T,\ T \rightarrow T * F \mid F,\ F \rightarrow a \mid (E)$.
c) $S \rightarrow AS \mid A,\ A \rightarrow (S) \mid ()$.
d) $S \rightarrow SA \mid A,\ A \rightarrow (S) \mid ()$.

Which of these parsers are deterministic? Which have the correct prefix property?

**5.46**  Show that, if the simple precedence parser for a grammar $G$ loops forever on some input string, then $A \Rightarrow^+ A$ for some nonterminal $A$ of $G$.

**5.47**  Show that the converse of Corollary 5.70 need not hold: specifically, a simple precedence grammar (as defined in this book) need not satisfy the condition $(< \cap \doteq) = \varnothing$.

**5.48**  An $\varepsilon$-free grammar $G$ is a *weak precedence grammar* if the following conditions are satisfied:

a) $(\leqslant \cap >) = \varnothing$.
b) For all symbols $X$ and rules $A \rightarrow \alpha X \beta$ and $B \rightarrow \beta$, $X \leqslant B$ is impossible.
c) $S \Rightarrow^+ S$ is impossible.

Show that the class of reduced simple precedence grammars is properly contained in the class of invertible weak precedence grammars.

5.49 Show that it is possible to construct for any invertible weak precedence grammar $G = (V, T, P, S)$ a deterministic right parser of size $O(|V| \cdot |T| \cdot |G|)$.

5.50 Show that any language generated by an invertible weak precedence grammar is also generated by a grammar that satisfies the conditions stated in Corollary 5.70.

5.51 Design a technique for implementing simple precedence parsers as high-level language programs. Apply your technique to the grammar $G_{\text{dblock}}$ given in Section 5.7. Can you simplify the implementation if the grammar satisfies the condition $(< \cap \doteq) = \varnothing$? Does your technique also apply to the parsers considered in Exercise 5.49?

5.52 Can you extend the precedence parsing method to grammars containing $\varepsilon$-rules?

## Bibliographic Notes

The concept of a pushdown automaton comes from Oettinger (1961) and Schützenberger (1963). Our definition of pushdown automaton is a slight generalization of the "extended pushdown automaton" defined by Aho and Ullman (1972), who also demonstrated the equivalence of these automata and conventional (i.e., normal-form) pushdown automata (cf. Proposition 5.5). The equivalence of (normal-form) pushdown automata and context-free grammars (Theorem 5.7 and Proposition 5.8) was demonstrated by Chomsky (1962) and Evey (1963). The polynomial time bound given in Proposition 5.8 comes from Goldstine, Price and Wotschke (1982). The theory of deterministic context-free languages originated in Haines (1965) and Ginsburg and Greibach (1966). The concept of a pushdown transducer comes from Lewis and Stearns (1966, 1968). Our formalization of parsers is essentially that used by Aho and Ullman (1972). The Greibach normal-form, and Proposition 5.22, come from Greibach (1965). The polynomial time bound given in Proposition 5.22 was established by Rosenkrantz (1967) (see also Harrison (1978)).

The relative succinctness of various kinds of pushdown automata, finite automata and context-free grammars has been studied by Meyer and Fischer (1971), Geller, Hunt, Szymanski and Ullman (1977), Schmidt (1978), and Goldstine, Price and Wotschke (1982). Proposition 5.4 comes from Meyer and Fischer (1971). Geller, Hunt, Szymanski and Ullman (1977) showed that nondeterministic pushdown automata can be nonrecursively more succinct than deterministic pushdown automata. Goldstine, Price and Wotschke (1982) showed that deterministic pushdown automata can be more succinct than context-free grammars.

Deterministically top-down parsable grammars were first considered by Lewis and Stearns (1966, 1968), Korenjak and Hopcroft (1966), Knuth (1967, 1971), Kurki-Suonio (1966, 1967, 1969), Culik (1968), Wood (1969a, 1969b, 1970, 1971), and Rosenkrantz and Stearns (1970). The concept of an $s$-grammar comes from Korenjak and Hopcroft (1966). The theory of LL$(k)$ parsing and LL$(k)$ grammars originated in Lewis and Stearns (1966, 1968). LL$(k)$ grammars were first called "TD$(k)$ grammars" (Top-Down grammars) in Lewis and Stearns (1966); the term "LL$(k)$" was suggested by Knuth (1967, 1971). The class of strong LL$(k)$ grammars discussed in this chapter was introduced by Kurki-Suonio (1969) and Rosenkrantz and Stearns (1970); the term "strong LL$(k)$" comes from Rosenkrantz and Stearns (1970), who established most of the formal properties of LL$(k)$ and strong LL$(k)$ grammars. The proper hierarchy of LL$(k)$ languages (Proposition 5.36) was first observed by Kurki-Suonio (1969). The sequence of languages given in Proposition 5.36 is from Aho and Ullman (1972).

The efficient construction of LL(1) parsers has been considered by Hunt, Szymanski and Ullman (1974, 1977) and Johnson and Sethi (1975, 1976). The relational expressions used in Section 5.5 come from Hunt, Szymanski and Ullman (1974, 1977), and from Sippu and Soisalon-Soininen (1985). The time bound given in Theorem 5.55 first appeared in Johnson and Sethi (1975). The recursive descent technique used in Section 5.6 to implement strong LL(1) parsers is attributed to Lucas (1961) and Conway (1963). Lewis and Rosenkrantz (1971) describe an Algol compiler the syntax analysis of which is based on LL(1) parsing.

The Wirth-Weber precedence relations are from Wirth and Weber (1966). Simple precedence grammars (in their original form) were defined by Pair (1964) and independently by Wirth and Weber (1966). Weak precedence grammars (Exercise 5.48) come from Ichbiah and Morse (1970). Other precedence-oriented parsing techniques are discussed in Floyd (1963), McKeeman, Horning and Wortman (1970), and Aho, Denning and Ullman (1972). The properties of precedence grammars and languages are studied in Fischer (1969), Graham (1970, 1971), and Aho and Ullman (1972). The method given in Section 5.7 for constructing the precedence relations comes from Hunt, Szymanski and Ullman (1974, 1977). For techniques for implementing precedence parsers, see Aho and Ullman (1973). The simple precedence parsing technique was used in several early compilers, including compilers for Euler (Wirth and Weber, 1966), AlgolW (Bauer, Becker and Graham, 1968), and PL360 (Wirth, 1968).

An important parsing method not discussed in this chapter is the method of LR$(k)$ parsing, invented by Knuth (1965). LR$(k)$ parsing will be treated in depth in Volume II of this monograph.

Several general texts on parsing and compiling have been published. Among them are Gries (1971), Aho and Ullman (1972, 1973), Bauer and Eickel (1976), Lewis, Rosenkrantz and Stearns (1976), Aho and Ullman (1977), Backhouse (1979), Waite and Goos (1984), and Aho, Sethi and Ullman (1986).

Extensive bibliographies on parsing are given in Nijholt (1983). Bibliographies on syntax error handling (Exercises 5.40 to 5.42) are given by Ciesinger (1979) and Hammond and Rayward-Smith (1984).

# Bibliography to Volume I


Aho AV, Corasick MJ (1975) Efficient string matching: an aid to bibliographic search. Commun. ACM *18*: 333–340

Aho AV, Ullman JD (1972) The theory of parsing, translation, and compiling, vol. I: parsing. Prentice-Hall, Englewood Cliffs, NJ

Aho AV, Ullman JD (1973) The theory of parsing, translation, and compiling, vol. II: compiling. Prentice-Hall, Englewood Cliffs, NJ

Aho AV, Ullman JD (1977) Principles of compiler design. Addison-Wesley, Reading, MA

Aho AV, Denning PJ, Ullman JD (1972) Weak and mixed strategy precedence parsing. J. Assoc. Comput. Mach. *19*: 225–243

Aho AV, Hopcroft JE, Ullman JD (1974) The design and analysis of computer algorithms. Addison-Wesley, Reading, MA

Aho AV, Hopcroft JE, Ullman JD (1983) Data structures and algorithms. Addison-Wesley, Reading, MA

Aho AV, Sethi R, Ullman JD (1986) Compilers: principles, techniques, and tools. Addison-Wesley, Reading, MA

Arbib MA, Kfoury AJ, Moll RN (1981) A basis for theoretical computer science. Springer, New York, Heidelberg, Berlin

Baase S (1978) Computer algorithms—Introduction to design and analysis. Addison-Wesley, Reading, MA

Backhouse RC (1979) Syntax of programming languages: theory and practice. Prentice-Hall International, London

Backus JW (1959) The syntax and semantics of the proposed international algebraic language of the Zurich ACM-GAMM conference. In: Proc. Internat. Conf. on Information Processing, June 1959. UNESCO, pp. 125–132

Bar-Hillel Y, Perles M, Shamir E (1961) On formal properties of simple phrase structure grammars. Z. Phonetic Sprachwiss. Kommunikationsforsch. *14*: 143–172

Bauer FL, Eickel J, eds. (1976) Compiler construction: An advanced course, 2nd ed. Springer, Berlin, Heidelberg, New York

Bauer H, Becker S, Graham SL (1968) ALGOL W implementation. Report CS98, Computer Science Department, Stanford University, Stanford, CA

Blum N (1982) On the power of chain rules in context-free grammars. Acta Inf. *17*: 425–433

Chomsky N (1956) Three models for the description of language. IRE Trans. Inf. Theory *2*: 113–124

Chomsky N (1959) On certain formal properties of grammars. Inf. Control *2*: 137–167

Chomsky N (1962) Context-free grammars and pushdown storage. Quarterly Progress Report, no. 65, Research Laboratory of Electronics, Massachusetts Institute of Technology, Cambridge, MA

Chomsky N (1963) Formal properties of grammars. In: Handbook of Math. Psych., vol. 2. Wiley, New York

Chomsky N, Miller GA (1958) Finite state languages. Inf. Control *1*: 91–112

Ciesinger J (1979) A bibliography of error-handling. ACM SIGPLAN Notices 14, no. *1*: 16–26

Conway ME (1963) Design of a separable transition-diagram compiler. Commun. ACM *6*: 396–408

Culik K II (1968) Contribution to deterministic top-down analysis of context-free languages. Kybernetika *4*: 422–431

DeRemer FL, Pennello TJ (1982) Efficient computation of LALR(1) lookahead sets. ACM Trans. Program. Lang. Syst. *4*: 615–649

Deussen P (1979) One abstract accepting algorithm for all kinds of parsers. In: Maurer H (ed.) Automata, Languages and Programming. Sixth Colloquium, Graz, July 1979. Springer, Berlin, Heidelberg, New York, pp. 203-217 (Lecture notes in computer science, vol. 71)

Earley J (1968) An efficient context-free parsing algorithm. Thesis, Carnegie-Mellon University, Pittsburgh, PA

Earley J (1970) An efficient context-free parsing algorithm. Commun. ACM *13*: 94–102

Ehrenfeucht A, Zeiger P (1976) Complexity measures for regular languages. J. Comput. Syst. Sci. *12*: 134–146

Eve J, Kurki-Suonio R (1977) On computing the transitive closure of a relation. Acta Inf. *8*: 303–314

Even S (1980) Graph algorithms. Computer Science Press, Rockville, MD

Evey RJ (1963) Applications of pushdown-store machines. In: Proc. AFIPS Fall Joint Computer Conference. AFIPS Press, Montvale, NJ, pp. 215–227

Fischer MJ (1969) Some properties of precedence languages. In: ACM Symp. on Theory of Computing. ACM, New York, pp. 181–190

Floyd RW (1963) Syntactic analysis and operator precedence. J. Assoc. Comput. Mach. *10*: 316–333

Garey MR, Johnson DS (1979) Computers and intractability: a guide to the theory of NP-completeness. Freeman, San Francisco

Geller MM, Hunt HB III, Szymanski TG, Ullman JD (1977) Economy of description by parsers, DPDA's, and PDA's. Theor. Comput. Sci. *4*: 143–153

Ginsburg S (1966) The mathematical theory of context-free languages. McGraw-Hill, New York

Ginsburg S, Greibach SA (1966) Deterministic context-free languages. Inf. Control *9*: 620–648

Goldstine J, Price JK, Wotschke D (1982) A pushdown automaton or a context-free grammar—which is more economical? Theor. Comput. Sci. *18*: 33–40

Graham SL (1970) Extended precedence languages, bounded right context languages and deterministic languages. In: 11th Annual IEEE Symp. on Switching and Automata Theory, 1970. IEEE, New York, pp. 175–180

Graham SL (1971) Precedence languages and bounded right context languages. Thesis, Department of Computer Science, Stanford University, Stanford, CA

Graham SL, Harrison MA, Ruzzo WL (1980) An improved context-free recognizer. ACM Trans. Program. Lang. Syst. *2*: 415–462

Gray JN, Harrison MA (1969) Single-pass precedence analysis. In: 10th Annual IEEE Symp. on Switching and Automata Theory, 1969. IEEE, New York, pp. 106–117

Gray JN, Harrison MA (1972) On the covering and reduction problems for context-free grammars. J. Assoc. Comput. Mach. *19*: 675–698

Greibach SA (1965) A new normal form theorem for context-free phrase structure grammars. J. Assoc. Comput. Mach. *12*: 42–52

Gries D (1971) Compiler construction for digital computers. Wiley, New York

Haines LH (1965) Generation and recognition of formal languages. Thesis, Massachusetts Institute of Technology, Cambridge, MA

Hammond K, Rayward-Smith VJ (1984) A survey on syntactic error recovery and repair. Comput. Lang. *9*: 51–67

Harrison MA (1978) Introduction to formal language theory. Addison-Wesley, Reading, MA

Heilbrunner S (1981) A parsing automata approach to LR theory. Theor. Comput. Sci. *15*: 117–157

Hopcroft JE (1971) An *n* log *n* algorithm for minimizing the states in a finite automaton. In: Kohavi Z (ed.) The Theory of Machines and Computations. Academic Press, New York, pp. 189–196

Hopcroft JE, Ullman JD (1969) Formal languages and their relation to automata. Addison-Wesley, Reading, MA

Hopcroft JE, Ullman JD (1979) Introduction to automata theory, languages, and computation. Addison-Wesley, Reading, MA

Huffman DA (1954) The synthesis of sequential switching circuits. J. Franklin Inst. *257*: 3–4, 161–190, 275–303

Hunt HB III (1979) Observations on the complexity of regular expression problems. J. Comput. Syst. Sci. *19*: 222–236

Hunt HB III, Rosenkrantz DJ, Szymanski TG (1976) On the equivalence, containment, and covering problems for the regular and context-free languages. J. Comput. Syst. Sci. *12*: 222–268

Hunt HB III, Szymanski TG, Ullman JD (1974) Operations on sparse relations and efficient algorithms for grammar problems. In: 15th Annual IEEE Symp. on Switching and Automata Theory, October 1974. IEEE, New York, pp. 127–132

Hunt HB III, Szymanski TG, Ullman JD (1977) Operations on sparse relations. Commun. ACM *20*: 171–176

Ichbiah JD, Morse SP (1970) A technique for generating almost optimal Floyd-Evans productions for precedence grammars. Commun. ACM *13*: 501–508

Johnson DB, Sethi R (1975) Efficient construction of LL(1) parsers. Technical Report no. 164, Computer Science Department, Pennsylvania State University, University Park, PA

Johnson DB, Sethi R (1976) A characterization of LL(1) grammars. BIT *16*: 275–280

Johnson WL, Porter JH, Ackley SI, Ross DT (1968) Automatic generation of efficient lexical analyzers using finite state techniques. Commun. ACM *11*: 805–813

Kasami T (1965) An efficient recognition and syntax algorithm for context-free languages. Scientific report AFCRL-65-758, Air Force Cambridge Research Laboratory, Bedford, MA

Kfoury AJ, Moll RN, Arbib MA (1982) A programming approach to computability. Springer, New York, Heidelberg, Berlin

Kleene SC (1956) Representation of events in nerve nets and finite automata. In: Automata studies. Princeton Univ. Press, Princeton, NJ, pp. 3–42

Knuth DE (1965) On the translation of languages from left to right. Inf. Control *8*: 607–639

Knuth DE (1967) Top-down syntax analysis. Lecture Notes, International Summer School on Computer Programming, Copenhagen

Knuth DE (1971) Top-down syntax analysis. Acta Inf. *1*: 79–110

Knuth DE, Morris JH Jr, Pratt VR (1977) Fast pattern matching in strings. SIAM J. Comput. *6*: 323–350

Korenjak AJ, Hopcroft JE (1966) Simple deterministic languages. In: 7th Annual IEEE Symp. on Switching and Automata Theory, October 1966. IEEE, New York, pp. 36–46

Kurki-Suonio R (1966) On top-to-bottom recognition and left recursion. Commun. ACM *9*: 527–528

Kurki-Suonio R (1967) A note on LL(1) Languages. International Summer School on Computer Programming, Copenhagen

Kurki-Suonio R (1969) Notes on top-down languages. BIT *9*: 225–238

Lesk ME (1975) LEX—a lexical analyzer generator. CSTR 39, Bell Laboratories, Murray Hill, NJ

Lewis HR, Papadimitriou CH (1981) Elements of the theory of computation. Prentice-Hall, Englewood Cliffs, NJ

Lewis PM II, Rosenkrantz DJ (1971) An ALGOL compiler designed using automata theory. In: Proc. Symp. on Computers and Automata, Polytechnic Institute of Brooklyn, NY, pp. 75–88 (Microwave research institute symposia series, vol. 21)

Lewis PM II, Stearns RE (1966) Syntax-directed transduction. In: 7th Annual IEEE Symp. on Switching and Automata Theory, October 1966. IEEE, New York, pp. 21–35

Lewis PM II, Stearns RE (1968) Syntax-directed transduction. J. Assoc. Comput. Mach. *15*: 465–488

Lewis PM II, Rosenkrantz DJ, Stearns RE (1976) Compiler design theory. Addison-Wesley, Reading, MA

Lucas P (1961) Die Strukturanalyse von Formelübersetzern. Electron. Rechenanlagen *3*: 159–167

McKeeman WM, Horning JJ, Wortman DB (1970) A compiler generator. Prentice-Hall, Englewood Cliffs, NJ

McNaughton R (1982) Elementary computability, formal languages, and automata. Prentice-Hall, Englewood Cliffs, NJ

McNaughton R, Yamada H (1960) Regular expressions and state graphs for automata. IEEE Trans. Electronic Computers *9*: 39–47

Meyer AR, Fischer MJ (1971) Economy of description by automata, grammars and formal systems. In: 12th Annual IEEE Symp. on Switching and Automata Theory, October 1971. IEEE, New York, pp. 188–190

Meyer AR, Stockmeyer LJ (1972) The equivalence problem for regular expressions with squaring requires exponential space. In: 13th Annual IEEE Symp. on Switching and Automata Theory, October 1972. IEEE, New York, pp. 125–129

Moore EF (1956) Gedanken experiments on sequential machines. In: Automata Studies. Princeton Univ. Press, Princeton, NJ, pp. 129–153

Myhill J (1957) Finite automata and the representation of events. In: WADD TR-57-624, Wright Patterson AFB, OH, pp. 112–137

Naur P et al. (1960) Report on the algorithmic language ALGOL 60. Commun. ACM $3$: 299–314, revised in Commun. ACM $6$: 1–17

Nerode A (1958) Linear automaton transformations. Proc. Am. Math. Soc. $9$: 541–544

Nijholt A (1983) Deterministic top-down and bottom-up parsing: historical notes and bibliographies. Mathematical Centre, Amsterdam

Oettinger A (1961) Automatic syntactic analysis and the pushdown store. In: Structure of Language and Its Mathematical Concepts. Proc. 12th Symposium on Applied Mathematics. American Mathematical Society, Providence, RI, pp. 104–129

Pair C (1964) Arbres, piles et compilation. Revue Francaise de Traitement de l'Information $7$: 199–216

Parikh RJ (1966) On context-free languages. J. Assoc. Comput. Mach. $13$: 570–581

Rabin MO, Scott D (1959) Finite automata and their decision problems. IBM J. Res. $3$: 115–125

Rosenkrantz DJ (1967) Matrix equations and normal forms for context-free grammars. J. Assoc. Comput. Mach. $14$: 501–507

Rosenkrantz DJ, Stearns RE (1970) Properties of deterministic top-down grammars. Inf. Control $17$: 226–256

Salomaa A (1969) Theory of automata. Pergamon Press, New York

Salomaa A (1973) Formal languages. Academic Press, New York

Savitch WJ (1982) Abstract machines and grammars. Little, Brown, Boston

Schmidt EM (1978) Succinctness of descriptions of context-free, regular, and finite languages. DAIMI PB-84, Department of Computer Science, University of Aarhus, Denmark (also: Thesis, Cornell University, Ithaca, NY)

Schützenberger MP (1963) On context-free languages and pushdown automata. Inf. Control $6$: 246–264

Sippu S (1982) Derivational complexity of context-free grammars. Inf. Control $53$: 52–65

Sippu S, Soisalon-Soininen E (1985) On the use of relational expressions in the design of efficient algorithms. In: Brauer W (ed.) Automata, Languages and Programming. Twelfth Colloquium, Nafplion, Greece, July 1985. Springer, Berlin, Heidelberg, New York, Tokyo, pp. 456–464 (Lecture notes in computer science, vol. 194)

Stearns RE, Hunt HB III (1981) On the equivalence and containment problems for unambiguous regular expressions, grammars, and automata. In: 22nd Annual Symp. on Foundations of Computer Science, October 1981. IEEE, New York, pp. 74–81

Stockmeyer LJ, Meyer AR (1973) Word problems requiring exponential time. In: 5th Annual ACM Symp. on Theory of Computing, April-May, 1973. ACM, New York, pp. 1–9

Tarjan RE (1972) Depth-first search and linear graph algorithms. SIAM J. Comput. $1$: 146–160

Thompson K (1968) Regular expression search algorithm. Commun. ACM $11$: 419–422

Valiant LG (1975) General context-free recognition in less than cubic time. J. Comput. Syst. Sci. $10$: 308–315

Waite WM, Goos G (1984) Compiler construction, Springer, New York, Berlin, Heidelberg, Tokyo

Warshall S (1962) A theorem on Boolean matrices. J. Assoc. Comput. Mach. $9$: 11–12

Wirth N (1968) PL-360: A programming language for the IBM 360 computers. J. Assoc. Comput. Mach. $15$: 37–54

Wirth N, Weber H (1966) Euler—a generalization of ALGOL and its formal definition. Commun. ACM $9$: 13–23 (part 1), 89–99 (part 2)

Wood D (1969a) A note on top-down deterministic languages. BIT $9$: 387–399

Wood D (1969b) The theory of left factored languages, part I. Comput. J. $12$: 349–356

Wood D (1970) The theory of left factored languages, part II. Comput. J. $13$: 55–62

Wood D (1971) A further note on top-down deterministic languages. Comput. J. $14$: 396–403

Wood D (1987) Theory of computation. Harper & Row, New York, NY

Younger DH (1967) Recognition and parsing of context-free languages in time $n^3$. Inf. Control $10$: 189–208

# Index to Volume I